The Mentally Ill Chemical Abuser

Whose Client?

Jacqueline Cohen, M.S.W.
Stephen Jay Levy, Ph.D., C.A.S.

Lexington Books
An Imprint of Macmillan, Inc.
New York

Maxwell Macmillan Canada
Toronto

Maxwell Macmillan International
New York Oxford Singapore Sydney

Library of Congress Cataloging-in-Publication Data
Cohen, Jacqueline
The mentally ill chemical abuser: whose client? / Jacqueline Cohen, Stephen Jay Levy.
p. cm.
ISBN 0-669-27671-5
1. Narcotic addicts—Mental health. 2. Alcoholics—Mental health. 3. Mentally ill—Substance use. I. Levy, Stephen J. II. Title.
[DNLM: 1. Mental Disorders—rehabilitation. 2. Substance Abuse—rehabilitation. WM 270 C67753m]
RC564.C6243 1992
616.86′001′9—dc20
DNLM/DLC
for Library of Congress 92-6217
CIP

Lexington Books
An Imprint of Macmillan, Inc.
866 Third Avenue, New York, N.Y. 10022

Maxwell Macmillan Canada, Inc.
1200 Eglinton Avenue East
Suite 200
Don Mills, Ontario M3C 3N1

Macmillan, Inc. is part of the Maxwell Communication Group of Companies.

Printed in the United States of America

printing number
1 2 3 4 5 6 7 8 9 10

The authors acknowledge use of material from Sheldon B. Koop, *If You Meet the Buddha on the Road, Kill Him!* (Palo Alto, Calif.: Science and Behavior Books, 1972). Quoted with permission of Science and Behavior Books.

To our parents

Irene Doctor Cohen
Hyman Cohen

Dorothy Cohen Levy
Marvin Levy

To all of our clients who had the strength and courage to share their lives with us

It is from them that much of the wisdom of this book has evolved and grown

Contents

Figure and Tables

Figure

Tables

Preface

The purpose of this book is to provide a critical analysis of the relationship between two forms of painful human conditions: mental illness and substance abuse. We review and carefully examine the complex definitional and pragmatic problems which define the two conditions. This book is about real people—the mentally ill chemical abuser (MICA) client and the clinical staff whose responsibility it is to treat them. The authors are a clinical social worker and a psychologist who have spent the combined equivalent of forty years working in the three fields of alcoholism, drug abuse, and mental health.

After reviewing the current literature, interviewing others doing this type of work, and reflecting upon our own clinical work, it is our contention that both mental illness and substance abuse fall along a continuum of psychopathology which cries out for clear assessment and rational treatment interventions. We begin with an appraisal of the linguistic problems in translating from one field to another. In chapter two we provide a chronological history of the development of the three fields with a summary of the relative state of the art in each. We then examine how each field has fared in its attempts to work with mentally ill chemical abusers and identify gaps in the treatment of MICA clients. We also present a number of alternative frameworks for understanding the variety of approaches to the MICA and other clients. In chapter three we ask directly: Who is responsible for the problems and who is responsible for the solutions? The chapter addresses a number of complex clinical issues such as diagnostic procedures, organic mental states, client assessment, abstinence, relapse, the use of psychotropic medications, and the need to attend to individual differences. Finally, in chapter four the authors review recommendations made by others as well as their own for the three fields.

We would like the reader to understand and appreciate our bias. We stand for a holistic and comprehensive treatment in which systems and issues that have been historically and traditionally considered separate are joined in a true integration of clinical technology. We cite examples of programs and approaches that aspire toward this ideal. This is not a cookbook of how to work with the MICA client. We maintain that there is no unique or singular MICA model any more than there is a singular MICA client (they cover the entire range of psychopathology). Instead we address this book to that which is much older and wiser—good treatment in all care systems. This book is intended to stimulate dialogue and brainstorming. We do not hesitate to criticize poor clinical work and narrow dogmatic perspectives. We believe that a holistic and comprehensive approach provides a scientifically supportable, clinically sound, and cost-effective approach to quality care for MICA clients in which clients get better and staff get validated for their hard work.

The identification of the MICA client in all systems is actually a recognition of a phenomenon which has existed for many decades—substance use by mentally ill individuals and the onset of such illness due to substance usage. Recent increases in the number of MICA clients in all systems has finally prompted a need to do something now. We have observed how many recommendations have gone unheeded and that agencies have failed to integrate existing knowledge into actual clinical programming. The idea of "client resistance" has become an excuse for "agency resistance." We also acknowledge several fine, existing agencies which have already demonstrated the kind of quality care that can be rendered when people move toward a holistic and comprehensive perspective. This book issues a challenge to alcoholism, drug abuse, and mental health agencies to join with those who already provide comprehensive, holistic, and integrated care. Clients have shown again and again that they can and will respond, improve, and get better when you give them what they need.

We wish to thank our editor at Lexington Books, Margaret Zusky, and our production supervisor, Loretta Denner. Their skills and wisdom were invaluable to us.

1
Basic Issues

Who Is the MICA (Mentally Ill Chemical Abuser) Client?

MICA, an acronym for the mentally ill chemical abuser, identifies persons who are suffering from a diagnosable mental disorder and who also use and abuse alcohol and other drugs (sometimes combined with psychotropic medications). Standard definitions of both abuse of and dependence on psychoactive substances in *The Diagnostic and Statistical Manual of Mental Disorders* (1987, third revised edition, commonly referred to as the *DSM–IIIR*) note continued use despite negative consequences (167–69). For the MICA client, even a single episode of psychoactive substance ingestion can lead to complications of mental functioning. Repeated episodes may even cause mental breakdown of a chronic or acute variety (McLellan, Woody, and O'Brien, 1979).

A review of the clinical literature on the MICA reveals few conclusive studies of the relationships between the mentally ill patient and substance use or abuse. However, informed researchers and clinicians in the MICA field agree on the following:

> Whatever the etiological role of substance use or abuse in the onset of mental illness (or vice versa), alcohol and drug use has been found to hinder almost every aspect of care for young adults with chronic mental illness. (Brown et al., 1989:566)

Ridgely, Goldman, and Talbot (1986) in their extensive review of the literature on chronic mentally ill young adults (aged 18–40) who have substance abuse problems conclude:

> There is little agreement about the relationship of drugs and alcohol to psychopathology and the pathogenesis of mental disorders. Existing research is flawed by overly simplistic models of cause and effect, samples drawn from already affected individuals in treatment settings, and the lack of prospective designs. (38)

Brown et al. (1989), in commenting on the review conducted by Ridgely et al. (1986), state:

> The literature review revealed a number of limitations in current research. For example, the lack of uniform definitions and methodologies makes it impossible at this juncture to compare or aggregate findings. Furthermore, the target population is very heterogenous—adding to the dangers of generalization. Almost none of the studies were found to be sufficiently large and nationally representative to permit reliable statements to be made about the group as a whole. (566)

Way and McCormick (1990) in their review of the MICA literature conclude:

> Information on the correlations between psychiatric diagnoses and substances of abuse is far from conclusive, indicating a need for further research in this area. . . . Do the mentally ill abuse drugs with the intent to relieve their psychiatric symptomatology (i.e., to self-medicate)? Does substance abuse precipitate mental illness or vice versa (i.e., what is the temporal relationship? Do common vulnerabilities underlie both substance abuse and mental illness? Numerous theories have been studied over the years, but the results are still inconclusive and causal relationships remain unclear. One issue that is clear is that the mentally ill are at a high risk for substance abuse and that substance abusers are at a high risk for mental illness. (14–15)

The authors of this book favor a pragmatic, multivariate, and holistic model. Having worked in all three fields: alcoholism, drug abuse, and mental health, we bring an insider's perspective to this study. As used in this book the term MICA serves as a convenient shorthand for describing a diverse and multivariate population. Its use does not attribute specific etiology (cause) as to which is primary or secondary (mental illness or substance use/abuse), but does directly imply that mental illness and substance use/abuse interact in synergistic ways. As previously indicated, these interactions are not well understood. For example, cases have been amply documented in which those suffering from major affective disorders—forms of depression—have used alcohol and other drugs with deleterious consequences; in such cases, depression causes alcohol/drug abuse. Other cases have shown that the chronic ingestion of substances such as ethanol can lead to full-blown depressive-spectrum disorders; in such cases, alcohol abuse causes depression.

Osher (1989) delineates three subgroups of clients who can be considered dually diagnosed (see figure 1–1). The entire MICA population is contained within the two circles. Area 1 indicates the primary psychiatric diagnosis of some MICA clients; area 2 indicates the primary substance abuse disorder of other clients, which is causally related to some form of psychiatric disturbance. Area 3 shows two separate illnesses or diagnoses, each exacerbating the other and each being driven by different genetic, biochemical, or social factors.

Clients as represented in area 3 have also been called dual-diagnosis patients. This term has its origin in the mental health system and springs mainly from investigations of those labelled the *young adult chronic* mentally ill patient, or *YAC*. However, the term is imprecise, because "dual" could equally refer to mental illness and mental retardation or other conditions and disorders. YAC patients are people aged eighteen to forty who meet the criteria for a variety of mental disorders (including schizophrenia, affective disorders, and personality disorders) and for whom such disorders cause some degree of lasting disability (Brown et al., 1989). This terminology is unique to the current mental health system vocabulary but it is too often taken to imply a primacy of the mental disorder in etiological thinking. This incorrect inferencing occurs even when authors like Vivian Brown and her colleagues take great pains to avoid such stereotyping.

Some terminology is unique to the medical model view of serious mental disorder as primarily *psychiatric*. In Philadelphia, for example, it is common to hear the MICA client referred to as a PISA, an acronym for the *psychiatrically ill substance abuser*. In New York State, MICAA is used to refer to the *mentally ill chemical abuser and addicted*. This is a term coined primarily by the mental health system (Office of Mental Health) and the alcoholism treatment system (Division of Alcoholism and Alcohol Abuse). Another term used in New York City, more unique to the substance abuse field (Division of Substance Abuse Services), is CAMI, the chemically abusing mentally ill person. With rare exception, all of the terminology is derivative of ideas concerning etiology.

In this work, the focus on the MICA client is not limited by age or diagnostic nosology or drug of choice. Our definition is inherently generic and springs from a comparatively more comprehensive and holistic base. Among other workers and writers in the three services systems there has always been a tendency to overemphasize biological factors and medical factors in mental health issues, all too often to the exclusion of other,

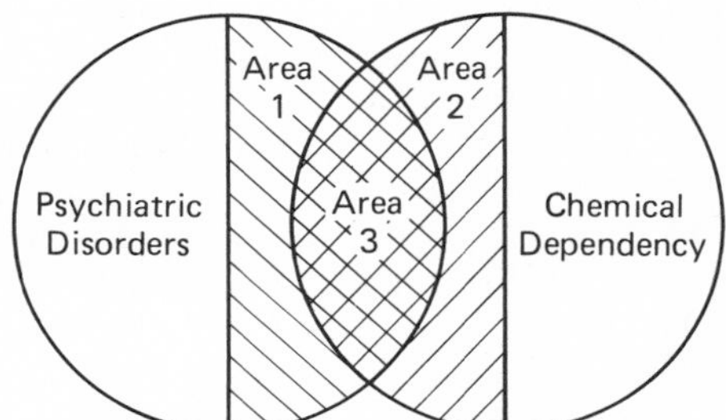

Figure 1–1. Subgroups of the MICA Population
Adapted from Osher (1989). Used with permission.

equally salient aspects, such as psychological, cultural, economic, and political factors. But the focus in defining the MICA client, in our view, should instead be based on a rational description of client behavior and symptomatology. What all three fields have failed to study is the phenomenology of the MICA client: that is, a bias-free description of the client's world—in the client's own words, thoughts, feelings, and actions. There has also been a severe lack of emphases on practical day-to-day life-style issues such as housing, physical health, poverty, the drug trade, and other realities of the street.

Some practitioners, biased and influenced by their own ideas concerning causality, may try to fit clients into intellectual pigeonholes, as aptly described in the following:

> Like the mythical blind men with their hands on various parts of an elephant, mental health and chemical dependency practitioners cling to their differing beliefs in regard to the etiology, diagnosis, and treatment of dually diagnosed patients. These differing views of the relationship between psychopathology and chemical dependence often result in fragmented and inadequate care, with the patient being shunted back and forth between mental health and chemical dependence treatment facilities. (Wallen and Weiner 1989:161)

Given the same set of behaviors, each system is likely to arrive at its own unique diagnosis and course of treatment. In a presentation entitled "Psychological Suffering and Substance Dependence: Unravelling the Cause/Consequence Controversy," Dr. Edward J. Khantzian, principal psychiatrist for the addictions at Cambridge Hospital and associate professor of Psychiatry at Harvard Medical School, states:

> All of us depend on concepts to understand and respond to complex problems. Alcoholism and addiction certainly are no exception and, in fact, concepts and theories have abounded to explain this maddeningly elusive and tragic problem in our society. The problem is that we have not worked out a means to strive towards and achieve a consensus on what the various concepts, and the approaches that grow out of the concepts, teach us. Despite each of our disclaimers that alcoholism is no one thing and that it has multiple determinants, we almost invariably, if not necessarily, fall prey to the problem of reductionism wherein we employ and consider our formulations, concepts, and data to the exclusion of other perspectives. *Nowhere is this more evident than in the controversy over whether psychological or psychiatric dysfunction is a cause or consequence of substance abuse.* (Khantzian 1987:9; emphasis added)

The following example of differential diagnoses provides a case in point.

> A 22-year-old white female, presents with alcohol on her breath, appears malnourished, is apparently delusional, complaining of auditory halluci-

nations (voices which command her to kill herself), and is found with three crack vials in her pocketbook. Efforts to take a recent history are useless and the patient becomes increasingly agitated, panicky, and paranoid.

The mental health practitioner diagnoses might be *paranoid schizophrenic break with substance abuse.*

The alcoholism treatment practitioner diagnoses might be *alcohol hallucinosis with multiple substance abuse.*

The drug abuse treatment practitioner diagnoses might be *crack/ cocaine–induced psychosis.*

The label that a prospective client receives can determine whether or not the person receives treatment and into which treatment system he or she is tracked. The suffering individual described above could be placed in any of the following: 1) drug detoxification unit; 2) alcohol detoxification unit; 3) psychiatric emergency room; 4) inpatient psychiatric unit; 5) dual-diagnosis unit (assuming one exists); 6) acute care medical unit (if one can handle alcohol/drug abusers); or 7) corner of the reception area of a conventional emergency room, where the client may be left to "freak out." This determination of placement not only has powerful implications for meeting immediate acute care needs but it can also begin a process of "labelling" that tracks the client's care system for many subsequent years.

This labelling process presents a serious impediment for investigators committed to studying the multifaceted nature of the MICA population. A literature review conducted by Way and McCormick (1990), of the Bureau of Evaluation and Services Research of the New York State Office of Mental Health (NYSOMH), describes this problem. Estimates of MICA prevalence rates found in the literature *ranged from a low of 7 percent to a peak of over 60 percent.* Some authors have reported even higher figures. Attia (1988), for example, notes: "Eighty percent of patients in both inpatient and outpatient mental health facilities present with drug and alcohol abuse." She does not, however, present a definition of "abuse" nor describe whether it was continuous or episodic.

Way and McCormick (1990) attribute their discovery of widely divergent rates to such definitional problems, as well as to other factors such as "different study designs, samples sizes, and study sites, regional, and population differences, and research undertaken in different time periods." Brown et al. (1989) concur with these criticisms and further point out:

> The lack of uniform definitions and methodologies makes it impossible at this juncture to compare or aggregate findings. Furthermore, the target population is very heterogeneous—diagnostically, functionally, and possibly geographically—adding to the dangers of generalization. (566)

Similar research problems, these writers note, characterize a literature review done by Ridgely et al. (1986): *almost none of the studies* had large enough samples or were geographically diverse enough to allow for national representation; and therefore little of a reliable nature could be stated about the MICA group as a whole.

MICA clients are not new clients. They have been in the three treatment systems (alcoholism, drug abuse, and mental health) for a long time. They are identified in many ways and all too often "fall between the cracks" within all three systems. Most are not totally dysfunctional. In fact they are clever at disguising or otherwise altering their symptomatology, in an attempt to manipulate workers in the various systems. They usually know all the acceptance/rejection criteria for most modalities of care. The more severely disturbed and debilitated are left to fend for themselves on the street.

The following list notes the major factors that have contributed to an increase in the MICA population:

- deinstitutionalization of mental health hospital
- greater acceptance of substance use in society
- decreased funding for alcohol, drug, and mental health treatment
- increased homelessness—the growing numbers of YAC patients, for example, are vagrant street people
- increasing rates of HIV infection and AIDS
- increased use of crack, smokable heroin (combined with crack), and smokable amphetamines
- failure of the mental health system to provide community-based services delivered in an outpatient format
- Refusal of psychiatric halfway houses to admit substance-using/abusing clients
- Refusal of most residential substance abuse and alcoholism treatment programs to admit mentally ill clients
- Poor coordination between treatment agencies and little cooperation between treatment agencies and other parts of the bureaucracy that serves social needs (welfare, housing, etc.)

We will elaborate on the interrelationships among these factors throughout this book, many of which may account for poor estimates of the MICA population and definition of its characteristics. Clients, many of whom live an antisocial, streetwise life-style, may alternate between systems and/or modalities, behaving in ways that are likely to meet their current needs. Appearing one day, for example, as primarily alcohol abusers, another as addicts, and yet another as mental patients, patients can manipulate admissions personnel into giving them what they refer to as "three hots and a cot." For many MICAs being *on the program* means an avenue to survival needs of food, shelter, and clothing. Social services programs motivate them to receive social welfare and medical benefits rather than stop using alcohol and other drugs or be otherwise treated for their mental disorders. Clinicians and investigators of the MICA population are further frustrated by the fact that clients (or patients) present differently in the variety of settings they are likely to interact with—public psychiatric facility, private psychiatric facility, veterans' hospital, emergency room, general hospital psychiatric unit, and the like (Galanter, Castaneda, and Ferman 1988:211).

Undocumented numbers of people have been mislabelled and misdiagnosed due to a lack of practical as well as clinical knowledge of practitioners. Not only has proper treatment not been prescribed or administered, but lives have been severely damaged by poor practice in all three systems. The following are examples of ineffective treatment of the MICA patient population:

- Harsh encounter group confrontation, unique to some drug treatment agencies, can further destroy self-esteem and weak ego structures. Those with major mental disorders are deprived of appropriate psychiatric evaluations, medications, and sensitive individual counseling which could render more tractable their ability to tolerate this modality.
- Alcohol-dependent persons with schizophrenia are forced to follow the dictum: "Don't drink and go to AA meetings," as well as be deprived of needed psychotropic medications due to the dogmatic "no mood-altering substances" bias found among older members of Alcoholics Anonymous.
- Psychiatric emergency workers fail to identify drug ingestion as the cause for psychotic episodes and, as a result, decompensation among chronic patients is rarely attributed to drug usage.
- A total of 20 percent of client depressions do not lift after abstinence from alcohol use, yet these clients are told to believe that the depression is caused *solely* by alcohol and they are therefore denied access to psychiatric assessments and antidepressant medication.
- Significant numbers of methadone-maintained clients are in fact being *medicated* against underlying and/or co-existing psychoses and mood disorders instead of also undergoing psychiatric evaluations and consideration of more appropriate medications.
- Many MICA clients in drug-free therapeutic communities or methadone maintenance programs are revealing sexual abuse histories, but the clinical skills and the personal sensitivity required to counsel these clients is sorely lacking among treatment staff. Failure to address these issues contributes to high dropout and relapse rates.

Some Recent Developments in the Treatment of the Mentally Ill Chemical Abuser

The federal, state, and local bureaucracies which deal with alcoholism, drug abuse, and mental health issues grew out of completely separate traditions. Efforts to mobilize government and private resources for the mentally ill predate the institutions and agencies that organized, separately, around the alcohol and drug abuse issues. To understand these different pathways one must appreciate the historical and cultural context of their development and must equally understand the highly emotionally charged atmosphere that often replaces a fuller scientific understanding of these complicated issues.

Dr. Howard Shaffer, director of the Center for Addiction Studies at Harvard Medical School, cautions us:

> The field of the addictions is very young, and marked by controversy, zealous emotion, and confusion. It is precisely this chaotic state of affairs that Shaffer observed when he argued that the field of addictions is in a preparadigmatic period and in the midst of a conceptual crisis. The developmental immaturity of the addiction field is evident by the presence of intensely conflicting and polarized explanations of its identity and purpose, anomalous research findings, and few facts.

The field of mental health is similarly undeveloped. Dr. Dale L. Johnson (1989) of the University of Houston describes, as one result, the stigmas and controversies surrounding schizophrenia:

> Families have adopted a belief that schizophrenia is a brain disease because they feel less stigmatized with that explanation than one that attributes cause to family behaviors. Even without regard to etiology, the family is often stigmatized by the public behaviors of their mentally ill family member. This is difficult to accept, but it is worse to feel guilty that one has caused such a dreadful condition . . . Most of the major etiological models of mental illness are too incomplete to cover adequately the complexities of schizophrenia, and they do not provide a good fit with current data . . . The medical model is also too limited. It does not deal adequately with [the] complex social and cognitive phenomena of schizophrenia. (553)

Those well versed in the real world of funding and politics know that when the scientists are confused, others move in quickly to influence prevailing social attitudes and demand that something be done. Even when scientific findings are clear, it takes time (often many years) for facts to be accepted by the public and even that acceptance doesn't diminish the ardor of vested interest groups. Walt Kelly recognized this when his famous cartoon character, Pogo Possum, exclaimed, "WE HAVE MET THE ENEMY AND HE IS US!"

Some have attempted to develop theoretical understanding of addictive behavior and disease. Dr. Stanton Peele, (1989) in his *Diseasing of America: Addiction Treatment Out of Control,* challenges our ability to think logically about addictive behaviors. He poses the question, "What are real diseases?" and provides the concepts of first, second, and third generations of disease, summarized as follows:

> *First generation diseases:* consist of disorders known through their physical manifestations (such as, malaria or cancer) and causal evidence (such as microbes that cause the disease).
>
> *Second generation diseases:* are mental or emotional disorders known not by what we measure in people's bodies but by the feelings, thoughts, and behaviors they produce in people. Problem behaviors are called *symptoms* and are organized into syndromes called *disorders* or *diseases.* The causes of the disorders are not well understood.
>
> *Third generation diseases:* are epitomized by the addictions. These so-called diseases are known by the very behavior that they describe (for example, a person's compulsively drinking or drugging). In other words, biology = behavior and behavior = disease. One has the disease even when he is not engaging in the behavior. To date, no specific or unitary cause can be scientifically attributed to addictive behavior.

Peele concludes:

> What is most striking about modern disease theories of behavior is that they militate against such human potentialities in favor of hypothetical disease mechanisms . . . It is as if, in the words of psychologist/physician Henry Murray, we were trying to "reduce the concept of human nature to its lowest common denominators," and then were "gloating over having done so." (29)

In his earlier analysis of compulsive behavior, Peele (1985) states:

> Addiction is best understood as an individual's adjustment, albeit a self-defeating one, to his or her environment. It represents an habitual style of coping, albeit one that the individual is capable of modifying with changing psychological and life circumstances. While in some cases addiction achieves a devastating pathological extremity, it actually represents a continuum of feeling and behavior more than a distinct disease state. Neither traumatic drug withdrawal nor a person's craving for a drug is exclusively determined by physiology. Rather, the experience both of a felt need (or craving) for and of withdrawal from an object or involvement engages a person's expectations, values, and self concept as well as the person's sense of alternative opportunities for gratification. (2)

In the following, Dr. Levy recounts what he refers to as his favorite story of human renewal. It describes Sam A., whom Levy terms his first teacher in the field of drug abuse.

Three Strikes Doesn't Have to Mean You're Out. . . . A Case Study of Sam A.

I first met Sam in the fall of 1967 when he was working as the director of a hospital-based therapeutic community run by the Phoenix House program (then part of the Addiction Services Agency of New York City). My wife was a nurse working in the program and Sam became my "outside" mentor while I was working toward my Ph.D. in psychology at Yeshiva University. The faculty told me I was wasting my time working with heroin addicts but I was not to be discouraged. Sam was a profoundly unique teacher.

Sam grew up in the Appalachian mountains. Both his parents had been alcoholics. He soon exhibited similar behavior and began mainlining heroin to accompany his pathological drinking behavior. He looked like a big Irish cop or a linebacker for the New York Giants. He was charming, suave in his own country manner, and highly manipulative. He also had a very big heart. He eventually ended up in Saint Elizabeth's Mental Hospital in Washington, D.C., where he was diagnosed as a catatonic schizophrenic. When I asked him about those five years in the "back ward" he said he was genuinely crazy but that he had also played a social withdrawal game when he could not be bothered dealing with people. He was sometimes in control of his social contact.

Sam was an accomplished jazz pianist. One day Louie Bellson, the sensational jazz drummer, and his orchestra came to entertain the patients at Saint Elizabeth's. Sam, dressed in pajamas, bathrobe, and scuffs, asked Bellson if he could sit in with the band. Bellson said he could play one tune and if he wasn't up to snuff he'd pull him off the bandstand. Sam ended up playing an entire set. Afterwards, Louie Bellson challenged Sam: "What are you doing in this hospital?" When Sam replied that he was crazy, Bellson accused him of hiding from real life and suggested that maybe it was time to think about getting out.

Sam had heard about an innovative drug abuse treatment program in New York City called Daytop Village. So he wrote a letter to the clinical director of the agency asking about employment. The director replied by suggesting that Sam might want to enter Daytop for a period of time as a resident. He reasoned that Sam had never really been treated for his substance abuse problem. Sam consented. The rigors of therapeutic community life took some adjustment but eventually Sam thrived in this tribal, extended family environment.

When I encountered Sam, he was running a similar program for Phoenix House. He had successfully graduated from Daytop and embarked on a journey of helping other addicts. I learned a lot from this man who had survived alcoholism, drug abuse, and serious mental illness. Unfortunately, despite years of abstinence, Sam's liver finally gave out and he died a relatively young man. But not before he came to enjoy friendship, marriage, and the joys and pains of life in the "square" world. Amazingly, before his death Sam had returned to Saint Elizabeth's—this time to run a program for drug addicts. He had always said "What goes around, comes around!"

Sam's story is a constant reminder to me that dealing with mentally ill chemical abusers is always a story about human renewal. It is also about pluck, innovation, counterculture, outrageousness, and belief in the human spirit. Although he had attended AA, Sam had never thought of his problems as biological. He had always assumed that all people have to wrestle with themselves to keep moving in a positive direction.

Caring for Their Own

Many, if not most, of the staff working in alcoholism treatment programs are "recovering" alcoholics. That is, they have the "disease" of alcoholism (or, according to the *DSM–IIIR,* are *alcohol dependent*). The theory suggests that people in remission serve as positive role models for alcoholics entering treatment. They represent proof that while a cure is not possible since the cause remains unknown, remission of symptoms through continuous abstinence, is possible. Even when the target behavior—that is, drinking—is absent, traditionally these people consider themselves victims of the disease and for the remainder of their lives must remain vigilant against relapse. Their relative ability to accomplish this is held out to patients as proof that an abstinent life-style can be achieved.

Of no less significance is the fact that many, if not most, of the staff working in certain drug abuse treatment (as distinguished from alcoholism treatment) programs, are ex-addicts. This staffing pattern is more characteristic of drug-free therapeutic communities (such as Synanon, Daytop Village, Phoenix House, and Gateway House) than it is of methadone maintenance treatment programs. However, some methadone maintenance programs do employ ex-addicts, who may be either drug-free or maintained on methadone. Once again the working theory is that persons who have suffered the problem and overcome it present positive role models to the client entering and undergoing treatment. They represent a powerful message: namely, that change is possible.

The difference between the concept of being "in recovery" and being an "ex-addict" is both overt and subtle. We will have more to say about these important distinctions later on. The major point we wish to make here is that, heretofore, traditional mental health and medical providers (both agencies and private practitioners) have either (1) totally ignored the plight of addicted persons, (2) aggravated a bad situation through mistreatment, (3) failed to diagnose addictive behavior, or (4) relegated them to a kind of treatment "Siberia."

Many new successful treatment programs had their origins apart from mainstream American medical and mental health practices. Those familiar with the historical beginnings of Alcoholics Anonymous (AA) know that a physician (the famous "Dr. Bob") and a businessman ("Bill W.") came to rely on one another in their struggle toward continuous sobriety because there was no one else to understand or help them. From those humble beginnings, the "miracle" of AA now claims to encompass some 800,000 members in the United States, and one-and-a-half million members worldwide. The impact of AA and its belief system have powerfully influenced the field of alcoholism treatment, much as the psychoanalytic movement once held sway over American psychiatry and psychology for many decades. But by not wanting to have itself associated with "mentally ill" people, and by viewing alcoholism as somehow separate from issues of mental health and illness, the new field of alcoholism treatment grew up apart from the mental health field.

While the federal government conducted research with drug addicts at its research facilities in Fort Worth, Texas, and Lexington, Kentucky, the treatment field emerged from non-governmental beginnings. The residential therapeutic community movement was begun in the 1950s when Charles (Chuck) Diederich founded Synanon on the West Coast. Daytop Village and Phoenix House followed on the East Coast. These programs make almost exclusive use of ex-addicts as staff. Once again, the origins and practices are split off from the mainstream of American medicine and mental health.

It is vital that the reader understand why and how the recovering alcohol abuser and the ex-addict came to be the core staff caring, as it were, for their own. Below we describe some of the ways in which the fields of medicine and mental health and traditional mental health and medical providers (both agencies and private practitioners) have failed addicted people. Case illustrations drawn from the authors' professional experiences are used to indicate how they have been ignored, misdiagnosed, mistreated, and sent to what can be termed *treatment Siberia.*

Traditional Treatment of Addicted Individuals

They Were Ignored. Prior to the 1950s the private sector in the United States as well as public agencies had failed to create treatment settings in which addicts and alcoholics could receive any treatment, much less, effective, humane, and compassionate care. The few that existed for addicts (like Riverside Hospital in New York and the Federal Center at Lexington) had published recidivism rates of over 90 percent (Brecher 1972).

Case Illustration 1: Joe

Joe called seventeen hospitals in New York City looking to be detoxified from heroin in 1956. Finally, he got into Riverside Hospital after his brother-in-law learned about it from the New York City Department of Health. This same brother-in-law smuggled in some heroin to the ward after Joe called him and said "there was money to be made."

Case Illustration 2: Hector

Hector told us a similar story about Lexington, Kentucky—known on the street as "KY." His federal probation officer sent him to KY after yet another drug arrest. When he got off the train in Lexington, he told us, he hid a hypodermic needle, syringe, cotton balls, bottle cap, and several bags of heroin in the wall of the train station. He removed several bricks and hid the drugs and works behind them. He said he got high on the train on the way down and after several months of obviously ineffective treatment, removed his stash from the wall and got high all the way back to New York City.

They Were Misdiagnosed. Addicted people do not usually volunteer the information that they are misusing licit or illicit substances. And many professionals are not trained to ask: they do not take drinking or drugging histories, and often they are afraid of offending the patient and losing revenue. However, in the past they were eager to apply their otherwise keen diagnostic skills to the clients' *symptoms,* such as sleep and appetite disturbance, nervousness, depression, anxiety, and numerous vague complaints of pain. The doctors quickly applied diagnoses designed to lead to the alleviation of suffering, usually by prescribing medicine. How many physicians have been "scammed" in this way? How many addicts got legitimate "scripts" for pain killers, tranquilizers, sleep medication, stimulants, and depressants to add to their pharmacopeia of street drugs? And how many alcoholics became dually addicted to alcohol and other sedatives (in pill form)? This practice, in particular, has led Dr. Stanley Gitlow to conceive of a form of addiction he has labelled "sedativism."

Case Illustration 3: Sandra

Sandra boasted about the many "docs" on Park Avenue she had strung along and how many pharmacies she had used (in the days before computers and triplicate forms). She bragged how she had as many different kinds of pills in her medicine cabinet as brands of liquor sitting on her bar. The stories stopped being funny after she suffered a series of jarring seizures while withdrawing from barbiturates.

Case Illustration 4: Jerry

Jerry had gone through a one-week detoxication program for heroin before he was admitted to the longer-term ward treating addicts. He had been screened by physicians and pronounced drug-free. He had been similarly screened by an ex-addict staff of the extended stay program in 1967. In the middle of an encounter group session, on the thirteenth day in the hospital he suffered a grand mal seizure. The "crash cart" was called and the medical staff stabilized him. He was returned to the medical unit. If he had not been in the hospital, he would have died. No one, it seemed, had picked up on Jerry's goofball (barbiturate) habit which co-existed with his heroin addiction.

They Were Mistreated. Mental health practitioners often see substance abuse as a symptom of an underlying disorder and use "uncovering" therapy to get at the repressed or suppressed psychological material. Uncovering painful life situations and memories can raise anxiety thresholds to intolerable proportions and induce further drug taking to suppress these painful effects. Psychodynamically oriented psychotherapists (among others) do not see the substance abuse as a problem in its own right, one worthy of being placed first in the order of things to be addressed. Furthermore, they are used to being directive with patients.

Case Illustration 5: Barbara

Barbara had been abusing cocaine for six months when she entered psychotherapy. She admitted her drug use to her therapist, who strongly encouraged her to cut down. As she grew increasingly anxious and distraught, her therapist again suggested she cut back on her cocaine use and perhaps just have "a drink or two." When she was brought to the emergency room by her sister in the midst of a paranoid psychotic episode brought on by cocaine, the staff immediately admitted her to the psychiatric unit. The psychotherapist told the admitting psychiatrist she had been resistant to therapy. Neither the sister nor the therapist mentioned cocaine use, but when the psychosis subsided, Barbara did.

Case Illustration 6: Ed

Ed was drinking heavily and kept complaining to his therapist that his marriage was in shambles and his work productivity was going down. Ed had been discussing his passive dependence on his parents and the therapist felt that they needed to explore this more deeply. He asked Ed to stop drinking and gave him a prescription for Valium. Now Ed had a powerful admixture of chemicals with which to further assault his brain. Ed choked to death on his own vomit one night. What really killed Ed?

They Were Sent to Treatment "Siberia." Many poor clients are ping-ponged around treatment systems. Not having money or insurance puts them outside the realm of the "for-profits." If they have Medicaid they stand a better chance of getting some kind of care. But many MICA clients cannot keep their paperwork up to date and end up living among the indigent homeless. They may wander from flops to shelters to hospital emergency rooms to jails to occasional hospitalization. Often due to their drinking/drugging histories, the mental health system excludes them. Similarly, the drug and alcohol programs may exclude them because they are deemed too "crazy."

Case Illustration 7: Jamie

Jamie wanders the streets, and appears lost in his schizophrenic reveries. Sometimes drinking, often taking whatever drugs he can afford or share with other street people, he drifts in and out of deep psychotic delusions and hallucinations. Social workers try to get him into psychiatric hospitals but he resists them and runs away. He tells us that he has been thrown out of some of the "best joints" in town. When he smokes crack or marijuana he becomes dangerously violent. Jamie says an emergency room nurse told him that they have a name for people like him: SPOS (pronounced "s'pōz"). He says it stands for subhuman piece of shit!

Case Illustration 8: Elvira

Elvira is subject to deep depressions. She often drinks or smokes crack to try to "feel better." Psychiatric units have provided her with decent care, but after release there are no outpatient facilities to care for her. She complicates matters by not taking her antidepressant medication on a regular basis. She tried going to AA but was told she needed to be totally drug free. She says that's why she doesn't take the medication. She wants to be drug free like the nice people she met at the meetings.

In various parts of the country one may find a more enlightened attitude at some local AA groups. There are a growing number of "double trouble" or "triple trouble" groups. These groups tend to cluster around urban centers and include AA members who also participate in psychotherapy and/or take psychotropic medications in appropriate ways. But too many groups still seek to stifle those who wish to qualify because of their drug use or their mental illness. And in some parts of the country, particularly in suburban and rural areas, it is possible to find that AA is the only service available. In these settings, "old-timers" are more likely to cling to the older traditions and rigidities.

If medicine and psychiatry (and psychology) have failed to provide for addicts and alcoholics who do not also have complicating psychological disorders, how well can one expect the MICA client to fare? Mental health practitioners often espouse negative attitudes toward substance abusers of all kinds. In 1975, Dr. Levy, while serving as director of research and evaluation at the Community Center for Mental Health, Inc. (CCMH) in Dumont, New Jersey, conducted a survey of drug and alcohol use among patients at this Northern New Jersey suburban community mental center serving a fourteen-town area. The CCMH operated a day hospital and provided outpatient mental health services. Levy (1975) found that, using strictly mental health diagnostic codes (DSM–II), the staff was reporting 1 percent admissions for alcoholics and drug abusers respectively. When staff were queried more directly concerning substance abuse and addiction, the incidence jumped to 3 percent for drug and 8 percent for alcohol abuse (which were comparable to the national rate then being reported by the National Institute for Mental Health).

More revealing in this study, however, were *staff attitudes* toward alcoholics and drug addicts. The typical, prevailing attitudes shared by many mental health personnel may be summarized as follows:

- 30% "always" or "often" avoided using alcohol or drug abuse as a primary diagnosis when doing intakes.
- 67% had "little" or "no" clinical experience with drug abusers or addicts.
- 54% had "little" or "no" clinical experience with alcohol abusers or alcoholics.
- 63% said they had no interest in having drug abusers or addicts on their case loads.

- 46% said they had no interest in having alcohol abusers or alcoholics on their case loads.
- 63% had never visited a drug abuse treatment program.
- 54% had never visited an alcoholism treatment program.
- 66% felt the CCMH did not provide adequate treatment for people with substance abuse problems.

(Adapted from Levy 1975)

The CCMH operated a day hospital program for chronic adult patients (who were primarily diagnosed as schizophrenics). This was an extremely energetic and positive program. The staff and patients got along well. However, as more young adult chronic (YAC) patients began entering the system, problems developed. Immediately perceived as different and troublemakers these clients (who ranged in age from seventeen to twenty-eight) were both overtly and subtly pushed to the periphery of day hospital activities. They, on the other hand, made fun of the older patients, some of whom had developed tardive dyskinesia, which is associated with taking phenothiazine medications. They drank, used illicit substances, and sometimes came to the center flagrantly intoxicated. Dr. Levy and a young entry-level worker began a group for these YAC folks, who complained bitterly of the prejudicial treatment they felt they received from other patients and staff. Dr. Levy perceived this as the hardest work he ever had done in the clinical arena. However, these clients were able to respond to kindness mixed with behavioral confrontation, and even developed significant insight into themselves.

Some problems to the service delivery system posed by MICA clients can be summarized as follows:

- MICAs are heavy users of services, especially crisis services.
- They typically resist continuing treatment.
- They often display disruptive behavior.
- They have frequent but brief psychiatric inpatient stays.
- They use emergency rooms on a continual crisis basis as their primary source of care.
- Their substance abuse is viewed as exacerbating and complicating their psychiatric and social needs.
- They often deny their substance abuse problem and resist abstinence messages.

(Adapted from Way and McCormick 1990)

MICA clients most often present in a crisis orientation, and repeatedly use psychiatric emergency rooms to seek short-term relief of troubling symptoms (Solomon and Gordon 1986; McCarrick et al. 1985; Wolfe and Sorensen 1989). By age twenty-nine, the typical young adult MICA client experiences at least eight psychiatric hospitalizations, and those with ongoing substance abuse problems have an annual psychiatric hospitalization rate of more than two-and-a-half times the rate of non-abusing young adult chronic psychiatric patients (Safer 1987). However, while hospitalization rates are higher for MICAs than for non-abusing psychiatric patients, their inpatient tenure is substantially shorter (Lyons and McGovern 1989).

According to the literature in many cases involving MICA clients of any age group, there are profound unmet assessment issues (Cohen 1989). No one knows how much of the presenting psychoses and other mental problems are substance-induced. Mental health clinicians often have expertise in assessment of mental illness or of substance abuse but rarely of both (Hall et al. 1977; Levy 1975). Young adult clients need *more* empathic understanding. Instead they are met with hostility and rejection. Is it any wonder that substance abusers (with and without major psychological complications) turn to one another for the understanding and compassion so dramatically lacking in the mental health field?

Contributions of the Ex-Addict

Previously addicted staff members serving young adult clients can be invaluable resources. In addition to having insights derived from direct life experiences with addiction, they have usually also gone through a treatment experience. Most importantly they stand as living examples that addictive behaviors can be stopped and a drug-free life-style can be achieved. Moreover, some of them have "hit bottom." They have lived the nightmarish consequences of addiction: jail, prison, mental hospitals, kicking drugs, violence, physical illness, loss of jobs, destruction of families, HIV infection and AIDS, and many psychic traumas, which are often perpetrated within their own families. They have an undeniable knowingness and folk wisdom. Previously addicted staff members have the ability to care passionately and deeply for people living at the edge of life. They can accept addicts or alcoholics for the very reasons that all others may reject them. And they are brave, going into communities and working in places where most of us would not even venture, due to our own fears and our own prejudices.

Ex-addicts often despise mental health professionals, whom they see as arrogant, uninformed, aloof, uncaring, and responsible for a part of the stigma that addicted people suffer in our society. Devlin (1975) states: "The professional is viewed as an intellectual giant but an emotional dwarf, who will expect to freely explore the depths of the ex-addict's psyche but who will not permit a reciprocal probe by the ex-addict of his hang-ups" (25). Ex-addicts *know* that most people fear and hate addicts. And they passionately believe that *they* are often the only ones capable of offering to other addicts the hope of positive change. Wepner (1973) provides us with some understanding of why ex-addicts can be effective helpers:

> The ex-addict knows the belief and value system of the addict, and he is conversant with the street code of addicts. The ex-addict counselor intuitively knows the reasons for using drugs such as the enjoyable effects, peer pressure, status seeking, or escape from a meaningless life style, and can understand the addict's self-reported motivations. In this respect, he does not communicate the negative attitude of those who may see addiction only as deviant, illegal, wrong, or psychopathological. . . . Since the ex-addict knows about addiction first-hand, he knows many of the cons and hustles which addicts use to manipulate others. He is able to prevent or stop these hustles. An example of this is the prevention of phony "insights" in therapy groups which can be used to gain advantages such as increased stature in the group or perhaps an early release from the treatment program. (103)

Ex-addicts have felt compelled to close themselves off from professionals, who often have punitive attitudes and fail to empathize with the plight of the addict and his/her family. They comprise a minority group, politically, but they are well attuned to the political scene. They know that in the last ten years this nation has turned its back on poor people, on racial and ethnic minorities, on women, on children, and on addicted people and the mentally ill. They, together with other keen observers, know that the so-called crack epidemic has really only affected minority older adolescents and young adults in the poorest of neighborhoods (Reinarman and Levine 1989). It is true that middle class and wealthy Americans engage in addictive behaviors but they have never been subject to an epidemic. Just as the field of mental health is divided between the "haves" and the "have-nots," so in the fields of alcoholism and drug abuse treatment there are two completely different service systems for the poor (read *no cash* and *no insurance coverage* except Medicaid) and those who have the financial means to pay for care. We will say more about this discrepancy later.

One can not overstate the problem of the stigma that the addict faces. Despite the seemingly heroic posture conveyed by the "celebrity" recovering addicts and alcoholics so common on radio and television talk shows, the average ex-addict or addict in recovery is not viewed as a hero or heroine or as an object of sympathy. Instead people tend to view addicts as behaving in ways that they think should have been avoidable. The slow but painful realization is only now creeping into the public consciousness that many addicts just do not make it to treatment or else relapse or leave treatment AMA (against medical advice).

Dr. Dan Casriel (1963), in *So Fair a House: The Story of Synanon,* summarizes the views of many professionals:

> In 1962, the *New York Herald Tribune* contained a quote relative to the treatment of the drug addict: "Put him away either in hospitals or jails for the rest of his life—or give him all the heroin he wants."
>
> *I was the author of that statement.*
>
> Ten years of contact through community psychiatry with the problem of drug addiction had left me deeply pessimistic about the rehabilitation and control, much less *cure* of the addict—an opinion shared with most of the professionals who worked in the field of drug addiction. (3)

These views, although presented almost thirty years ago, still hold strong sway in the professional community. Addicts *are* seen as chronic and incurable. The disease concept of alcoholism reinforces this view by maintaining the rigid stance that alcoholism is a chronic, lifelong, incurable condition. Even twenty years after the last drink, one still has the disease: it is simply in remission. The disease concept of addiction helps to explain outcries for the legalization of drugs like heroin and cocaine.

Dr. John Enright (1970) presents the provocative challenge that innovative counterculture programs like Synanon address to the mental health professional:

> 1. Whose ends are you serving in this program? Yours? Society's? Those of science? The client's? Naturally goals will be mixed and some will be "selfish," but it is extremely important to be clear with yourself and others.
>
> 2. Do you know, respect, and care for some members of your population *as people?* Can you set aside your professional props and get down ("relate") with them, touching their common humanity with yours? . . . If you would be acceptable as a role model, are you sufficiently available to him as a whole person, so that he (the addict) could model himself effectively after you? "You can only teach what you are." Are you satisfied with the lesson that your life will teach? (259–60)

Enright points out that the answers to these questions are not easy and it is not a purely cognitive task. Dr. Levy, who began his career in 1967 as a volunteer at Phoenix House—a drug-free therapeutic community for heroin addicts in New York—remembers clearly that in his first encounter group, the residents wanted to know why he wanted to work with them. He recalls:

> After answering how unique the program was and how intellectually stimulating and emotionally exciting the encounter group was, I finally got to my own truth. To my amazement I found myself saying simply, "I just want you guys to like me. I know I'm a *square* (non-addict) but I want to be accepted." It was a hell of an introduction to dealing with addicted clients. After all, I as the psychologist was supposed to ask the questions (and have all the power)! There was a great comfort in being "real." After all, what

> could I possibly have known about helping them back then? They were the teachers, I the student. But we shared a common humanity and a desire to learn about ourselves.

Despite cries of inadequate training, the place of former addicts or recovering alcoholics is assured by their willingness to feel for and act on behalf of the addicted individual. They have the "heart" that professionals so often lack. They have created treatment programs where none had existed, and have done so in the belief that "the heart has a mind that the brain does not comprehend." They resent efforts of mental health professionals to move in on their hard-won territory. They choose their alliances with great care, working only with those who share their mission and their zeal and who strongly reinforce their often anti-scientific and anti-professional biases. They do not read journals and books, but instead work and learn in the vineyard of the streets.

It may have already occurred to you that it is easy to slide on the "slippery slope" of the very words that one uses to describe these issues. For the record, we wish to state what we consider the logical and scientifically supported terminology to be, in regard to the term *alcohol and other drugs*. Alcohol is a hypnotic-sedative and anesthetic drug which has many psychological and physical consequences. In this sense it is like many other drugs. However, in this work we will continue to make a distinction between the fields of drug abuse treatment and alcoholism treatment. While this may represent an artificial, intellectual distinction, it does more accurately represent what has taken place and continues to take place in the real world of addiction treatment.

Problems Caused by Turf Battles

In purely practical terms the historical development of the three separate clinical and administrative worlds of alcoholism, drug abuse, and mental health has led to turf battles resulting in the following problems:

- Exclusionary criteria for acceptance of patients in each system have been implemented. These are often arbitrary and capricious and fail to account for the multifaceted nature of the MICA client. Rigid criteria regarding abstinence from alcohol and other drugs set by traditional substance abuse programs, for example, fail to recognize the need for innovative strategies and flexible criteria for engaging preabstinent clients who have major mental disorders.
- Findings of narrowly focused research projects appear in disparate literatures and have rarely filtered down to the practitioner's level. Good studies have been ignored or "trashed" because they challenge prevailing beliefs.

- Provisions are made only for short-term funding of treatment approaches. These trials lack evaluation criteria and the time necessary for the types of longitudinal studies that could yield more thorough understanding both of causality and of effective treatment
- There has been an unwillingness of what Dr. Seymour Halleck (1971) has termed the "pretorian guard of the status quo" to relinquish authority to those who hold a more holistic and comprehensive point of view. A quest for new knowledge will threaten sacred cows in all three fields, and may even suggest a more generic approach in which the fields can be merged. Issues of money and power figure largely as well.
- MICA clients have often been refused treatment because they fall outside the highly exclusionary criteria set by alcohol, drug abuse, and mental health agencies. That is: which is the *primary* substance abuse or the *primary* mental disorder? A false dichotomy between behaviors is introduced, and represents a refusal to work with the whole person.
- MICA clients have rarely been studied by researchers who are knowledgeable about the multiplicity of issues to be examined. The field needs to include more sociological, social psychological, and anthropological perspectives. There has been a tendency to overfocus on individual psychopathology and ignore important contextual issues. Currently, a biopsychosocial model is best supported by *all* available evidence in the three fields.
- The NIMBY (*not in my backyard*) phenomenon has been commonly voiced. A public attitude toward clinical facilities may be summed up: "It's O.K. to treat those alcoholics/addicts/mental patients—but not in *my* neighborhood!"
- There has been a general refusal to understand that the MICA client will often fail to follow through on therapy and treatment. Close-knit relationships must be forged between practitioners and families.
- No single agency has been willing to act as a broker for all the client's needs, despite talk about comprehensive treatment plans. Good case management models in fact tend to come primarily from the fringe of the community mental health movement and have not been embraced by mainstream mental health and addiction workers.
- State and federal regulations have not required most addiction treatment programs to maintain mental health professionals on staff. These programs prefer to use recovering addicts or ex-addicts. Despite other credentials, however, many of these people do not have formal education beyond high school and lack training in mental health issues. Community mental health centers have usually hired a specialist to handle their mandate in the substance abuse area but they have failed

to educate the rank and file clinicians who handle the bulk of the client caseload.

- Despite growing concern about MICAs, there has been no political constituency working expressly for these clients' needs. In many parts of the country, very few projects have been jointly funded by the several state agencies now dealing with MICA issues, and whose combined financial and moral support might lead to innovative solutions. The MICA issue remains a cause without effective leadership.
- There has been a failure on the part of many treatment agencies to utilize alcohol and drug surveillance. This could be accomplished by doing "stat" urines (drug toxicologies) or using breathalyzers on site. Such surveillance would help to monitor usage and explain symptom flare-ups.
- There has been a failure to cross-train staff members from the three fields. In New York State, mandates to do this type of training were created by the fields' three state agencies in 1987 and 1988, but as of 1991 have yet to be carried out.

Real World Problems

The issues of AIDS (and other immunodeficiency disorders), homelessness, and crack/cocaine are among the real world problems which have profoundly affected our society in the last several years. There is also an interplay between these issues; for example, crack/cocaine has exacerbated the homelessness problem. We will consider each briefly below.

AIDS

Here are some sobering facts about the AIDS epidemic, as it affects the country's entire population:

- In 1981 fewer than 100 people died of AIDS; by the end of 1990, approximately 160,000 in the United States have been diagnosed with AIDS and 100,000 have died. One million Americans are infected with the HIV virus. The Centers for Disease Control (CDC) estimates that by the end of 1993 there will be between 285,000 and 340,000 deaths.
- Intravenous (IV) drug users make up approximately 25 percent of all AIDS cases in the United States and this number is doubling every 14 to 16 months. Of this percentage 8 percent also have homosexual activity as another risk factor.

- The greatest concentration of AIDS IV drug use cases is in the New York metropolitan area. In New York City, almost 90 percent of the heterosexual transmission cases of AIDS involve transmission from an IV drug user to a heterosexual partner who did not inject drugs, and over 80 percent of the perinatal (mother to child) cases involve IV drug use by the mother or a sexual partner of the mother.
- Pediatric AIDS, along with child abuse and substance abuse, have replaced traditional infectious diseases as the major causes of death in poor children. The CDC estimates that in each year of the 1990s, at least 2,000 babies will be born infected with the AIDS virus.
- Nationally, the number of syphilis cases rose nearly 30 percent from 1985 to 1987 and is continuing to increase. The increase is centered in large urban areas where crack has appeared. According to Dr. Stephen Joseph, former New York City health commissioner: "The logical chain goes: crack, syphilis, HIV. There are now some very strong indications that crack and other forms of cocaine are a driving force in HIV transmission." These increases in HIV transmission and in the spread of syphilis are owing to the now more common IV injection of cocaine and to indiscriminate sex in crack houses. A study in San Francisco has shown that identifying those who inject cocaine provides better identification of persons infected with the HIV virus than does confining identification to those who inject heroin. Dr. Arnold Washton estimates that as many as 70 percent of cocaine addicts who enter treatment are dually addicted both to cocaine and to sex.
- AIDS has begun to produce a generation of orphans. In New York City, in this generation alone, experts estimate that by the year 2000, 100,000 children will lose at least one parent to AIDS. By 1990, 20,000 children have already lost one or both parents to AIDS.

The effort to combat chronic degenerative diseases has led to a reallocation of health resources. In the late 1970s only 5 percent of the federal health budget was committed to combating infectious diseases. As the AIDS epidemic worsens, however, the rise in funds needed to successfully combat the problem has failed to keep pace. Government financing of health care has been neither comprehensive nor coordinated. And as apparently runaway health care costs have soared, health care finance specialists (rate setters and managed care personnel) have become important managers of health care. This trend has prevented Americans both from caring for and paying for the care of AIDS and HIV patients. According to Dr. Michael S. Gottlieb, a physician specializing in patients with AIDS and HIV infection:

> The tragedy, of course, is that the AIDS epidemic was preventable. The war could have been won early if there had been a commitment at the highest

> levels of government. . . . It is likely that in three or four years every American will know someone who has AIDS. Maybe that is what it will take to change attitudes and make every American an AIDS activist.
>
> (*New York Times,* 5 June 1991:A29)

MICA clients are among the most vulnerable populations in terms of contracting sexually transmitted diseases (STD) and immunodeficiency disorders, including AIDS. Their mental illness, combined with their substance abuse, makes them prime candidates for IV drug use and sexual behavior that would put them at risk. They have fewer defenses and are harder to reach educationally about health risks effected by their life-style. We need to be aware that many MICAs suffer from nonpsychotic disorders (Group for the Advancement of Psychiatry 1986), and that many are young adults (aged 18–40) and sexually active. They join in their peer subculture which includes both drug use and sexual activity (Bergman and Harris 1985). Many people think of mentally ill persons as older, highly dysfunctional psychotics who do not engage in sex. This, too, is a mistaken stereotype. Mental health personnel working in psychiatric hospitals can tell many stories of older patients' efforts to engage in sexual activity. The sexual motive remains powerful, even in chronic and acute mental illness.

In many cases of AIDS, neurologic or psychiatric symptoms are the first to become evident, which further complicates the differential diagnostic picture. Research conducted by the National Institute of Mental Health (NIMH) in 1989 has shown that the HIV virus can enter the central nervous system early in the course of the disease and produce a range of nervous system impairment. Some HIV-positive individuals have memory losses, as well as a slowing in the ability to process specific types of information. NIMH investigators have also identified the specific strain of the AIDS virus in the brain which is associated with AIDS dementia complex. In addition, there is some evidence that acute and chronic alcoholism can suppress immune functions, and thus is among the important factors that predispose people to the development of AIDS (*ADAMHA* 1989).

Crack/cocaine

MICA clients are vulnerable to aggravated mental dysfunction which can be induced by injesting even small amounts of a wide variety of psychoactive substances. They suffer from what Dr. Bert Pepper (Pepper and Ryglewicz 1984) has labelled an "exquisite sensitivity" to psychoactive substances. Of all the drugs available to MICAs, crack/cocaine (often called simply crack) has no parallel in terms of exacerbating existing mental problems and of causing additional, debilitating mental states. Emergency room personnel around the country have noted that crack has replaced phencyclidine (PCP, or angel dust) as a primary precipitant of drug-induced psychoses (Wolfe and Sorenson 1989). They have also commented on the increased violence associated with the drug. Their patience has been worn thin by the "crack heads" who have begun to inundate ERs.

Crack first appeared on the streets of New York City in December 1984. It was first called "rock cocaine" on the West Coast; but because of the crackling sound made when smoked in a glass pipe, it was given the East Coast street name "crack." Cocaine, freed from its hydrochloride salt (HCl), has a lower melting point and the fumes can be inhaled. Creating "free base" cocaine once required expensive and dangerous chemicals, such as ether, which were difficult to obtain. But crack can now be made in anyone's kitchen sink or blender by mixing cocaine HCl with water and common baking soda (sodium bicarbonate). It only takes four to six seconds for the drug to reach the brain because of the greater size of the mucous membranes of the human lung, compared to the smaller nasal membranes. The duration of the high from a single dose is from three to twelve minutes. Purity may range from 40 to 85 percent, which is significantly higher than cocaine HCl (which is usually 30 to 40 percent). This greater volume of cocaine, ingested more rapidly, leads to a greater degree of dependence among its users. Cocaine IV users inject with greater frequency than heroin addicts due to the short high obtained from cocaine. They also use "speedballs"—a mixture of cocaine and heroin. All of these practices increase the possibility of HIV transmission.

Cocaine's extraordinary impact on individuals is due to its multiple neuropharmacological effects coupled with the subjective sense of personal power, omnipotence, suppression of fatigue and appetite, euphoric mood, increased self-confidence, and heightened senses of sexual power and enjoyment. Feelings such as these are often referred to as drug-induced illusions. Cocaine causes a general arousal of the central nervous system (CNS) with an accompanying increase of the neurotransmitters norepinephrine and dopamine in synaptic sites in the brain stem, the limbic system, and the cortex. Cocaine also depletes serotonin. Cocaine, in all its forms, blocks the *reuptake* of these neurotransmitters. Reuptake is a neurochemical conservation process, in which the chemicals are returned to their original sites (or vesicles).

During periods of intoxication or the ensuing *crash,* crack can cause: paranoid ideation; acute psychotic states; extreme hostility and belligerence leading to violent and volatile behavior; serious, short-term memory problems; dementia and confusion; serious sleep disruption; acute anxiety and panic attacks; and depression with suicidal ideation and behavior. Furthermore, MICA clients tend not to be in good physical health. This makes them more vulnerable to the physical effects of cocaine and the considerable biomedical risks it presents to them. Among these risks are: *cardiac complications,* including hypertension, arrythmia, angina, and coronary artery spasm—these problems have been noted in young, healthy individuals as well as in older, debilitated patients; *central nervous system complications,* which can include cerebrovascular accidents and seizures possibly resulting in death; *pulmonary problems,* which include emphysema and pneumonia, edema and respiratory failure; *nasal problems,* which include nasal irritation, rhinitis, sores, infections, ulcers, and perforation of the septum. In addition to these risks, the use of cocaine can complicate *preexisting medical problems,* such as heart disease, hypertension, seizure disorders, circulatory problems, and liver dysfunction; in women cocaine interferes with the menstrual cycle, and can cause *obstetrical complications,* pre- and post-natal complications, and fetal damage, as well as developmental problems in the child; and problems brought on by sexual marathons and "freak shows" have led to a rise in *syphilis* and other sexually transmitted diseases or STDs.

One can readily see how and why crack can have such a devastating effect on those who have a tendency toward psychotic disorders, affective disorders, or the severe personality disorders that characterize MICA clients. Both authors have worked with clients who, although having no histories of *axis one* mental disorders (as defined in *DSM–IIIR*), became psychotic after repeated cocaine ingestion (particularly by smoking the drug). Our experience closely mirrors the clinical reports by McLellan and his associates (1979). Most had acute episodes and returned to premorbid mental states. Others developed chronic mental health problems, most of these resembling paranoid and schizophrenic conditions.

Because crack smoking can cause serious mental disruptions, involves criminality, tends to exhaust a person's financial resources, and tries the patience of one's family and friends, crack has uniquely contributed to the growing problem of homelessness, of both MICA and non-MICA drug addicts. In many instances, the rent does not get paid, money and other property are stolen, and landlords and relatives react by evicting tenants/relatives.

Cocaine, particularly when smoked, is an incredibly powerful substance, which produces both reinforcing and debilitating effects. Users tend to try to boost, balance, counteract, or sustain the effects of other drugs with the sedative drug, alcohol, as noted by Carroll et al. (1977:296). In fact, these researchers' review conservatively estimated that 80 percent of the heroin addict population had self-reported problems related to drinking *prior to using heroin.* Barr and Cohen (1979:44) reported that problem drinking heroin addicts were "more deeply disturbed, and their disturbance can be traced to the earlier periods of life." In addition, heavy drinking and problem drinking, both before and after admission to treatment for opioid drug abuse, were found to be associated with poorer treatment outcomes.

Similar patterns have been reported for alcoholics who abuse cocaine and for cocaine addicts who abuse a variety of substances. In the Rockland County crack/cocaine program (an outpatient treatment program in New

York State), over a three-year period, alcohol, marijuana, and Valium were the drugs most frequently associated with cocaine abuse (Levy and Doering 1990). Crack smokers also use barbiturates, benzodiazepines (particularly Valium/Librium), and heroin (in any manner—smoking it, snorting it, or injecting it) to try to prevent or counteract the "crashing" associated with high volume cocaine usage. We have interviewed MICAs who have used psychotropic medications such as MAO inhibitors, tricyclic antidepressants, and phenothiazines in an attempt to smooth out the effects of cocaine and cocaine crashing. These are not "garbage heads"—that is, people who indiscriminately use whatever mood-altering substance is available. They are following a pattern of sequential drug taking: drug elation followed by drug sedation. Sometimes the pattern involves the simultaneous use of both substances (Gardner 1980; Levy 1982). Both of these patterns of multiple substance abuse—simultaneous or sequential—have been found to be associated with elevated levels of poor physical and mental health.

Homelessness

MICA clients are overrepresented among the homeless. There are sixty thousand homeless people in New York City alone. Experts estimate that between 25 percent and 40 percent of these homeless people have psychiatric problems that require frequent hospital care (*New York Times,* 28 Feb. 1991). As affordable housing in the inner city and surrounding suburbs diminishes, many MICAs, dependent upon public assistance, are priced out of the housing market. Their sometimes aberrant behavior makes them unattractive to motel and hotel owners and other residents. They may spend their available funds on alcohol and other drugs and be unable to pay their rent. This contributes to their reality as a transient population and makes them even harder to engage in treatment. Furthermore, many alcohol, drug abuse, and mental health agencies consistently have full-bed occupancy and MICAs can not hope to enter them. Instead, they drift into homelessness and deeper despair and pathology. Even state mental hospitals will often not accept them back unless they demonstrate clear indications of harming themselves or others.

Clearly, options for shelter are becoming more limited. In addition, clinicians in all mental health settings have become concerned about writs of habeas corpus ("show cause" release orders) and malpractice suits, from clients to whom they have provided shelter. Partly as a result of this concern, it can be noted that, for example, the number of psychiatric inpatients in 1961 in New York State was 90,000, whereas in 1991 the number has decreased to 15,559. As budget pressures in the state result in more hospital closings, it thus becomes imperative to understand the relationship between mental illness, substance abuse, re-hospitalization, and homelessness. Yet another part of the problem in New York State was described in the following editorial:

> *Money that once supported patients in hospitals was supposed to follow them to support their treatment in the communities where they settled after their release. It didn't. Tens of thousands came to New York City, where the evaporation of cheap housing eventually forced them into the streets.*
>
> (*New York Times,* 1 Jan. 1991; emphasis added)

In 1989 the National Institute of Mental Health (NIMH) established the Office of Programs for the Homeless Mentally Ill. Ten studies of the homeless mentally ill had been undertaken by the NIMH between 1982 and 1986. Sargent (1989) summarized the findings as follows:

- Approximately one-third of the homeless population suffer from severe mental illnesses, such as schizophrenia, manic-depression, or severe depression.
- Between 35 and 40 percent of homeless mentally ill individuals *also have an alcohol or other substance abuse problem.*
- A sizable number have had some involvement with the criminal justice systems, more often due to homelessness than to antisocial or criminal behaviors.
- Roughly three-fourths of the homeless population have never received mental health treatment, and many who were formerly in treatment are no longer disabled by mental illness.
- A significant proportion are interested in receiving help, but their perception of needs differs from that of service providers. The first priority of mentally ill homeless individuals is to have their basic subsistence needs met, while service providers tend to make mental health treatment a top priority.

A further analysis of the data from the same studies also revealed:

- The majority of the homeless and the homeless mentally ill populations are male, although women are overrepresented among the mentally ill subgroup.
- Across all studies the median age of the homeless mentally ill ranges from twenty-nine to thirty-eight years old.
- Blacks and Hispanics are overrepresented among the homeless.
- Only 40 to 50 percent of homeless people have graduated from high school, and most are underemployed.

- Only one-third receive public benefits such as Social Security, although many more are eligible.
- The five studies that investigated veteran status found that 18 to 51 percent of the homeless were veterans of the armed services.
- Homeless people in the Midwest and West are more mobile than those in the Northeast, who tend to remain in one place.
- Most homeless people have poor medical health, and most face threats to themselves and their belongings.
- Housing and case management are priority needs of homeless mentally ill persons.

(Adapted from Sargent 1989)

It should be pointed out, however, that most people working with the homeless to whom the authors have spoken assess the alcohol and other drug problems among the homeless mentally ill as much higher than the 35 to 40 percent figure noted by the NIMH. Estimates vary widely but cluster around 50 to 60 percent. In addition, many of the homeless MICAs are considered *chronically* mentally ill. This has serious implications, according to a number of research findings. For example, Drake and Wallach (1989) studied a group of 187 chronically mentally ill patients living in the community. They note, according to ratings by aftercare clinicians, that about one-third abused alcohol or street drugs or both in the six months prior to evaluation; and those who were "dually diagnosed" with substance abuse and mental illness differed from those suffering only from mental illness. Among the characteristic differences of the dually diagnosed were the following:

- They often were younger and more often male.
- They were less able to manage their lives in the community in terms of eating regularly, having adequate finances, stable housing, and regular activities.
- They often exhibited greater hostility, suicidal tendencies, and speech disorganization, and had poorer medication compliance.
- They were twice as likely to be re-hospitalized during their one year follow-up. (1043)

Drake and Wallach conclude that "substance abuse appeared to add to the problems of disruptive, disinhibited, and noncompliant behaviors to chronic mental illness" (1045). Mental health practitioners clearly link substance use with increased severity of mental dysfunction. And Pepper (1985) has found that substance use not only exacerbates mental illness but may confound underlying psychiatric issues as well by "masking, complicating, or mimicking psychiatric illness."

A study of the state of care provided to the mentally ill was released in 1990 by the Public Citizen Health Research Group and the National Alliance for the Mentally Ill. The two groups had questioned mental health officials and patients' families and had examined health agencies' records in each of the fifty states. As reported by the *New York Times* (1990), the following findings appeared in their report:

- Not since the 1820s have so many mentally ill individuals lived untreated in public shelters, on the streets, and in jail.
- More than 250,000 people have schizophrenia or manic-depressive illness but only 68,000 of them are in mental hospitals.
- Of this group, 100,000 are estimated to be incarcerated. In, for example, the Los Angeles County Jail, the largest in the country, there are 3,600 inmates who are seriously mentally ill. This is 700 more people than are in the nation's largest hospital. The study termed the Los Angeles County Jail the largest "de facto mental hospital" in the United States.
- Waiting lists may be as long as six months, such as at South Florida State Hospital; and in Boston, the Pine Street Inn, a shelter for street people, houses 500 mentally ill people per night (which makes it Massachusetts' largest mental institution).
- From 1955 to 1984 the number of patients in mental hospitals declined from 552,000 to 119,000. The study pronounced deinstitutionalization a "disaster" and describes a "near total breakdown in public psychiatric services in the United States."

One has to wonder, how much does homelessness contribute to mental illness and drug taking? Homeless people live in a world of despair barely comprehensible to most of us. When one can not find affordable housing, a job, and other staples for living, who is "ill": the unstable individual or the society that permits these conditions? Answers must be found to help rectify this situation in which the homeless, mentally ill chemical abuser daily suffers.

In this brief review of real world problems, it becomes quite apparent how many issues overlap and affect the MICA population. Substance issues, psychological issues, and real life issues interact in myriad ways, although few details about these interactions are clearly delineated and understood. Available frames of reference all have failed to capture the essence of the MICA problem. Extremely complicated issues confront all those who try to help MICA clients; there is no single or simplistic model of care.

Two case illustrations are provided below to demonstrate the complexities of issues involved in caring for the MICA. Both clients were treated by Jackie Cohen at a continuing mental health program in New York City. A *continuing treatment program* is an informal day treatment model where clients may interact and recreate in a variety of group settings.

Case Illustration 9: Mary

Mary, now age twenty, had been a resident of Covenant House (a program for runaways and street kids) but at eighteen had "aged out." She now shares an apartment with another woman. The apartment has been provided by the continuing care treatment program where she has been a member since age eighteen. She was one of the youngest members of the program. This treatment program is a highly regarded continuing care mental health program, and has day and evening program components. It provides a low stress environment. Clients usually have had lengthy histories of schizophrenic disturbance and have not been expected to work or function normally in society.

Mary is a black woman who is tall, lanky, energetic, and personable. She was well liked by the staff and other clients who found her to be both witty and friendly. She is a great dancer and a talented cartoonist. She could often be found drawing in the dayroom while other clients rocked themselves or did whatever else was soothing to them. Mary identified herself as gay.

Her family history includes a heroin-abusing mother, who was also alcoholic. She was raised mostly by her grandmother. She remembers her mother trying to care for her and her four significantly younger siblings. Invariably she and the other children returned to live with her grandmother. She recalls being a very young child and living with her grandmother. She also recalls living in a residence with her mother (Odyssey House's MABON facility for addicted women and their children in New York City) and once falling out of bed and getting a lot of attention from the staff. She was five years old at the time.

Mary's relationship with her mother has been deeply troubled. Her mother's current boyfriend had tried to abuse her sexually. When Mary told her mother about this, the child was not believed. Both the mother and the boyfriend drank heavily and would engage in physical assaults upon one another. In tears, Mary recalled how she would physically place herself between them in an effort to break up the fights. She hated seeing her mother getting hit.

Mary's diagnosis of record was borderline personality disorder. She exhibited no thought disorder or hallucinations. Her capacity for insight was good and she is quite intelligent. She was able to maintain a therapeutic relationship with her therapist, Jackie Cohen. She did exhibit tremendous mood swings and would become quite angry at times. At other times she exhibited depressed behavior, seemed unmotivated, and would miss the program. She had short-lived sexual relationships with other women.

Given her history, it was surprising to see her ability to maintain relationships with the staff and other clients. She was able to have fun in a healthy way, though sometimes to the point of appearing to have regressed into a very childlike state. She would play basketball, baseball, and often dance around the dayroom. It appeared as if Mary were trying to make up for the fun she did not have as a child. It was remarkable to see her striving for intimacy and safety. She demonstrated an innate strength of will to survive. She exhibited no fear of the sicker clients (many of whom are schizophrenic) and enjoyed being around them.

Several of the clients were using street drugs. The staff was not trained in substance abuse issues and did not routinely assess clients for drug usage. They were not aware of other clients who were getting high, and were able to discern Mary's use of crack/cocaine only because she confided in them. This occurred at a time when the media were concentrating heavily on the "instantly addictive" qualities of crack. Although little about such effects of crack use was known scientifically, the media were "hyping" the problem. As a result, clients' use of the drug aroused great consternation in staff members, who were trained to focus only on mental health issues.

When confronted by her therapist, Mary admitted to using crack several times a week. She was certainly not addicted. The apartment provided to her by the treatment program was on 115th Street, and drugs were sold openly in her building and on the street. She spoke of drug dealing and middle-of-the-night gunfights. To expect her to live drug-free in this milieu was highly unrealistic.

When clients' use of crack cocaine was reported to the agency's governing board, they reacted strongly. The board members, in concert with the agency director, moved to remove Mary and another client from both their apartments and the clinical program. They feared that "crack-crazed" clients would intimidate and steal from the more vulnerable schizophrenics. This was the first time that the board had recommended such an intervention. Both clients were indeed asked to leave the program. This in effect is a clear example of how unscientific media reports may influence naive but otherwise deeply caring professionals toward taking unwise action.

After several meetings in which Mary's case was reviewed the clients were invited into the program, with the realization that there had been a failure to properly serve the clients' multiple needs. For one of them, it was too late. She had begun to use crack on a regular basis and was unmotivated for treatment. Crack smoking had exacerbated her psychosis: and this had been in fact the real reason for her original dismissal from the program. Mary did not become addicted. She was readmitted to the program and allowed to return to her apartment. She began to address her drug usage, and entered weekly therapy with another therapist and saw Jackie Cohen only for informal contacts.

When Jackie Cohen was preparing to leave the agency to take a position elsewhere, Mary came to her and told her she once again feared being asked to withdraw from the program. She was getting high and experiencing great personal difficulties. She felt that the rest of the staff did not understand her and did not want to help her. The only person with whom she had felt safe and comfortable talking about her drug usage had been Jackie. Mary knew no one else could or would help her with her drug problem and she knew it was Jackie who had gotten her reinstated in the program. All of her fears of abandonment were confirmed.

Working with Mary had been a bitter learning experience for Jackie. Below she summarizes her impressions of the effects of the treatment agency's policy, staff attitudes, and the clinical dynamics involved in Mary's case.

Agency Policy. The agency's professionals were not prepared for drug use and abuse by clients and were untrained in assessing and treating such behavior. Most importantly, they simply did not understand the powerful connections between drug usage and psychopathology. Instead of learning the correct assessment and treatment tools, they developed a simplistic policy of rejecting or terminating drug-abusing clients. They had taken the media accounts to heart and felt a genuine threat to the integrity of their clinical program for mentally ill clients. They were unwilling to adopt objective and clear policies that reflected a true understanding of the problems indigenous to their own surrounding community, which included the growing drug culture.

Staff Attitudes. Staff responded very differently to higher functioning clients with personality disorders than they did to lower functioning patients with psychoses. Substance usage by borderline personalities is quite common (it actually appears as one of the diagnostic criteria in the DSM-IIIR) and should not have been ignored. Although the "acting out" of seriously disturbed patients was not treated punitively, in Mary's case it was. It seems that Mary was too healthy and bright, capable of anger and questioning authority. Borderlines ask questions and demand answers. They have higher cognitive functioning, want to problem solve, and be actively involved in making decisions. They are far less compliant and malleable than the chronic schizophrenics the agency was used to dealing with. As a result, persons like Mary are punished rather than treated, rejected instead of understood.

Staff members are far more comfortable relating to and controlling the behavior of patients with psychosis. The routine of a mental health program like this is more like babysitting a group of chronic and docile patients. Working with a client like Mary is more dynamic, difficult, and frustrating. Street-wise clients who have unmet dependency needs present a real challenge for any staff person but more so to one who is unschooled in working with them. The staff was also unaccepting of the reality of young blacks getting high as part of a peer street culture. A more energetic approach to all clients would have required a major change in the ethos of this program.

Clinical Dynamics. Borderlines are hard to work with but caring, empathy, and consistency, combined with limit-setting, can work. Given Mary's sad history, it is easy to suggest why crack was used—she sought to escape, through self-medication, the painful affects associated with sexual abuse, abandonment, and unsettled issues of sexual identity. Mary was a huge vacuum of unmet needs—she demanded a great deal of staff time (more than they were prepared to give or felt comfortable giving). By dismissing her from the program, the staff reinforced all the painful feelings Mary associated with being "ping-ponged" back and forth between her mother and grandmother. It was important not to lie to Mary since her reality testing was healthy. Therefore, at their last meeting, she had to be told that she had assessed correctly the program staff's outright refusal to work with her drug and other problems as the motivation for dismissing her from the program.

Mary's case is not one of a resistant client who heavily abuses drugs. Her drug use was not great enough to place her in a therapeutic community (yet she needed a domicile). She had a self-medicating depression that was not appropriately treated. Instead this is an example of an agency whose orientation, assessment skills, and clinical resources were just not equal to the task of helping clients like Mary. She might have fared better in an outpatient drug counseling program but such a facility could not have helped her with her housing problem. This is a frank example of serious, pragmatic service gaps in many modalities of care. Jackie concludes:

> There were too many gaps in services and too much lack of knowledge on the part of staff. This was a client who wanted and needed help and who could have responded well to it. This was hard to watch and hard to

experience. My own frustration was in knowing that Mary could have had a better life experience with diminished psychic pain and sorrow. If only we could have helped her differently—a human being was not being helped when we should and do know better.

Case Illustration 10: Willie

Willie is a black man in his late forties. When Jackie Cohen met him he had already been participating at a continuing mental treatment program for several years. He lived alone, being able to maintain an apartment in a housing project in Harlem, New York, where he had grown up and spent his life. Willie had been a professional boxer in his youth and had sustained many blows to the head, which may have contributed to his mental disturbance. He was diagnosed as a chronic paranoid schizophrenic. He was known to have an addiction history. Several times each day he would walk into Jackie's office and remind her that he had been enrolled in a methadone maintenance program in the past. It was almost impossible to get a full addiction or any other kind of history from Willie owing to his severe thought disorder.

At about the time that Willie began his daily announcements about having been in a methadone program, his behavior began to deteriorate. Naturally, Jackie wondered about the meaning of this communication. Willie was being maintained on a high dose of Thorazine. He now had begun yelling hostile and abusive statements at other clients. When asked to explain his behavior, Willie stated that he was having trouble hearing. This was found to be true and a hearing aid was secured. However, the nastiness persisted, particularly in group therapy sessions. Jackie expelled him from the group on several occasions in an effort to get him to control his behavior.

At the same time Willie began to state that he needed more medication. Medication management is a standard issue in mental health settings which serve clients like Willie. Staff members want all clients to be in compliance with their medication regimes as defined by their treatment plans. In fact, in order for their symptoms to remain in remission many do need to be medicated. It is properly feared that if clients do not take their medications as prescribed, their psychoses could *flare up* and they could become destabilized. Therefore, it is widely accepted that no clients should ever be without their medications and, if more is required, then it should be given. But when Willie was given more Thorazine he would continue to request even more.

Something about Willie's case had begun to disturb Jackie—it had an all-too-familiar ring of drug abuse. His hostile behavior toward other clients and previously undetailed addiction history made current drug problems (with his prescribed medication) a real possibility. Most clients complain bitterly about taking Thorazine: It was hard to picture a client actually wanting more Thorazine than was clinically necessary. Nevertheless, at about that time it was discovered that Willie was "borrowing" Thorazine from other clients in the program. Willie had indeed transferred his former heroin-abusing behavior patterns to abuse of antipsychotic medications: in effect, Willie was now a Thorazine junkie! The reasons remain unclear at this point.

Clients were barred from the program only if they became violent, not for other forms of rule breaking. Willie's hostility and disruptive behavior continued to escalate. Jackie barred him from the program over a weekend in an effort to help him understand limit setting and to protect the other patients who were now overtly afraid of him. She knew that he liked coming to the program and would shape his behavior accordingly. Her supervisor was suspicious of this type of intervention, however, and feared for Willie's well-being on the streets. Nevertheless, Willie did just fine: he kept himself out of trouble and was far less abusive to the other clients upon his return.

Soon afterwards, however, calls began to come into the program from the psychiatric emergency room at Bellevue Hospital reporting that Willie had come there several times demanding more medication. Later, the program was notified that Willie had really *gone off* and had had to be confined at the hospital in four-point restraints. Jackie went to visit Willie and met with the primary care psychiatrist for the first time. Willie was known to this physician, who had been following him for several years. Willie steadfastly refused to admit that he was taking too much medication. Jackie persisted in confronting him with this behavior, believing that she might get through to him if he saw that she understood his problems. She informed the psychiatrist that she believed that Willie was seriously abusing his medication—periodically taking too much and at other times going into a precipitous withdrawal experience. She stated that his manipulative behavior around the Thorazine was characteristic of drug addicts. In addition, she informed him of Willie's taking medications from other clients prior to his coming to the emergency room at Bellevue asking for even more medication, and of his disruptive and hostile behavior.

Nevertheless, the doctor told her point blank that she was wrong. Willie, he insisted, did not have a substance abuse problem. Willie's psychosis was growing worse, probably as a function of his age; his medication simply was not "holding him." He also stated that he could not give Willie any more Thorazine since he was already at the maximum dosage level. As protocol dictates, the doctor's opinion should not be questioned. Jackie's opinions and recommendations were rejected out-of-hand by the doctor.

It was later learned and verified, however, that Willie had been buying Valium in the street. He had destabilized the therapeutic benefits of his medication both by taking extra doses and also ingesting Valium. Jackie's instincts had proven correct. Willie was indeed still a drug addict. Clearly, the accepted modes of caring for the mentally ill had fallen short of addressing the needs of the MICA patient. The effects of the treatment agency's policy, staff attitudes, and the clinical dynamics involved in Willie's case are reviewed below.

Agency Policy. That the agency viewed all behavior with the exception of violence as tolerable at first appears to be a humane policy. Clients cannot be expected to rise to the height of their own healthier capacities, however, if they do not have to comply with the rules of civility. Psychiatric disabilities occur over a range of human functioning and many clients have real strengths they can evince, as long as the staff works to bring these out. To permit a drug-abusing client to operate without limit setting simply provides the impetus for further acting out and limit testing.

Staff Attitudes: There was no critical thought applied to the truism "The doctor is always right!" Nevertheless, most clinicians know that the best clinical work usually results from a team approach, which values the input and insights of all staff. In this case the doctor seemed to describe Willie's psychosis as having a life of its own, somehow completely detached from any of his own willful acts. The staff held stereotyped beliefs about mentally ill clients which did not allow for the fact that Willie was readily able to live on his own, negotiate the streets, buy and use illicit drugs, and in a number of ways exhibit genuine street savvy: they saw poor Willie as too crazy to carry out this type of life-style. He was viewed as too disturbed and vulnerable to being ripped off. The staff's shortsightedness resulted from a lack of relevant training in caring for the MICA patient, and an adherence only to theories of psychopathology. It also reflects the dangers of a middle-class orientation being applied to a poor, inner-city minority population.

Clinical Dynamics. Obtaining a clear addiction history is essential for assessing cases like Willie's. Without one, Jackie had to wonder whether his talk of past involvement with a methadone program was some sort of ploy or a real cry for help. Urine analysis would have helped to establish Willie's actual pattern of drug taking. Addicts have a great deal of trouble managing anger and rage: this largely accounts for the fury regularly displayed at therapeutic community (TC) encounter groups and the relative success of methadone as a sedating medication. There was something about Valium that Willie liked. Perhaps it helped control his anger better than the Thorazine. However, in the absence of good, controlled studies it is difficult to understand the psychopharmacological effects: the interactive and/or synergistic effects of combining Thorazine and Valium are not known. Jackie concludes:

> The doctor was completely devoted to a medical model of psychosis. He could not integrate a substance abuse client assessment into his treatment rationale. The idea of a Thorazine junkie was new to both of us. Our different training and orientation made it almost impossible for us to communicate. The field of mental health does not yet seem ready for this type of integration. In addition, the staff at the treatment program could not see what they were not willing to see—their orientation, like that of the psychiatrist, was overly focused on a view of mental illness which must be completely separated from substance abuse and a street life-style.

2
History and Systems

A Brief History of the Three Fields—Mental Health, Alcoholism, and Drug Abuse

Horatio. O day and night, but this is wondrous strange!
Hamlet. And therefore, as a stranger give it welcome./ There are more things in heaven and earth, Horatio,/ Than are dreamt of in your philosophy.

—Shakespeare

The Mental Health Treatment Movement

According to Alexander and Selesnick (1966), in their informative text, *The History of Psychiatry: An Evaluation of Psychiatric Thought and Practice from Prehistoric Times to the Present,* there are three basic trends in psychiatric thought that can be traced to earliest times. They are: (1) the attempt to explain diseases of the mind in physical terms—known as the organic approach; (2) the attempt to find a psychological explanation for mental disturbances; and (3) the attempt to deal with inexplicable events through magic. For the reader interested in a detailed review of how these trends developed from ancient times to the modern era we suggest their book. Wender and Klein (1981) provide a briefer review, beginning with the end of the nineteenth century, in *Mood, Mind and Medicine: A Guide to the New Biopsychiatry.* For those interested in a review of the history and systems of psychology, we suggest Rieber and Salzinger (1980), *Psychology: Theoretical and Historical Perspectives,* and Smith (1983), *Ideas of the Great Psychologists.* Torrey (1988) provides, in *Nowhere to Go,* a searing review of the results of deinstitutionalization.

An overview of the development of the mental health movement in the United States is presented below. From this account one realizes that in mental health, as in many other fields, a great deal has transpired in a relatively short period.

Chronology of the Mental Health Movement in the United States

1693: The prominent Puritan clergyman Cotton Mather publishes *Wonders of the Invisible World,* in which he describes how the mentally ill are possessed by Satan and are his "evil agents." This possession is viewed as a punishment for an individual's immorality and justifies the insane person's being ridiculed and punished in public whippings and beatings.

1753: With Benjamin Franklin as one of its prime sponsors, the Pennsylvania Hospital begins to admit mental patients, placing them in basement cells.

1792: Phillipe Pinel unchains and unshackles inmates in an asylum in Paris, and treats them with kindness. They have previously been treated inhumanely, no better than unwanted animals. In 1806 he will publish *A Treatise on Insanity* in which he expresses the humanistic ideals of the Enlightenment.

At about the same time in Northern England, a Quaker named William Tuke, believing that the most beneficial therapeutic environment for the mentally ill would be a quiet and supportive religious setting, founds York Retreat. There patients talk out their problems, work, pray, rest, and go for country walks. From York Retreat the first high recovery rate is reported. Tuke's approach will become known as "moral therapy." It views mentally ill people as ordinary people with extraordinary problems and seeks to boost their morale.

1812: Benjamin Rush, a physician, publishes the first American psychiatric textbook, entitled *Medical Inquiries and Observations upon Diseases of the Mind.* Like Pinel, Rush advocates humane treatment of the disturbed, and uses leeches and ice packs as treatment. Rush will later be referred to as the Father of American Psychiatry.

1833: The State Lunatic Hospital opens in Worcester, Massachusetts, becoming the first public institution devoted to the therapeutic treatment of the insane. It will make unsubstantiated claims of an 80 percent cure rate. The optimism of this era will never be repeated.

1834: An Ohio court establishes the "irresistible impulse" ruling. Defendants are acquitted if, as a result of mental illness, it is judged they could not resist the impulse to do wrong. This is the first "insanity defense."

1843: Some states and courts prefer to use the "M'Naughten rule" handed down by an English court. Defendants are ruled legally insane if, as a result of a "disease of the mind" and consequent impairment of reason, they either (1) did not know what they were doing, or (2) did not know that what they were doing was wrong.

1844: The American Association of Medical Superintendents (later the American Psychiatric Association) is founded, marking the beginning of a powerful sociopolitical movement in mental health.

1848: Social reformer Dorothea Dix submits a petition to Congress describing how she has observed over ten thousand mentally ill and retarded people being maltreated in this country. Dix will be instrumental in the founding and funding of thirty-two public mental hospitals. These hospitals are understaffed from their inception, however, and owing to the staffs' lack of training, the 70 percent recovery rate anticipated from moral therapy declines along with the practice of moral therapy itself. A leadership vacuum also develops. Reformers like Pinel, Tuke, and Dix are in short supply.

1879: In Germany, Wilhelm Wundt establishes the first laboratory for the scientific study of psychology. This marks the beginning of modern psychology. One of Wundt's students, Emil Kraepelin, performs some of the first investigations into psychopathology, and furnishes the first comprehensive classification system in his *Textbook of Psychiatry,* published in 1883. All later classification schema would be strongly influenced by this taxonomy, including the *Diagnostic and Statistical Manual of Mental Disorders* (*DSM*) of the American Psychiatric Association, developed in 1952.

1880: There are seventy-five public mental hospitals in the United States, treating 36,780 patients.

The National Association for the Protection of the Insane and the Prevention of Insanity (NAPIPI) is founded by those interested in preventing insanity. The organization will disband four years later owing to disagreements between the neurologists and social workers who were among its leaders, but the idea of prevention of mental illness has been publicly promoted for the first time.

1887: Pliny Earle, superintendent of Northampton State Hospital in Massachusetts, publishes his statistical study *The Curability of Insanity,* which refutes the exaggerated claims of cures by pre–Civil War era asylum superintendents. He is the first to document the decrease in the number of recoveries (which sometimes had been falsely claimed) and the increase in the number of chronic cases.

1892: The American Psychological Association (APA) is founded. The two most influential groups within APA are those committed to basic research (and teaching) and those involved in delivering services (clinical psychology). This alliance becomes a powerful sociopolitical force in mental health and remains an uneasy one right up to modern times.

1896: Sigmund Freud first uses the term *psychoanalysis* and begins a true revolution in attempts to understand and treat mental disorders. Perhaps Freud's most profound contribution is not that he founded a new school of therapy but that so many lay people will be influenced by his ideas and use them in everyday language. His views will come to hold positions of great power in American psychiatric circles (and in clinical psychology and social work as well). This, despite the fact that his basic ideas regarding id, ego, and superego remain unproven. It is only in the last ten years or so that the zeitgeist has shifted away from the psychoanalytic point of view. Many schools of psychodynamically oriented psychotherapy will emanate from Freud's original psychoanalytic model, which emphasizes individual psychology and instinctual drives, primarily sexual and aggressive in nature. Freud, however, strongly repudiates those who disagree with him (such as Carl Jung and Alfred Adler).

1900: Psychologists William James and G. Stanley Hall, two of the leaders of the now well-established field of psychology, espouse a philosophy supporting the malleability of human personality. This is in direct opposition to theories of social Darwinism. James and Hall are interested in psychopathology; they also advocate progressive asylum care and work to promote psychology in the treatment and prevention of mental disorder.

1904: Ivan Pavlov receives the Nobel Prize for his work in classical conditioning behavior, which, coupled with operant conditioning, forms the basis of understanding how people learn. From Pavlov's original work will spring the school of behaviorism and the cognitive-behavioral models of change.

1907: The influential psychiatrist, Dr. Adolf Meyer, introduces psychoanalytic theory and technique into the New York State mental hospital system.

1908: Clifford Beers's book *A Mind That Found Itself* describes his recovery from a mental breakdown in a way that will lead to increased public support for the treatment of mental illness and the founding of the National Committee for Mental Hygiene in New York City.

1909: Sigmund Freud delivers a series of lectures at Clark University in Worcester, Massachusetts. William James tells him, "The future of psychology belongs to your work." (Freud's work had never been greeted with such enthusiasm in Europe.)

The National Committee for Mental Hygiene is founded, its goal being "to act as a clearinghouse for the nation on the subject of mental health, the prevention of nervous and mental disorders, and the care and treatment of the insane."

1923: The number of inpatients in mental hospitals has risen to 255,245.

1931: The number of inpatients in mental hospitals has risen to 318,821.

The first American psychoanalytic institute is founded in New York. Although psychoanalysis does not involve the practice of medicine, physicians (primarily psychiatrists) try to claim that only they can practice this form of therapy. Thus, the stage is set for a continuing dispute between psychiatry and non-medical psychotherapists. The disputes sometimes erupt into public view and one can only wonder at the psychiatric name-calling that goes on.

1935: In Portugal, the neurologist Antonio de Egas develops the first effective techniques in psychosurgery. Of all the techniques developed in psychiatry, the lobotomy evokes the most fear and misunderstanding. It is usually employed only when all other medical efforts have failed, and is rarely the treatment of first choice. However, lobotomies remain popular until the 1950s, when psychotropic medication will become widely employed.

1938: In Italy, clinicians Ugo Cerletti and Lucio Bini develop the first effective electroshock therapy (now called electroconvulsive therapy or ECT). Shrouded in fear and mystery, this technique is feared by the public. In modern times, the addition of sedatives and anticonvulsive drugs have made this a more humane form of treatment for serious depression. The use of antidepressive medication in the 1960s will greatly reduce the use of ECT.

1943: The number of inpatients in mental hospitals has risen to over 450,000.

A group of conscientious objectors, working with the mentally ill, "go public" in the *Cleveland Press* regarding the dismal state and inhumane treatment of mental patients in the Cleveland State Hospital. More than two thousand such reports are compiled by a national network of conscientious objectors, who issue reports through the National Mental Health Foundation.

1946: Major General Lewis Hershey, director of the Selective Service system, testifies before both houses of Congress on the rejection of men for military service. Mental illness accounts for 18 percent of the rejections (856,000 our of 4,800,000); mental deficiency for 14 percent (676,000); and neurological diseases for 5 percent (235,000). Thus, some 38 percent of the otherwise qualified men have been rejected due to "mental disease."

The National Mental Health act of 1946 (Public Law 79–487) is passed. The passing of the act provides the impetus for the shift from hospital-based to community-based care (a decision that will be followed by subsequent laws). The same year, President Truman signs the act into law and creates the National Institute of Mental Health (NIMH). Three divisions are established within the institute: research, training, and service assistance to the states. Funds are not actually made available until 1948.

1947: A shortage of psychiatrists and psychologists in the Armed Forces results in practitioners' experimenting more with group therapy approaches. At about the same time the National Training Laboratories (NTL) develop the "T" (training) group. Doctors working with tuberculosis patients in Boston also experiment with group approaches.

1949: Lithium is introduced. It is used to treat those who suffer from mania or from bipolar (manic-depressive) disorders. Doses are highly individualized. With careful monitoring of blood levels and thyroid functions, it is demonstrated that Lithium can be taken over extended periods.

1952: The first edition of the *Diagnostic and Statistical Manual of Mental Disorders* (*DSM*) is published by the American Psychiatric Association. The manual provides the first glossary of descriptions in diagnostic categories. It owes its origins to the work of Emil Kraepelin.

In his challenging book *The Effects of Psychotherapy,* Hans Eysenck reviews seven thousand therapy cases in the literature, and concludes that the data fail to prove that any form of psychotherapy has facilitated recovery in patients with abnormal behavior. He maintains that therapy "works" because it takes so long: in effect, enough time elapses for remission to occur spontaneously. His work creates quite a stir. It helps to promote a more careful review of psychotherapy and a search for objective measures of therapy outcomes.

Chlorpromazine is introduced. It is the first of a long series of phenothiazines, which were originally referred to as major tranquilizers or neuroleptics; however, they are most accurately known as antipsychotic medications. The drugs become widely used in the treatment of schizophrenia, and represent a major impetus for deinstitutionalization. Unfortunately, when taken on a chronic basis, these drugs can produce a neurological disorder called tardive dyskinesia, which involves involuntary movements of the tongue, cheeks, mouth, and lips. Patients taken off the medication often slip back into psychosis. The drug therefore poses a difficult problem for doctor and patient alike.

1954: Dr. Nathan Kline publishes a major paper describing the success of the drug reserpine (Rauwolfia) in the treatment of schizophrenia. The research institute on mental disorders in Rockland County, New York, will later be named after this pioneering researcher.

1955: The number of hospitalized mental patients in the United States reaches an all-time high of 550,000, and 47 percent of hospital beds are occupied by mental patients. Dr. Robert Felix, director of NIMH, reports that "by the time the patient has been in the hospital for two years (75 percent of the total) his chances of getting out alive . . . are about 16 to 1." It is not uncommon at this time to find only one psychiatrist per every 2,000–3,000 patients in many state hospitals. Rockland State Hospital and Pilgrim State Hospital in New York have over 9,000 and 14,000 patients respectively. The Mental Health Study Act of 1955 (Public Law 84–182) is passed, which creates the Joint Commission on Mental Illness and Health. The Commission is authorized to evaluate the needs of the mentally ill and to make recommendations to Congress for future programs.

1956: Dr. Harry Stack Sullivan promotes the importance of society and social interaction in human behavior; he will later be known as the Father of Social Psychiatry. Until now analysts primarily emphasized "individual psychology." Years will pass before Anna Freud announces agreement with Sullivan's point of view. Sullivan tries to use psychotherapy with schizophrenics.

The first decrease in the population of mental hospitals occurs between 1955 and 1956 (from 558,922 to 551,390 patients).

1958: Dr. Harry Solomon, president of the American Psychiatric Association, publicly calls for the abolishment of state mental hospitals.

1959: Imipramine, in the form of Tofranil, is introduced as the first tricyclic antidepressant. It becomes the first successful chemical treatment for depression: until now, only electroconvulsive therapy has been helpful in treating serious depressions.

1961: Monoamine-oxidase (MAO) inhibitor drugs such as Parnate are introduced and are used in the treatment of severe depression. Patients must observe dietary restrictions and be willing to tolerate side effects such as flatulence, retarded orgasm, memory disturbance, and weight gain. Those suffering with severe depression or panic disorder, however, may gladly trade their symptoms for such side effects.

The appearance of *The Myth of Mental Illness* by Dr. Thomas Szasz creates a stir in the psychiatry community. Szasz maintains that mental illness is a "myth"; he claims that deviations from norms are signs of "problems in living" rather than of illness. Calling people "sick" does not mean they really are. Szasz views psychiatry as a force which restricts personal freedoms, a theme he deals with in another of his books, *Psychiatric Justice*.

Erving Goffman's *Asylums* describes how patients in mental hospitals become "totally institutionalized" by learning how to adjust to hospital life.

Dr. Gerald Caplan's study *An Approach to Community Mental Health* expounds upon the better alternative of providing psychiatric treatment within the community, and it sets the stage for the community mental health center movement.

Since 1955, the NIMH budget for research has increased sixfold and the budget for training ninefold, while that of psychiatric services has only doubled.

1962: The American Law Institute (ALI) recommends a new Model Penal Code in which the following would be adhered to: (1) A person is not responsible for criminal conduct if at the time of such conduct, as a result of mental disease or defect, he lacked substantial capacity either to appreciate the criminality of his conduct or to conform his conduct to the requirements of law; (2) as used in the article (of the code), the terms "mental disease" or "defect" do not include an abnormality manifested only by repeated criminal or otherwise antisocial conduct. [The ALI test will be adopted by all federal circuit courts of appeal and by about half of the states. Other states will use the M'Naughten test, with or without a supplemental "irresistible impulse," test].

Ken Kesey's novel *One Flew over the Cuckoo's Nest* becomes an underground hit in which the "heroic" McMurphy is pitted against the "evil" Nurse Ratched.

1963: Valium, a member of the benzodiazepine family of drugs, is introduced. Labelled a minor tranquilizer, it is destined to become the most widely used drug of its kind, reaching its peak in 1975, when over eighty million prescriptions will be written. In fact, it will become the most widely prescribed of all drugs in the United States. In 1980, Americans will spend $293 million on Valium (that's $800,000 a day!). It is used primarily as an antianxiety compound.

The Mental Retardation Facilities and Community Mental Health Centers Construction Act of 1963 (Public Law 88–164) is passed in order to help initiate up to 650 community mental health centers (CMHCs).

In January, in his State of the Union Address, President Kennedy speaks of the "abandonment of the mentally ill and the mentally retarded to the grim mercies of custodial institutions." He proposes community mental health centers as a "bold new approach" and promises that "when carried out, reliance on the cold mercy of custodial isolation will be supplanted by the open warmth of community concern and capability."

The federal government provides benefits to mentally ill individuals in the form of the Aid to the Disabled program, which later will become part of the Supplemental Security Income (SSI) program and the Social Security Disability Insurance (SSDI) program.

1964: The director of NIMH calls Dr. Gerald Caplan's second book *Principles of Preventive Psychiatry* a "primer" and a "bible" for the community mental health worker. It creates additional theoretical underpinnings for the community mental health movement (closely following the ideas of Freud).

Additional federal legislation expands support to cover CMHC operations and staffing, since Public Law 88–164 covers only capital costs like construction.

1965: B. F. Skinner publishes *Science and Human Behavior* in which he spells out the theoretical basis of behaviorism and describes how the environment is filled with reinforcing consequences.

The federal Medicaid insurance program is established, providing help for poor mentally ill persons.

1966: The federal Food Stamps program is enacted, which aids the mentally ill in community living.

The federal Medicare program is enacted, which helps older mentally ill persons.

1967: Dr. Aaron Beck, in his *Depression: Clinical, Experimental, and Theoretical*

Aspects, describes the cognitive-behavioral approach to understanding and treating depression. This therapeutic approach will later be shown to create benefits comparable to antidepressant medications.

1968: The second edition of the *Diagnostic and Statistical Manual of Mental Disorders (DSM–II)* is published. Its descriptions are made consistent with the eighth edition of the *International Classification of Disease* (CD–8). Professionals in American psychiatry wanted to use diagnostic categories which were consistent worldwide.

1969: More than half (55 percent) of the expenditures for mental health organizations in the United States are devoted to state and county mental hospitals and 7 percent to private psychiatric hospitals.

Esalen Institute at Big Sur, California was the first "growth center." By 1969, more than ninety such centers are scattered across the nation. People like Abraham Maslow, Carl Rogers, Erich Fromm, and others are breaking new ground in the so-called "third force" in psychology. (The "first force" was psychoanalysis, and the "second force" behaviorism). The third force is called the "human potential movement."

The community mental health center at Lincoln Hospital in the South Bronx closes its doors following a strike by two hundred staff members. Founded in 1964, it was known for its indigenous staff and Neighborhood Service Centers (storefronts which provided outreach to the community). It was designated as one of eight model centers around the country. The local members of the board of directors, made up of blacks and Hispanics, fired the directors, Drs. Peck, Roman, and Kaplan, who had preached community control.

1970: NIMH Director Dr. Stanley Yolles resigns under duress, claiming that, by withholding funds, the Nixon administration's policies are harming mental health policies.

1971: *Wyatt v. Stickney* becomes the landmark case upholding the mentally ill person's right to treatment. It holds that "involuntary committed patients unquestionably have a constitutional right to receive such individual treatment as will give each of them a realistic opportunity to be cured or to improve his or her mental condition." It also rules that patients have the right to refuse ECT, aversive conditioning, and psychosurgery or other major surgery.

A survey conducted by NIMH reveals that there are only 196 psychiatric halfway houses in the United States, with a total capacity of only 6,170 persons. By now, as a result of deinstitutionalization, some 433,000 former patients have been released from mental hospitals.

1972: In *Lessard v. Schmidt,* the judge rules that the only ground for hospitalizing patients on an involuntary basis is the dangerousness of the person to self or others. The American Civil Liberties Union (ACLU) was determined to abolish "involuntary hospitalization."

1975: In another landmark case, *Donaldson v. O'Connor,* the Supreme Court rules that non-dangerous persons who were not receiving treatment should be released if they could survive outside the hospital. This is a "right to liberty" ruling. It prohibits keeping people indefinitely in "simple custodial confinement." Mr. Donaldson is awarded $20,000: this perhaps is an incentive for other mental hospitals around the country to discharge many in their custodial care.

In *Dixon v. Weinberger,* a judge in the District of Columbia rules that patients have the right to treatment in "the least restrictive setting."

Patients with the diagnosis of schizophrenia represent only 10 percent of the total CMHC population. In retrospect, Torrey (1988) notes in *Nowhere to Go: The Tragic Odyssey of the Homeless Mentally Ill* that "probably no more than 20 percent of the individuals seen in the CMHCs would ever have been treated in a state mental hospital." By 1975, he says, the CMHCs, which were set up to treat the seriously mentally ill, had instead begun to cater to the needs of what he calls the "worried well."

Congress passes new CMHC legislation. President Ford, following a path set down by President Nixon's hostility toward funding the mental health movement, vetoes the legislation. Four days later both the House and the Senate override the veto. The mandate of the CMHCs is expanded.

1976: The California Supreme Court rules in *Tarasoff v. Regents of California* that "when a therapist determines . . . that a patient presents a serious danger of violence to another, he incurs an obligation to use reasonable care to protect the intended victim against such danger. The protected privilege (of confidentiality) ends where the public peril begins."

Jimmy Carter is elected president of the United States, and First Lady Rosyln Carter becomes a champion of mental health by supporting both expansion and improvement of programs. She is made honorary chairwoman of the new Commission on Mental Health.

1977: Smith and Glass review four hundred studies of psychotherapy, using detailed statistical analyses, and conclude that all of the psychotherapeutic treatments were more effective than no treatment; only small differences are found to exist between the therapies; and group therapy is found to be as effective as individual therapy.

1978: During this year (the last for which such figures are available), the CMHCs conduct ten million counseling and psychotherapy sessions, which nationally represent 80 percent of all treatment activities. These sessions, according to the NIMH, do not include medication or drug maintenance, and only a small proportion include people with "serious mental illness."

The President's Commission on Mental Health issues a voluminous report (2,139 pages). It contains 117 recommendations. A thorough document, it contains something for everyone. It is sharply critical of care provided to the seriously mentally ill. It states: "Ironically, although [the seriously mentally ill] are the primary reason for the existence of many mental health services, they have too frequently been excluded from the service delivery system. The President's Commission on Mental Health has at this time a unique, and extremely important, responsibility to recommend this history of neglect be stopped." The report points to a lack of coordination among a multitude of agencies and a wide degree of poor implementation on mental health goals. It is evident that there exists no clearly stated mental health policy in the United States.

1980: The third edition of the *Diagnostic and Statistical Manual (DSM–III)* is published by the American Psychiatric Association. It attempts to move away from theory into more descriptive criteria and to maintain compatibility with the ninth edition of the *International Classification of Disease. DSM–III* will have a major impact on language usage in the mental health field and on insurance billing practices.

Close to one million mentally disabled persons live in nursing homes and boarding homes, in contrast to an inpatient population of 138,000. This is the major *transinstitutionalization* achieved by the dramatic transfer of care out of mental hospitals (Brown 1985). Press accounts of shocking living conditions are revealed in many of these new settings. They represent a new custodial private sector for the care of the mentally ill.

1981: The Reagan administration repeals the Mental Health Systems Act and establishes the Alcohol, Drug Abuse, and Mental Health Block Grant system. The federal government has thus relinquished its responsibility for the mentally ill by passing it along to the states, whose record in this area has at best been checkered. Like the Nixon administration, the Reagan administration also, as promised during its election, slashes the amount of federal funding allocated to the national institutes (NIAAA, NIDA, and NIMH) and to the block grants. Echoes of the Nixon years are heard.

1982: Across the nation, from 1970 to 1982, nearly half of the total stock of single-room occupancies (SROs) in hotels, some 1,116,000 units, cease to exist. This greatly complicates the plight of the homeless mentally ill, many of whom had come to depend on the affordable rooms.

1983: Expenditures for state and county mental hospitals drop to 38 percent (from 55 percent in 1969), while the figure for private psychiatric hospitals has grown to 12 percent (from only 7 percent in 1969). The block grant mechanism ushered in by President Reagan allows the states to ignore mental health issues, and does not, in addition, provide the states with desperately needed funds.

1984: The number of people in mental hospitals is down to 119,000 (from 550,000 in 1955), while the number of outpatient episodes continues to rise.

The number of registered nurses working full time in mental health organizations reaches 54,406 (up from 31,110 in 1976), according to the NIMH.

The number of psychiatrists in full-time positions in mental health organizations reaches 18,482 (which is up from 12,938 in 1976), according to the NIMH. In the public sector, 7,622 psychiatrists are employed, of whom 60 percent are foreign medical graduates. The number of American-trained physicians is about 3,053 (which is slightly less than twice the number that had been in such jobs in 1945). Torrey (1988) points out that although the population has doubled from 1944 to 1984, the number of American-trained psychiatrists in public sector jobs is virtually unchanged, despite forty years of federally supported training programs.

The number of psychologists in full-time positions in mental health organizations reaches 21,052 (which is up from 9,443 in 1976), according to the NIMH. More and more are entering private practice. Academic psychologists in the American Psychological Association (APA) are expressing concern over what is perceived as too much attention being given to clinical concerns. The national membership of APA is nearing sixty thousand. Lobbying efforts in the legislative and legal arenas are being stepped up in an effort to ward off attempts by the American Psychiatric Association to restrict the ability of psychologists to practice and receive insurance reimbursement for their services.

The number of social workers in full-time positions in mental health organizations reaches 36,397 (which is up from 17,687 in 1976), according to the NIMH. The National Association of Social Workers (NASW), never as powerful a lobby as the two APAs, develops more clout. Clinical social workers are being increasingly approved by insurance carriers for rendering psychotherapy services (lower fees charged by social workers play a role in this change).

1985: Approximately 64 percent of state mental health agency expenditures are allocated to state mental hospitals; and about 32 percent go to community-based programs. Although it is estimated that three-fifths of the nation's approximately 2.4 million chronically mentally ill persons live in the community, powerful labor unions are trying to save jobs in state hospitals. In some small towns where public sector hospitals are located, they are the mainstay of the towns' economy. As a result while the private hospitals are growing in number and influence, the public sector is deteriorating.

1986: The Comprehensive Mental Health Services Act of 1986 (Public Law 99–660) is passed, which mandates that the states plan and implement a comprehensive system of community-based care for the seriously mentally ill. It is based on evidence provided by Senate hearings in 1986 that stated that Community Support programs (funded on a modest scale by the government since 1977) help people experience fewer symptoms, greater life satisfaction, and more positive social relationships, and enable them to spend less time unemployed than do comparable people who remain in hospitals. The passing of the act also signals a return of more direct responsibility for the mentally ill by the federal government.

According to the NIMH, the whereabouts of 937,300 persons with a diagnosis of schizophrenia are unknown, having been lost to follow-up care.

1987: The revised third edition of the *Diagnostic and Statistical Manual* (*DSM–IIIR*) is published by the American Psychiatric Association. Greater emphasis is placed on describing the functional disability of various disorders and newly defined disorders are added, such as nicotine dependence.

Prozac (fluoxetine) is introduced and is used to treat a variety of mental disorders. It works effectively and produces fewer side effects than did the first generation of antidepressants. However, by the end of the decade, some one dozen homicide trials will have used the "Prozac defense," which claims that the drug induces violent behavior in some people. Once again, outrageous claims are being made for a psychotropic medication.

1988: The ADAMHA estimates that mental illness has cost the nation $129.3 billion for lost productivity, treatment, mortality, and non-health costs.

The General Accounting Office estimates that there are between 250,000 and three million homeless people in the United States. It also estimates that between one-sixth and one-half of this group may be mentally ill. In addition, between 20 and 45 percent of homeless persons suffer from alcohol and other drug-related disorders.

Through the Stewart B. McKinney Homeless Assistance Act of 1987, ADAMHA provides funds for services to the homeless mentally ill. In 1988 grants are let in twelve cities.

1989: The NIMH establishes the Office of Programs for the Homeless Mentally Ill: its primary function is to lead a national institute-wide research effort.

The NIMH reports that there are more than ten million Americans who suffer from depressive illnesses, including one million who suffer from bipolar illness (manic-depression). It is estimated that four out of five people could be effectively treated if they would seek help, but most do not. Without treatment, symptoms can continue for months, even years. Ten to 20 percent do not not recover. Over half who do recover will suffer a relapse. The suicide rate for those with serious depressions is 15 percent.

The NIMH also reports that thirteen million American adults (8 percent of the population) eighteen years and older experience some type of anxiety disorder, the most prevalent of mental illnesses.

More than two million Americans suffer from schizophrenia, the most chronic and disabling of the major mental disorders, as estimated by the NIMH. Schizophrenics still occupy 31 percent of mental hospital beds (that's more than seventy-six thousand on any given day). The NIMH estimates that more than eight million children and adolescents—13 to 18 percent of Americans under the age of eighteen—experience mental disorders.

The NIMH's budget, primarily devoted to research, is $450,294,000.

The American Psychoanalytical and the International Psychoanalytical Associations make an out-of-court settlement with four psychologists. As a result twenty-seven American analytic institutes must accept "non-physicians" for at least 28 percent of non-research clinical training spots. This is one example of the many turf wars between psychiatry and psychology. Why haven't psychologists simply formed their own institutes? After all, there are institutes that train non-medical analysts (even lay analysts). The answer seems to be tied up with both discriminatory practices and a desire to be permitted to attend the more "prestigious" older training institutes (those originally reserved only for the training of physicians). An attempt to get closer to the "source" (Freud and his direct disciples—all doctors!).

1990: William Styron (author of *Sophie's Choice*) describes his descent into near-suicidal depression in his book *Darkness Visible: A Memoir of Madness*, which makes the *New York Times* bestseller list in 1991. The book is a powerful tool for educating the public about depression, a problem that affects ten million Americans.

In *CAPP v. Rank* the California Supreme Court rules that psychologists are independent health practitioners, authorized by law to practice in hospitals, and do not require supervision or approval by other health professionals. This case represents one among many attempts by the American Psychiatric Association to exclude psychologists from working with mentally ill patients. Not competencies but turf, power, and money are at issue.

The Alcoholism, Drug Abuse and Mental Health Administration (ADAMHA) publishes a study on the relationships between mental illness and alcohol and/or substance abuse. Under the direction of Dr. Darrel Reiger, 20,291 adult individuals, age eighteen and older, living in five geographic areas (NIMH Epidemiological Catchment Areas—ECAs), were interviewed between 1980 and 1984. The findings include:

- Thirty percent who have *ever* had a mental disorder have also had a diagnosable alcohol and/or other drug abuse problem during their lives.
- Fifty-three percent who have had drug abuse disorders have also had one or more mental disorders.
- Anxiety and depressive disorders are more likely to precede the onset of substance abuse.
- A total of 22.5 percent have had at lease one mental disorder, 13.5 percent have had an alcohol abuse disorder, and 6.1 percent have had a drug disorder.
- Individuals with a mental disorder are three times more likely to have an alcohol or drug abuse disorder than those who do not have a history of a mental disorder.
- Nearly half (47 percent) of those with schizophrenia have had a substance abuse disorder at some time.
- A history of substance abuse is also found among 32 percent of persons with clinical depression, including 56 percent with bipolar (manic-depressive) illness.
- For persons who have had a drug abuse diagnosis during their lives the most common disorders are: anxiety disorders (28 percent); mood disorders (26 percent); antisocial personality disorders (18 percent); and schizophrenia (7 percent).
- For persons who have had either an alcohol or other drug abuse disorder, their chances of also having had the other addictive disorder are seven times greater than the rest of the population.
- Among those who sought treatment for a drug disorder, 64 percent have had a mental disorder in the previous six months.
- Among those who sought treatment for an alcohol problem, 55 percent have had a mental disorder in the previous six months.
- Twenty percent who have visited a treatment center for a mental disorder have had a substance abuse disorder in the previous six months.
- Among the institutionalized population, 72 percent have a co-morbidity rate twice that of the general population. Prison inmates, who comprise 66 percent of this population, have a history of both a mental disorder and substance abuse problem.
- Co-morbidity is found to be remarkably higher among those who seek help from outpatient substance abuse or mental health centers than among those who do not visit the centers.

Large companies are spending 7 to 15 percent of their annual health care dollars on psychiatric care, with alcohol and drug cases accounting for more than one-third of this total. Mental health diagnoses are now among the top five reasons for hospitalization. Self-insured employers and insurance carriers now seek ways to curb claims as health care costs continue to rise. Mental health benefits, including care for alcohol and substance abuse, are subjected to deep cuts or are eliminated.

Providers find themselves challenged in unprecedented ways: managed care representatives, Professional Provider Organizations (PPOs), and Health Maintenance Organizations (HMOs) begin to threaten independent practitioners by cutting fees and tightly reviewing all claims. "Caps" on benefits begin to rise. All of these are reactions to past abuses by agencies and individual practitioners. Once again, the shape of mental health care is undergoing convulsive changes.

Unprecedented cuts are occurring in the public sector with diminishing federal, state and local revenues being allotted for mental health needs. Legislation and court orders that have no realistic way of being funded offer little more than rhetoric.

Summary. It is clear from the brief historical review above that a sort of slow-moving pendulum has swung through the mental health care movement, beginning with the initial reforms which created inpatient care, primarily in government-supported mental hospitals. The next wave of reforms swung the pendulum in the opposite direction. Hospitalization has been discouraged as the concept of community-based care pushed itself into the zeitgeist and public policy domains of mental health care during the last several decades.

The brave new worlds promised by psychoanalysis, psychopharmacological treatment, community mental health centers, deinstitutionalization, and community-based care have failed to materialize, however. Each movement has been, in a very real sense, oversold as a sort of sociopolitical panacea. Governmental funding trends, subject to powerful fluctuations in the political arena, have proved themselves unreliable over the long haul. In addition, public policy has often been forged without regard for the scientific literature (from which could be drawn empirically supportable approaches) and often in the very face of a total paucity of evidence.

The founding of the community mental health movement provides an example of such an unscientific approach. It had been based on Freudian principles at a time when (1) the basic tenets of Freudian psychoanalysis remained unproven; (2) Eysenck's critique of psychotherapy offered no evidence that psychotherapy (psychoanalytically oriented or otherwise) was helpful; (3) there was no empirical evidence to support the use of psychoanalytic techniques as the treatment of choice for the chronically mentally ill (particularly schizophrenics; (4) such theories, supported by little evidence, further stigmatized the families of clients by referring to such theoretical concepts as "schizophrenogenic" parents; and (5) by way of contrast pharmacotherapies, family support, case management, and behavioral therapies were offering real hope and evidence of their efficacy.

The failure of community-based care for the chronically mentally ill has led to a natural tragedy. On April 19, 1991, ABC's documentary program "20/20" graphically depicted how our jails have replaced the old state mental hospitals as the institution of "no-choice." Focusing on courts and jails in Los Angeles and Miami, Tom Jerrold reported on how judges and jailers are being overwhelmed by the homeless mentally ill. The Los Angeles County jail has more mental patients than any single mental hospital in the country; yet there is only one psychiatrist for thousands of patients. Powerful psychotropic medications are distributed there just as they used to be in the state mental hospitals. The difference is that the jails are even less humane places for the mentally ill, and staff are not being trained to care for mental patients. Their mission includes the incarceration and processing of criminals. Judges are forced into making Solomon-like decisions despairing of the paucity of services offering more appropriate placement of these sick persons, who become prisoners both of mental illness and the criminal justice system.

Once again mental illness is being treated as if it were a crime and not an illness. It is as if Phillipe Pinel, Benjamin Rush, Clifford Beers, and Dorothea Dix never existed and the Supreme Court never made a distinction between a disordered mind and criminal intent. Nevertheless, these patients are not psychotic killers like Hannibal the Cannibal or Buffalo Bill of *Silence of the Lambs* fame. They are harmless souls lost in the helplessness of ravaged minds. Ironically, however, the only way many can receive hospital-based care is to become a "proven" threat to self or others. Chronic or acute mental patients' best hope for rehospitalization, then, is violence and total madness: Only by acting out in the street can they receive help.

Only those blessed with caring families with money or the right kind of health insurance will otherwise receive help. As the number of publicly funded hospital beds declines, the number of proprietary beds continues to increase. In addition, a two-tiered service system has emerged to treat the mentally ill and the dually diagnosed. The number of private hospital beds is increasing for alcoholism, drug abuse, and mental health, separately and together. The co-morbidity of the substance abuse and mental illness has led to a dramatic increase in the number of "dual diagnosis" units available in private institutions. The number of such units is still small in public psychiatric settings. It is once again, as is so common in American history, a case of one system for the "haves" and another system for the "have-nots." The United States spends less on its public health system than any of the industrialized nations. It seems where the fiscal incentives are strong the treatment of both disorders (addictive behaviors and mental illness) are easy enough to accomplish. Where funds are sparse incentives to innovative programming are weaker.

The newest approach, biopsychiatry, has indeed provided meaningful relief from suffering for mental patients. But not without a price (see Levy 1983). Each time psychotropic medication is prescribed, there exists a cost-benefit ratio. Patients, some without the mental capacity to judge rationally for themselves, are faced with a trade-off between intended therapeutic benefits and unwanted but predictable side effects. Adverse reactions can present more serious consequences. For example, a patient on an antidepressant medication benefits from the removal of symptoms but may also often experience blurred vision, dryness of the mouth, constipation, and impaired urination. In the case of the phenothiazines, which are used to treat schizophrenia, more dramatic adverse effects can occur. Among these is tardive dyskinesia, which causes involuntary movements of the lips, tongue, and mouth.

There are other drawbacks to this approach as well. When mental patients live in controlled environments—mental hospitals, day hospitals, family settings, or halfway houses—they are likely to conform to medication regimes. There are caring people available to supervise the taking of drugs that permit continued functioning in the community. It is not reasonable, however, to assume that when poor people, who are often without the benefit of caring families or needed housing and other subsistence resources, are discharged from public mental hospitals into the community, they will follow their medication regimes. In retrospect this assumption was the greatest failing of the deinstitutionalization movement. How can minds ravaged by major mental disorders, delusional and hallucinating, take their medications as prescribed? And who would be there to see to it that they did not add alcohol and street drugs to the pharmacologic soup? No one has any idea how many of these drug-to-drug interactions have contributed to the further disorganization and decompensation of these patients. For that matter, no one knows how many times non-psychotic individuals have been rendered permanently psychotic after ingesting repeated doses of crack or PCP.

Mental patients living in controlled environments also have their physical health needs attended to. The homeless mentally ill are already overrepresented among those who are HIV positive or who have AIDS, syphilis, diseased livers, and an almost endless list of other physical disorders and maladies. This should not come as a shock to anyone, as NIMH acknowledges that 937,300 persons previously in public mental hospitals have been lost to follow-up care. Their whereabouts remain unknown—except to the extent that we all step over them in bus terminals, parks, subways, and countless other places where we would not want a family pet, much less a human being, to live. Is there anyone in any American city or town of major size who has not witnessed their hallucinating, talking to imaginary people, ranting and raving, and staring catatonically into an unimaginable space? The most incredible thing is that as we hurry by and ignore them we render them "invisible." Does anyone want our taxes increased so we may better care for these, our lost brothers and sisters? Sadly, it is improbable.

During the 1960s and 1970s thousands of people received mental health care services provided by the CMHC movement, and for that we can all be proud. Many people who might never have been able to afford psychotherapy in all its forms—individual, group, marital, family, and couples therapy—then found affordable treatment in the community mental health centers. Because of public funding, centers were able to provide treatment either at no cost or on a sliding fee scale. Community outreach, together with consultation and education efforts, helped bring hope through treatment to many blue-collar people whose previous ethos taught survival and self-sufficiency: people were supposed "to tough things out and solve their own problems." CMHCs became places where society was able to identify social problems that had tended to remain hidden—child abuse and neglect, family violence, incest and other sexual assaults on children, and poverty among the elderly. In 1978, the last year for which such figures are available, some six hundred CMHCs had undertaken almost 10 million counseling and psychotherapy sessions: 8,120,344 individual sessions, 876,441 group sessions, and 727, 520 family sessions.

Nevertheless the majority of mental health professionals in the various alcohol, drug abuse, and mental health settings the authors have worked in preferred doing psychotherapy with verbal patients, who were highly motivated for treatment and conformed to practice schedules. Few of us have been trained to work with the seriously mentally ill and many of us fear these patients whom we do not understand and who do not easily or comfortably validate us as clinicians (by getting "better"). Minkoff (1987) described three sources of resistance by mental health professionals to working with chronically mentally ill individuals:

1. Affective barriers—including feelings of hopelessness, helplessness, dislike or disgust, and discomfort
2. Lack of adequate training in the skills required to overcome these barriers
3. Lack of peer support and validation

According to Dr. E. Fuller Torrey (1988), the CMHC movement failed in two main areas: namely, the provision of emergency services and services to the chronically mentally ill. CMHCs, he notes, emphasized the care of the "worried well" over that of the chronically mentally ill, particularly those who had been released from public hospitals. He points out that the state hospital systems and the CMHCs rarely communicated effectively or planned together for the benefit of the individual patient. In 1978, during the Carter administration, the President's Commission on Mental Health reported that, as of 1975, only 10 percent of CMHC admissions were diagnosed with schizophrenia. At the same time, 21 percent had "neuroses and personality disorders" and another 22 percent had "social maladjustment" or "no mental disorder." A survey by the NIMH (1977) revealed that 32 percent of the centers had no emergency service. Another 39 percent handled such calls by using a telephone answering service, which would then contact a professional. In 1985 only 9.5 percent of the research budget of the NIMH was dedicated to researching schizophrenia, despite the fact that schizophrenics occupied 50 percent of the psychiatric beds in the country and were (and remain) the most prominent group among the homeless mentally ill. This portion of the research budget rose to 13 percent in 1987.

Torrey lists eight outcomes which have resulted from the misguided policy of deinstitutionalization, summarized as follows:

1. There are at least twice as many seriously mentally ill individuals living on streets and in shelters as there are in public mental hospitals.
2. There are increasing numbers of seriously mentally ill individuals in the nation's jails and prisons.
3. Seriously mentally ill individuals are regularly released from hospitals with little or no provision for aftercare or follow-up treatment.
4. Violent acts perpetrated by untreated mentally ill individuals are increasing in number.
5. Housing and living conditions for mentally ill individuals in the community are grossly inadequate.
6. Community mental health centers, originally funded to provide community care for the mentally ill so these individuals would no longer have to go to state mental hospitals, are almost complete failures.
7. Laws designed to protect the rights of the seriously mentally ill primarily protect their right to remain mentally ill.
8. The majority of mentally ill individuals discharged from hospitals have been officially lost. Nobody knows where they are.

(Adapted from Torrey, 1988)

Torrey suggests that we develop new policies to aid the seriously mentally ill which emphasize the following:

1. The seriously mentally ill must get first priority for public psychiatric services.
2. Psychiatric professionals must be expected to treat individuals who have serious mental disorders.

3. Government responsibility for the seriously mentally ill must be fixed at the state or local level.
4. Housing for the seriously mentally ill must be improved in quantity and quality.
5. Laws regarding the mentally ill must be amended to insure that those who need treatment can be treated.
6. Research on the causes, treatment, and rehabilitation of serious mental illnesses must increase substantially.

(Adapted from Torrey 1988)

In *The Transfer of Care: Psychiatric Deinstitutionalization and Its Aftermath* (1985), Dr. Phil Brown, a sociologist at Brown University, provides us with a thoughtful analysis of the current problem of care for the mentally ill. He states:

> Mental health planners and providers have usually considered current trends in psychiatric services to be a path of continuing progress from a backward, dehumanizing past to a progressive, humanistic present. Good intentions, a belief in the progress of knowledge and practice and a clear vision of the pitfalls continue to hinder professionals' awareness of the mental health system. Caught in the middle of the system's workings and trying to function within so many constraints, providers and planners are unlikely to develop an accurate picture of the system's problems and limitations. To protect themselves and prevent burnout, they may emphasize the positive aspects of policy, even if those positive aspects are more likely goals than actual outcomes. . . .
>
> To the general observer, however, the psychiatric system looks very different. She or he is likely to perceive public mental health care as a continual failure which eats up large portions of state and federal spending, while resulting in a growing corps of urban bag people and an increase in ex-patient criminal activity. The average citizen may be bothered by homeless psychotics in bus stations and fear that community residences will reduce property values and threaten the safety of their children . . . Neither the relatively optimistic views of the professional nor the exaggerated anxiety of the public are accurate, though certainly each has some truth for the believer.

Dr. David Rochefort, associate professor in Political Science and Public Administration at Northeastern University and editor of the comprehensive *Handbook on Mental Health Policy in the United States* (1989), observes:

> Contemplating the discourse of public mental care in the 1980s—presented in the pages of professional journals, on conference programs, and in the

> expressed concerns of public officials charged with evaluating current programs—it is hard not to be impressed by the depth of soul searching, of painful collective self examination that is underway. It is also hard not to be impressed by the burgeoning of creative ideas that has taken place within this period of reflection and assessment . . . The exact shape of the public mental health system in the United States ten or fifteen years from now is unknown at present. What is plain, however, is that much ferment is indispensable to the process of renewal.

In 1986, Congress passed the Comprehensive Mental Health Services Act (Public Law 99–660). It mandates that states plan and implement a comprehensive system of community-based care for the seriously mentally ill. It authorizes federal grants to assist in planning efforts and requires that federal technical assistance be provided to states requesting it. The ADAMHA block grant mechanism has been in place since the early 1980s; the primary responsibility for planning (and implementation) falls to the states. The act of 1986 urges the development of new plans and treatment strategies. Will the individual states exercise clinical, programmatic, and fiscal wisdom based on lessons learned from the last four decades? Or will there be a continuing crisis in provision of services to the seriously mentally ill? The story will unfold one state at a time.

Senator Edward Kennedy (1990) has outlined the key features comprising effective community-based programs, as documented by programs that have met with success. These features include:

1. Qualitative analysis of the population to be served, so that the number of people to be helped and their specific needs can be determined.
2. Case management, making someone responsible for coordinating and monitoring necessary services.
3. A program of support and rehabilitation to provide services appropriate for each client's age, functional level, and individual needs. Psychotherapy, regular social contact to assist reintegration into the community, vocational training, supervised work, and assistance in obtaining and keeping competitive employment should be available to adults, and an appropriate range of services should also be available to children. The goal is to enable individuals to function at the maximum feasible level.
4. Medical treatment and mental health care, available on a continuum from day hospitalization to periodic appointments, to regulate medication and monitor mental status.
5. Assistance to families, who often provide the frontline care for the mentally ill in the community, and who are so often left to cope with the severe strains of mental illness without assistance from the society at large.
6. Housing services, ranging from halfway houses with staff in resi-

dence who provide continuous supervision to largely independent living. Outreach to the homeless mentally ill should be seen as an essential part of these services.

(Adapted from Kennedy 1990)

In this article in the *American Psychologist,* Senator Kennedy states that these programs will not be inexpensive but they can be financed by savings in expensive institutional care. States which have well-developed community-based programs, such as Colorado and Wisconsin, have reduced hospital days to less than 50 percent of the national average. Two other articles in this same issue, one written by two former patients (Judi Chamberlain, of the National Association of Psychiatric Survivors, and Joseph A. Rogers, of the National Mental Health Consumers Self-Help Clearinghouse), and another by a parent of a schizophrenic child (Dan E. Weisburd, chairman of the California Task Force for the Seriously Mentally Ill), stress the value and importance of involving such people in direct policy-making roles together with the professionals. This type of partnership can only make the system healthier, more diverse, and less prone to professional myopia and unenlightened self-interest.

All of this activity in the field serves as a backdrop against which to consider the emergence of the MICA client. We have purposely omitted any detailed references to the MICA issue at this juncture. It is our intention that the reader take a long moment to pause on the historical antecedents of each field—rich with its own traditions, controversies, and unsolved problems—before forging ahead into deeper waters. Nonetheless, it is remarkable, as one can note after reading the history of the mental health movement, that the field was never seriously involved in the identification or treatment of patients with alcohol or other drug problems (except as the sheer weight of client numbers dictated it). We next consider the highlights of the emerging alcoholism treatment movement.

The Alcoholism Treatment Movement

As background material to the alcoholism treatment movement, *Drinking in America* by Martin and Lender (1982) provides an important historical review; it is written with clarity and is free of the usual biases of the clinician. For a broad overview of the field, *Encyclopedic Handbook of Alcoholism,* by Pattison and Kaufman (1982), is quite helpful. Valliant (1983), *The Natural History of Alcoholism,* is a good review of the disease concept. An excellent overview of the disease concept may also be found in Heather and Robertson's *Controlled Drinking* (1981). A critical analysis of the research literature is contained in Peele's book (1985) entitled *The Meaning of Addiction* and Miller and Heather's (1986) *Treating Addictive Behaviors.*

For insight into Alcoholics Anonymous we suggest their own "Big Book" and *Twelve Steps and Twelve Traditions* (published by AA World Services). A historical overview of the treatment movement in the United States is provided below.

Chronology of the Alcoholism Treatment Movement in the United States

1662: The governor of Connecticut brews beer from Indian corn. Thomas Jefferson and Benjamin Franklin also brew beer.

1673: The Puritan leader, Increase Mather writes *Wo to Drunkards,* in which he warns colonists of the "worse than brutish sin of drunkenness." He refers to drink as a "good creature of God" but sees the abuse of drink as coming "from Satan." (It is precisely this type of moralizing that twentieth-century treatment professionals and members of AA will attempt to refute, and it helps to explain why the idea of alcoholism as a disease will have to compete against a harsh form of puritanical morality.

1700: The first American distillery opens in Boston, producing rum.

1790: Two physicians, Benjamin Rush in the United States and Thomas Trotter in England, write about the effect of "ardent spirits" and "spiritous liquors" on human behavior. They are the first to speculate that there is something about certain people—they have a "disease"—that causes intemperate drinking. For the first time, the cause is seen to lie within the person rather than within the "demon rum." Their views are the forerunner of the twentieth century disease concept. There was perhaps a medical cause for drunkenness. Rush is also the first to write about the progressive nature of alcohol addiction and the medical and social complications brought on by problem drinking. He is also a major public champion of temperance.

1804: In England, Dr. Thomas Trotter publishes *An Essay, Medical, Philosophical, and Chemical, on Drunkenness and Its Effects on the Human Body.* He states: "In medical language, I consider drunkenness, strictly speaking, to be a disease." In this one sentence, he challenges the prevailing moral code, threatens a basic church tenet, and confronts the failure of the medical community to work with alcoholism.

1840: The Washingtonian Movement is begun by six men in Baltimore. This is a fraternal association of reformed "drunkards" who seek to save fellow sufferers from their plight. This is the beginning of taking the total abstinence "pledge." Members believe that one has to avoid social situations where drinking occurred. The group focuses on the individual drunkard rather than on social reform. Their movement lasts only four years.

1864: Dr. Joseph E. Turner opens the New York State Inebriate Asylum in Binghampton, New York. A firm believer in the disease concept, Turner believes that humane treatment can be afforded the alcoholic in a facility such as his and that research can be conducted there as well.

1870: Drs. Joseph W. Parrish and Willard Parker found the American Association for the Cure of Inebriates. It is dedicated to research and humane treatment for the alcoholic. Many of its members are strong temperance advocates.

1874: The Woman's Christian Temperance Union (WCTU) is founded under the leadership of "Mother" Eliza Thompson (who has become famous for praying in saloons in Cleveland). The group's response to alcoholism is a "gospel temperance"—a moral suasionist attempt at a spiritual rebirth to get them to pledge total abstinence. They preach in private homes, jails, hospitals, and saloons, and they establish reform clubs similar to the Washingtonian Movement.

1880: Dr. Leslie Keeley announces the "Keeley" or "Gold" cure, as it came to be known. Using no scientific data, Keeley claims that a nonexistent "bichloride of gold" leads to miraculous cures. He becomes wildly successful. Other quacks, while quick to denounce Keeley, also make their own similarly unsubstantiated promises of miracle cures. Despite the fact that Keeley never supplies any proof for his claims, as many as four hundred thousand people are to take his "cure." This will not be the last time that people make claims for positive treatment outcomes and yet have no supporting data to back them up.

1899: Carrie Nation begins her famous campaigns of taking a hatchet into saloons and wreaking havoc. Although considered part of the "lunatic fringe," she helps popularize anti-saloon and prohibitionist sentiment in the United States.

1920: The National Prohibition Act, known as the Volstead Act, is put into full effect. This is the Eighteenth Amendment to the Constitution of the United States.

1933: The Volstead Act is repealed after a wave of public clamor and support. The mortality rate due to drinking and the rate of cirrhosis have gone down nationally during prohibition, while the crime rate has soared.

1935: "Dr. Bob" and "Bill W." meet in the Midwest and found the self-help (more strictly speaking, mutual help) fellowship of Alcoholic Anonymous. In the 1980s, Dr. Bob's son referred to the founding of AA and its future success as a "miracle." The twelve steps of AA are developed as a prescription for living a sober life, based upon a spiritual program of recovery. The first step says: "We are powerless over alcohol and our lives have become unmanageable." The second step says: "We came to believe that a power greater than ourselves could restore us to sanity." The third step says: "We made a decision to turn our will and our lives over to God as we understood Him."

1939: The "Big Book" is published. Its actual title is *Alcoholics Anonymous: The Story of How Many Thousands of Men and Women Have Recovered from Alcoholism.* When it is first published there are approximately one hundred members in AA. The foreword to the first edition states: "To show other alcoholics precisely how we have recovered is the main purpose of this book."

1940: The Yale University Center for Alcoholism Studies, founded in the late 1930s, inaugurates the *Quarterly Journal of Studies on Alcohol* (now called the *Journal of Alcohol Studies*). This is an important step in promoting research in the field. (The Center for Alcohol Studies will move to Rutgers University in 1962.)

1943: The Du Pont Company begins a unique program of helping alcoholic employees seek rehabilitation, as an alternative to firing them. This is the forerunner of modern-day employee assistance programs (EAPs). By the late

1970s there will be over 2,250 such EAP programs.

1944: The U.S. Public Health Service labels alcoholism the nation's fourth largest public health problem.

Under the leadership of Marty Mann, the National Committee for Education on Alcoholism is founded. The Committee will change its name to the National Council on Alcoholism (NCA) in the early 1950s. In the late 1980s NCA will change its name again to the National Council on Alcoholism and Chemical Dependencies. NCA estimates that there were three million alcoholics in the United States in 1943.

1948: Disulfiram, better known as Antabuse, is first used in the United States. Disulfiram is an inhibitor of aldehyde dehydrogenase. It is the first metabolic by-product of alcohol, and causes discomfort and toxicity in the user. It will be used as a behavioral reinforcer for maintaining sobriety.

1952: E. M. Jellinek, director of the Yale University Center of Alcohol Studies, publishes "Phases of Alcohol Addiction," in the *Quarterly Journal of Studies on Alcohol*. Based on questionnaires administered to ninety-eight members of AA, he introduces the idea that alcoholism progresses in phases. In his conception of alcohol addiction as a disease, he makes a distinction between the alcohol addict and the habitual, symptomatic, excessive drinker (or problem drinker). Although he speaks directly of excessive drinking as an attempt to reduce symptoms of an "underlying personality disorder," the field of alcoholism largely ignores this statement and seizes upon the central idea of alcoholism as a progressive disease, with an emphasis on biological factors. Perhaps the most important concept in Jellinek's writings is that of "loss of control."

The World Health Organization (WHO) issues a wide and imprecise definition of alcoholism.

1954: Al–Anon is incorporated as a separate fellowship from AA. Al–Anon is for family members and others close to the alcoholic. This group shares many similar beliefs and approaches to alcoholism. Alateen group meetings are sponsored by Al–Anon.

Lillian Roth's autobiography, *I'll Cry Tomorrow*, describes her descent into alcoholism; the book will be made into a movie.

1955: The second edition of AA's "Big Book" is published. There are now six thousand AA groups with over 150,000 members in attendance.

1956: The American Medical Association and the American Hospitals Association pass resolutions which recognize alcoholism as a disease. This formal recognition is paralleled by many other organizations, including the American Psychiatric Association. The NCA estimates that there are five million alcoholics in the United States.

1962: A major controversy is set in motion when an English physician named Davies reports that out of a group of ninety-three alcoholics, only seven have safely moderated their drinking, based on a ten-year follow-up study. This finding was not considered remarkable in England but was roundly criticized in the United States.

1965: The NCA estimates there are 6.5 million alcoholics in the United States.

Medicare is established in the United States. The hospital insurance component (part A) pays for treatment of alcoholism as a psychiatric disorder. Part B of Medicare pays for outpatient care.

The Medicaid program is also established. However, a great deal of discretion is left to the states regarding payment for alcoholism services, since alcoholism is not specifically mentioned in the regulations. As a result, payments for illness that are the physical consequences of alcoholism are more easily reimbursed than payments for the direct treatment of alcoholism.

The President's Commission on Law Enforcement and Administration of Justice reports two million arrests in this one year for the offense of public drunkenness. This figure represents one out of every three arrests in the United States.

1966: Two federal courts of appeals decisions, *Driver v. Hinnant* and *Easter v. District of Columbia,* support the idea of alcoholism as a disease.

1967: The Cooperative Commission on the Study of Alcoholism publishes its report, *Alcohol Problems: A Report to the Nation.* The commission recommends a change in American drinking patterns in order to "reduce rates of alcoholism and other types of problem drinking."

1968: In *Powell v. Texas,* the Supreme Court rules that Powell has failed to document that he could not avoid being intoxicated in public and upheld that the conviction for public intoxication stand. The court indicates that there are differences in medical opinion about whether alcoholism is a disease and rejects the argument that public drunkenness should not be considered criminal on the grounds that it represents an "alcoholism sickness."

Congress enacts the Alcoholism Rehabilitation Act (Public Law 90–574), thus setting the stage for a federal role in the support of treatment and research on alcoholism.

1970: The Comprehensive Alcohol Abuse and Alcohol Prevention, Treatment, and Rehabilitation Act (Public Law 91–616) is passed by Congress. This act leads to the creation in 1971 of the National Institute on Alcoholism and Alcohol Abuse (NIAAA)—which represents a full-blown effort to support research and treatment of alcoholism at the federal level.

1972: The criteria committee of the National Council on Alcoholism publishes major and minor criteria for the diagnosis of alcoholism in the *American Journal of Psychiatry* and the *Annals of Internal Medicine.* The criteria are divided into two tracks: (1) physiological and clinical, and (2) behavioral, psychological, and attitudinal.

1973: The NIAAA begins to function as a separate institute (from NIMH and NIDA). If alcohol is a drug, why a move to create separate agencies? The answers have to do with power and turf issues rather than clinical or social wisdom.

1975: The NIMH reports that there are 597 halfway houses for alcoholics in the United States. Their distribution is very uneven across the states.

The confidentiality of alcoholic patients is assured by new federal guidelines governing patient records (in Title 42, Code of Federal Regulations, Part 2).

1976: The third edition of AA's "Big Book" is published. AA now lists some twenty-eight thousand groups in over ninety countries with a total membership of more than one million.

Fetal Alcohol Syndrome (FAS) is identified. Physicians up until this time have often encouraged pregnant women to drink moderately during pregnancy.

1977: Some fifty different compounds, primarily tranquilizers and sedatives, are used around the country to manage withdrawal from alcohol. Phenobarbital, Valium, and Librium top the list. All are used to comfortably step the alcoholic down from the alcohol dependency. All such medication is meant to be stopped at the end of the detoxification period, so as to avoid a new sedative dependency.

The "unitary model" of alcoholism (which states that there is a single phenomenon that can be identified as alcoholism) is called into question. Pattison, Sobell, and Sobell (1977) describe a "multivariate alcoholism syndrome" that is supported by fifteen years of research evidence.

1978: The first of two Rand Reports in the United States is published in book form. These study the results of NIAAA treatment programs. The studies follow up 2,339 patients at six months after treatment and 597 at eighteen months. At the eighteen-month point, 22 percent are drinking "normally" and 24 percent are abstaining. The NCA criticizes the report, and many unfounded rumors are circulated. The follow-up is lengthened to four years. At that juncture the study finds that 40 percent of those in remission are drinking but with no reported problems. The alcoholism treatment establishment and the NCA in the end simply ignore these studies, and the NIAAA leaders again reiterate their support for abstinence as the "appropriate goal" in the treatment of alcoholism.

Medicaid provides only 6 percent (or $5 million) of payment costs of the total receipts from one hundred NIAAA-funded alcoholism treatment centers. Reimbursement under Medicaid varies among states: for example, only $45,000, in Mississippi, but $32.1 million in New York.

The FBI reports 1,176,600 arrests for public drunkenness in the United States. These account for approximately 11 percent of all arrests. In some locales, humane "sobering up" stations begin to replace the "drunk tanks" located in most jails. Many states rescind old laws making public intoxication a crime.

Alcohol is recognized as the single most important factor yet identified in traffic fatalities (Waller 1982). Laws begin to change around the nation as the Driving While Intoxicated (DWI) movement gathers strength. During the coming years several states will raise the legal drinking age to twenty-one.

It is estimated that 20 percent of alcoholics in the United States are women. As the estimate of the total number of alcoholics in the country is ten million, this means two million are women. Very little is known about these women, however. The vast majority of research has been on males. Of the studies done, it is clear that minority women are overrepresented in the population of alcoholics. This is more likely a reflection of an impoverished life-style than of anything unique to a given race or ethnic group. There is controversy as to whether or not the population of women alcoholics is increasing.

National studies of adolescent drinking practices show that three out of ten tenth to twelfth graders may be classified in the misuser category based on frequency of drunkenness and perceived alcohol-related negative consequences (Rachal et al. 1982).

1979: The NIAAA commissions a national survey of alcohol use and drinking problems. Two trend studies compare the 1979 survey with eight other drinking practice surveys funded by the NIAAA over a thirteen-year period. They reveal that there are no marked shifts in alcohol consumption or alcohol problems in the population. The percentage of drinkers versus abstainers is quite stable and the proportion of heavy drinkers has not changed in any way that suggests a trend. However, the 1979 survey provides "a glimpse of problem rates" for young adults, women, blacks, Hispanics, and older people (see Clark and Midanik 1982).

1980: New York State creates the Credentialed Alcoholism Counselor (C.A.C.), and defines criteria and requirements for his or her credentialing as an alcoholism counselor. One must have a minimum of a high school diploma, one year of full-time counseling experience under the supervision of a C.A.C. (or other qualified health care professional), and 450 clock hours of relevant "instruction," at least 150 hours of which are "alcoholism counseling specific," and one must then take a written examination. Prior to this time, many alcoholism counselors have had little training or experience (except perhaps their own recovery). Many other states will follow New York's initiative.

The New York State Division of Alcoholism and Alcohol Abuse develops specific regulations which define minimum standards of care, including staffing, physical plant, and staff credentials for a variety of treatment modalities. Other states will follow suit in establishing criteria.

Dr. Allen Marlatt, using the balanced placebo experimental design, demonstrates that alcohol's effects on behavior are as much a result of expectancy and belief as they are a product of pharmacological effects (Marlatt and Rohsenow 1980).

According to the National Drug and Alcoholism Treatment Utilization Survey (NDATUS), state governments have provided 21.9 percent of their total annual tax revenue funds to alcoholism treatment centers. Local governments contributed 10.3 percent of the total. Private insurance provided 19.6 percent of the total. The other half of the funds came from the federal government via the NIAAA, whose support has been a vital lifeline of funding for treatment services for poor people.

According to surveys by the National Association of Private Psychiatric Hospitals, admissions for alcoholism have risen from 11 percent in 1970 to 15 percent by 1980 (Moore 1982).

Marian Sandmaier's important book *The Invisible Alcoholics* documents the pain and suffering of women with drinking problems. This is the first major book on the topic. Most research, up to this point, has been done on male alcoholics.

1981: Despite his verbal support of alcoholism treatment, President Reagan slashes the budget of the NIAAA, thus reducing federal support for some programs and closing others. By switching to a block grant approach to allocations for alcoholism, drug abuse, and mental health funding, support for these services was found to be 20 percent *lower* than the levels of the preceding categorical programs (Saxe 1983). Administration officials claim that programs have failed to demonstrate their effectiveness.

The Surgeon General warns American women not to drink at all during pregnancy.

1982: The full fury of the "controlled drinking" debate explodes when an article in *Science* attacks one of the seminal studies conducted by Sobell and Sobell (1973; 1976). Strangely, the article addresses only the experimental (controlled drinking) group, reporting re-hospitalizations and death among alcoholics who tried to control their drinking. More patients in the control group (those who received traditional abstinence-oriented treatment) have been rehospitalized and died. Although the numbers in both groups are too small to allow for wider generalizations, only a blue ribbon panel of distinguished experts at the Addiction Research Foundation in Toronto, Canada can temporarily quell the controversy. When the smoke lifts, the authors of the *Science* article have been chided by the panel for their failure to take both study groups into account and to recognize the body of data regarding controlled drinking. This is another powerfully charged episode in a field filled with controversies.

"Polydrug" abuse is noted by many researchers as increasing among alcoholics (see Levy 1982). Estimates vary widely but the vast majority indicate that drug use by alcoholics is on the rise. Old-timers in the field begin to wonder where all the "alcoholics only" have gone. Alcohol now is seen to play a major role in the lives of drug addicts as well.

1983: Dr. George Valliant's book *The Natural History of Alcoholism* is published, and it becomes the rallying point around which the medical model is championed during the 1980s. Valliant's emphasis is on alcoholism as a unitary disease having a life of its own. His study shows that those exposed to medical treatment and AA fare no better than untreated alcoholics (even among those who choose to abstain, more than 60 percent have no contact with AA). His is the longest longitudinal study of alcoholism, his research spanning over forty years.

The National Association for Children of Alcoholics is established. According to Dr. Timmen Cermak (1985) one of the founders, "Children of alcoholics require and deserve treatment in and of themselves, not as mere adjuncts of alcoholics." *Adult Children of Alcoholics,* by Janet Woitiz, will become a *New York Times* bestseller. It contains no formal studies and does not compare children of alcoholics with any control or comparison groups. Yet many people in the burgeoning field of adult children of alcoholics (ACOAs) will quote from it.

The Effectiveness and Costs of Alcoholism Treatment (Saxe et al. 1983) is published by the Office of Technology Assessment of the United States Congress. The authors reviewed all existing studies and concluded as follows:

- Ten percent of the population account for 50 percent of national alcohol consumption.
- Eighty-five percent of alcoholics and problem drinkers receive no treatment for their condition.
- Alcoholism and alcohol abuse have multiple origins and affect diverse groups of individuals.
- In comparing reviews and studies of treatment programs, general statements must be offered with great caution.
- Treatment seems better than no treatment, but methodological problems render it difficult to conclude that any specific treatment is more effective than any other.
- There is some evidence to support the hypothesis that alcoholism treatment is cost-beneficial. It is difficult to determine the relative effectiveness or cost effectiveness of inpatient versus outpatient treatment.

Medicare proposes limiting reimbursement for hospital stays for alcoholism to eight days. An outpouring of protests from the field (NCA, National Association of Alcoholism Treatment Programs, AMA, NIAAA, American Psychiatric Association, Joint Commission of the Accreditation of Hospitals, and others) leads to a rescinding of the proposal. By 1986 the reimbursable stay is increased to fifteen days (despite the findings of congressional research by Saxe et al., which concludes that inpatient stays have demonstrated no superiority to outpatient care in terms of outcome or cost effectiveness).

Drunk drivers kill twenty-five thousand men, women, children, and babies each year on American highways. They injure another 750,000. In 1982, spurred on by organizations like Mothers Against Drunk Drivers (MADD), President Reagan appoints a national commission to study the issues (see Levy 1983).

The number of private, for-profit, hospital-based and free-standing, twenty-eight-day inpatient rehabilitation facilities is growing rapidly. The "twenty-eight-day stay" does not derive from any clinical wisdom but rather from the number of days that insurance companies are willing to reimburse. Many of these programs will make exceptional claims of success (such as 90 percent recovery rates). Few such claims are substantiated by any objective data. These programs are good for corporate growth, but claims of exceptional effectiveness go unproven.

The NIAAA reports that more than 500,000 Americans have been in treatment for alcoholism and alcohol abuse during this year.

An American Medication Association survey reveals a paradox: Practicing physicians regard alcohol abuse as a major problem, but the majority of them don't feel adequately prepared to treat it.

1985: Social psychologist Dr. Stanton Peele's book *The Meaning of Addiction: Compulsive Experience and Its Interpretation* is published. It challenges the overemphasis on biomedical views of alcohol and other addictive behaviors and provides a review of literature and a framework for understanding the powerful environmental, sociocultural, and psychological influences on drinking behavior. Peele rapidly becomes the most vocal of critics of the disease model of addiction.

It is estimated that over forty thousand babies born this year suffer from prenatal alcohol exposure, which will have permanent effects for many. According to Dr. Loretta Finnegan, alcohol is the most toxic of the drugs to which the fetus can be exposed. The government estimates that Fetal Alcohol Syndrome (FAS) has cost the United States $1.6 billion in 1985. Eighty percent of the cost is spent for residential care and support services for mentally retarded persons over the age of twenty-one who are impaired by this condition. FAS is believed to affect five thousand births per year, and Fetal Alcohol Effects (FAE) to affect another thirty-five thousand births. This estimate of FAS incidence represents a rate of 1.5 to 2.0 per ten thousand births. By 1991 FAS will be listed as the leading cause of mental retardation in the United States (more prevalent, for example, than Down's syndrome).

1986: Miller and Hester (1986) review the entire alcoholism treatment literature (totalling over nine hundred studies). They report four key "surprises": first, the sheer volume of research; second, the encouraging number of alternative treatments found (over twenty different methods of treatment); third, the copious amount of clinically relevant information published; fourth, the treatment approaches most clearly supported as effective have *rarely* been practiced in the United States.

Alcohol diagnoses are now among the top five reasons for mental health-related hospitalizations. Alarmed at escalating costs, insurance companies begin to impose cost containment strategies. The insurance firms readily cite for Congress the finding in the Saxe et al. (1983) study that there is no evidence to support the more expensive form of inpatient care over outpatient care. Inpatient alcoholism rehabilitation programs must deal with managed care screening personnel who closely question each admission. Competition between facilities reaches new heights.

Secular self-help groups (as opposed to spiritual ones like AA) begin to form in the United States. Save Our Selves (SOS) begins in Buffalo, New York under the leadership of James Christopher. There are now some three hundred grass roots SOS groups in the United States, Canada, Europe, and Asia. "SOS" also refers to the name "Secular Organizations for Sobriety. In the same year Jack Trimpey founds Rational Recovery in California. Within five years this group will claim two thousand members in over one hundred cities.

1987: Cox (1987) reviews the entire research literature on personality and alcoholism. He concludes that despite the important role played by personality, it is clearly interactive with biological and other psychological, environmental, and sociocultural determinants. Psychological factors alone are not sufficient to produce alcoholism. This is corroborated by the National Academy of Sciences, which concludes that there is no single set of psychological characteristics that embraces all addictions. Research does not support the idea of an "alcoholic" personality.

Dr. Lee Robins reports on the NIMH-sponsored Epidemiological Catchment Area (ECA) study which involves repeated interviews with twenty thousand people undertaken by five university research teams. Her findings are important for understanding why 85 percent of alcoholics go untreated. Among these findings are the following:

- Eighty-six percent believe that they should be strong enough to handle it alone.
- Eighty-one percent never told their doctors about drinking (or drug) problems.
- Seventy-seven percent believe they will recover without care.
- Forty-nine percent only sought care because of family pressure.

The most important finding is that those alcoholics whose family and friends voice their concerns about their drinking problems are most likely to seek treatment.

1988: The Supreme Court rules again on a case involving alcoholism. It has not heard an alcohol-related case in twenty years (since *Powell v. Texas*). In the current case, *Traynor and McKelvey v. Thomas K. Turnage, Administrator, Veterans Administration,* the court rules that the VA is within its rights to define primary alcoholism as a consequence of "willful misconduct" in determining educational benefits eligibility. The Court does not rule on the issue of whether alcoholism is a disease, stating that there exists "a substantial body of medical literature that even contests the proposition that alcoholism is a disease, much less that it is a disease for which the victim bears no responsibility." In addition, the Court asserts that "even among many who consider alcoholism a 'disease' to which its victims are genetically predisposed, the consumption of alcohol is not regarded as wholly involuntary" (*United States Law Week* 56:4319). A powerful point is being made: How can alcoholism be a disease whose primary symptom is loss of control when recovery is based on total abstinence, itself definitely a form of control?

The ADAMHA estimates that alcohol abuse has cost the nation $85.8 billion for such things as treatment services, reduced productivity, mortality, criminal justice expenditures, and other related costs.

1989: The United States is spending $2 billion per year for the treatment of alcohol and drug abuse: $1 billion to private hospitals, and another $1 billion spent by federal and state governments (Peele 1989). A one-month stay in a private rehabilitation center ranges from $5,000 to $35,000.

AA reports that the number of people attending AA who are addicted to drugs (in addition to alcohol) has grown from 38 percent in 1986 to 46 percent in 1989. They also report that the percentage of women in AA, which in 1969 was 22 percent, has grown to 35 percent by 1989.

The NIAAA estimates that there are approximately 10.5 million adult Americans affected by the "devastating disease of alcoholism." They also estimate that more than seven million others are alcohol abusers.

The NIAAA's budget is $125,245,000.

1990: The American Medical Association finally warns pregnant women not to drink alcohol in any amount despite the Surgeon General's warnings in the early 1980s.

In April, researchers at the University of Texas announce in the *Journal of the American Medical Association (JAMA)* that they have identified a genetic link between a predisposition to alcoholism and dopamine receptors. Researchers at the NIAAA in December of this same year announce in *JAMA* that they are unable to confirm such a link and are dubious that alcoholism can be so simply explained. The hunt for a biological marker continues.

The NIAAA reports that the estimated alcohol consumption per capita shows a clear downward trend from 1980 (about 2.75 gallons of pure alcohol per year) to 1990 (about 2.50 gallons per year).

Summary. The above chronology reveals that since its earliest beginnings, the use of the term "alcoholism" has been problematic. Many different terms have been used to refer to problems associated with the ingestion of alcohol. All too often, however, researchers and clinicians have failed to use adequate operational definitions for the concepts they so freely name. Terms like "heavy drinker," "problem drinker," "abusive drinker," "alcoholic," "alcohol dependent," "alcohol addicted," "excessive drinker," "true alcoholic," and "alcohol abuser" all have evolved over time. Each writer ascribes a different meaning to these diverse terms and, sadly, all too often fails to define them in an objective manner. So it is hard to know from report to report what meanings to draw from the same language universe. The field is cluttered with a language that lacks operational definitions and precision. It also engages in a great deal of circular reasoning: Who is the alcohol abuser? Someone who abuses alcohol!

Jellinek (1952) himself talked about a "habitual symptomatic excessive drinker"—someone we would now call a "problem drinker"—who was not addicted to alcohol. The difference in his theoretical formulation was the central idea that the alcohol addict was someone who eventually loses control over his ability to stop, once drinking is initiated. However, this was a theoretical idea, not a proven fact. Jellinek conceived of it, along with his other speculations about alcohol addiction, on the basis of a study of ninety-eight questionnaires filled out by members of AA (themselves a subgroup within the universe of all problem drinkers). In comparing the two types of drinking patterns he noted:

> In both groups, the excessive drinking is symptomatic of *underlying psychological or social pathology*, but in one group after several years of excessive drinking "loss of control" over the alcohol intake occurs, while in the other group this phenomenon never develops. The group with the "loss of control" is designated as "alcohol addicts". (674)

This seminal paper, entitled "Phases of Alcohol Addiction" appeared in the *Quarterly Journal of Studies on Alcohol.* In it Jellinek also spoke of the "occasional symptomatic excessive drinker" for whom "no psychological abnormality can be claimed." He continued:

> There is no intention to deny that the nonaddictive drinker is a sick person; but this ailment is not the excessive drinking, but rather the psychological or social difficulties from which alcohol intoxication gives temporary sur-

> cease. . . . "Loss of control" is a disease condition per se which results from a process that superimposes itself upon those *abnormal psychological conditions* of which excessive drinking is a symptom. . . . The fact that this "loss of control" does not occur in a large group of excessive drinkers would point toward a predisposing X factor in the addictive alcoholics. . . . The vast majority of users of alcoholic beverages stay within the limits of the culturally accepted drinking behaviors and drink predominantly as an expression of their culture, and while an individual expression may be present in these behaviors its role remains insignificant. (674)

Clearly, Jellinek, in describing these theoretical formulations—he referred to his own ideas as the "disease conception of alcohol addiction"—allowed for an unknown biological (X factor), in addition to the psychological, the social, and the cultural factors. As a researcher, he did not consider an *N* of ninety-eight subjects drawn from one subgroup (AA) to be a representative sample or proof positive of any one point of view. Nevertheless, he is often quoted as having stated that "loss control" was indeed a fact. Pattison et al. (1977) are quick to point out that what he was actually stating was nothing more than an opinion expressed by AA and not his own. They also point out that "his thoughts were presented modestly and cloaked in caution, lest some mistake his speculations for facts" (9–39). The concept of "one drink–one drunk" belongs to AA and not to Jellinek. Perhaps most interesting is that Jellinek never in his earlier or later writings mentioned total abstinence as a therapeutic requirement in the treatment of alcoholism (Heather and Robertson 1981). His writings instead suggest the need to alleviate the social and psychological problems of which the excessive drinking was a symptom.

It is sad to note that the psychological and sociocultural underpinnings of alcoholism are vastly understated, however, owing to a near exclusive emphasis on biomedical factors. This, even though the role played by medical doctors in the treatment of alcohol dependence is limited to its physical consequences (which represent a small part of most treatment programs). The vast majority of efforts by clinical staff are devoted to counseling. This counseling, nonetheless, generally fails to draw on traditional psychological and psychiatric sources; instead it elaborates on sentiments expressed by the "folk psychotherapy of Alcoholics Anonymous" (Alibrandi 1985). Ravitz (1971) described the consequences of this confrontation between "folk science" and empirical science:

> A folk science is a body of accepted knowledge whose function is not to provide the basis for further advance, but to offer comfort and reassurance to some body of believers . . . In an immature field of scientific development there is inevitable conflict which occurs when the result of disciplined scientific inquiry conflicts with the beliefs of a folk science, usually a popular one which is also adopted by the established cultural organs of society.

This problem is not limited to conflict between science and beliefs of the lay public or of members of a particular fellowship. It is also the focus of diverse opinions and interpretations by professionals in the field. We consider one such example below, which involves the important question of identifying the causes (etiology) of drinking problems. Valliant and Milofsky (1982), used a sample of inner-city youth originally studied by Glueck and Glueck (1950; 1968), and relocated the sample subjects at age forty-seven. Thus, a longitudinal-developmental framework which emphasized physiological, behavioral, and sociocultural variables regarding the development of problem drinking in later life was utilized. Zucker and Gomberg (1986), reporting in the same journal (*American Psychologist*), reviewed the exact same data and reached widely different conclusions. We compare the interpretations below and refer the reader to the original articles for more detail.

Valiant and Milofsky (1982) concluded:

1. Where association exists between alcoholism and any behavioral traits or symptoms, alcoholism is the *cause* of the behaviors or symptoms rather than the *result*. Alcoholism is not viewed as a disorder whose etiological antecedents include personality and early environmental factors.
2. Premorbid antisocial behavior contributes significantly to the etiology of alcoholism. However, antisocial behaviors that are manifest before the development of alcohol problems are not "specific personality facets"; in fact, "specific personality facets are not major factors in alcoholism." (500–502)
3. A great deal of emphasis can be placed on the genetic contribution to alcoholism. Genetic contribution presents a greater risk than does the actual presence and interaction contributed by growing up in an alcoholic family.
4. Finally: "Thus, the etiological hypotheses that view alcoholism as a symptom of psychological instability may be illusions based on retrospective study." (494)

Zucker and Gomberg (1986) concluded:

1. The relationship of premorbid antisocial behavior to alcoholism has been vastly underestimated. The relationship of childhood antisocial behavior to adult alcoholism has been too readily dismissed.
2. Antisocial behavior is a part of personality and it plays a significant etiological role.
3. The summary regression analysis of potential etiological variables underestimates the contribution of cultural and personality factors to the variance explaining alcohol-related problems. Their [Valliant and Milof-

sky's] analysis also potentially underemphasizes early environmental characteristics as etiological factors.

4. Childhood antisocial behavior is, in fact, consistently related to later alcoholic outcomes in other studies.

5. Finally: "In the study of schizophrenia, significant research advances were made when investigators moved away from a descriptive base that classified individuals primarily on the basis of existing symptoms and moved into the extensive use of history and course variables in understanding the multiple etiologies of schizophreniform problems. The alcohol field is in the early stages of making this distinction." (791)

Psychological investigations and counseling have often been overlooked in the treatment field. Indeed, prior to the establishment of the C.A.C. (alcoholism counselor certification) in the early 1980s, alcoholism counselors often functioned as little more than "sponsors" similar to the system used by AA. This prompted many to speculate why the inpatient rehabilitation programs, with their high costs and mirror image of AA principles, were even necessary. The point being, that AA provides the services of its fellowship at no cost and in the community setting where all problem drinkers must ultimately grapple with their sobriety. Much of the treatment in the field follows a psychoeducational model which also studiously avoids traditional psychology and psychiatry. Treatment workers abhor the use of "psychotherapy" using instead the term "alcoholism counseling" and thus making highly artificial distinctions between the two endeavors. Once again, there is a studious effort to underplay the role of psychopathology in alcohol dependence. The issues have more to do with folk science, belief, turf, power, and money than they do with actual clinical issues of human behavior and how to change it.

Where psychology is emphasized, sometimes in elaborate and fascinating detail (see, for example, Zimberg et al. 1985, *Practical Approaches to Alcoholism Psychotherapy*), there nevertheless exists little or no empirically derived data from which psychological theories and ideas can be substantiated and generalized. Such theoretical models deserve scientific scrutiny because in some ways they represent a nexus between the theoretical underpinnings of psychodynamic approaches of both psychotherapy and alcoholism counseling. Practice in the field could be enhanced by this theory based on therapeutic findings. According to Heather and Robertson (1981):

> It is difficult to overestimate the influence of Alcoholics Anonymous on medical theory and practice in the field of alcoholism. The fellowship has always been interested in popularizing its creed among the medical profession . . . [and] the conclusion can only be that this effort has been remarkably successful . . . A great many hospital rehabilitation programmes consist of little more than a formalized version of AA principles or make

> attendance at AA meetings compulsory . . . On a more theoretical level the parallelism between AA and dominant medical conceptions may be illustrated by the fact that Jellinek's seminal description of the phases of alcoholism was based on replies to a questionnaire constructed by AA and sent out to members through the official AA publication, *Grapevine*. (7)

It is quite clear that theoretical, biomedical underpinnings are the mainstay of considering alcoholism a disease. To have supported Jellinek in his full theoretical formulations would also have meant embracing his ideas about the sociocultural and psychological foundations of problem drinking. Members of AA wanted to be isolated from the mental health movement and from professional counseling. (Early AA history is fraught with an antiprofessional bias which still exists in many quarters of the field.) Neither did the National Council on Alcoholism, as the educational arm of the original Yale School, want the plight of the alcoholic confused with those diagnosed with mental disorders. As a result, that part of Jellinek's theoretical musings were almost totally ignored. The inclusion of the broad diagnostic entities of alcohol dependence and alcohol abuse in the *DSM–IIIR* allow for a diagnosis of either condition alone or in combination with other mental disorders. However, the diagnostic criteria reflect the negative consequences of drinking but do not include any comments about premorbid psychological states. The criteria sidestep the entire issue of etiology. As Pattison, Sobell, and Sobell (1977) point out:

> The traditional model of alcoholism often bears only a marginal relationship to the tentative ideas proposed by Jellinek. Keller (1972) has discussed many of the misuses and misinterpretations that have been made of Jellinek's formulations and suggested that the major source of misinterpretation was members of Alcoholics Anonymous, which had already formulated a physical allergy theory of alcoholism parallel to but not at all identical with Jellinek's model. Jellinek dispenses with such a conception by stating that it was adequate for the purposes of AA, "as long as they do not wish to foist it upon students of alcoholism" (1960, p. 87). What makes the origins of the traditional model of alcoholism so difficult to specify, however, is public and professional interpretation and misinterpretations of the Jellinek and AA models. (10)

Modern conceptions of alcoholism are beginning to replace the classic disease concept among workers in the field. But conceptions in the public eye change more slowly. The following, stated by Dr. Enoch Gordis, director of NIAAA, is excerpted from the fifteenth anniversary issue of *ADAMHA News* (1989):

> For many years, alcoholism was viewed as a unitary disease, with the main task facing the clinician [being] that of determining whether or not the

> patient was alcoholic. One of the primary advances in NIAAA alcoholism treatment research is the greater understanding today that there are many patterns of dysfunctional alcohol use which result in many kinds of disability. This knowledge points to the need for improved diagnostic criteria. (2)

However, the support of research by the NIAAA is clearly tilted toward the biomedical approach to alcoholism. As Gordis notes:

> While there are some who still regard the problem as "willful misconduct," due to our progress in medical research it is now widely accepted as a disease, with both genetic (heritable) and environmental factors involved in the disease process . . . [W]e plan to build upon our newly acquired research base on the genetic predisposition to alcohol abuse and alcoholism . . . Over the next five to ten years, the explosion in knowledge of the brain and new ways of looking at its functioning will, I predict, lead to a surge in medical understanding of alcohol abuse and alcoholism.

The search for a "biological marker" for alcoholism is, in fact, the top research priority of the NIAAA. It also invests heavily in the search for genetic variations in such areas as the liver's metabolism of alcohol. The organization describes two types of alcoholism—"one largely inherited, and one in which both inheritance and environment play a role" (*ADAMHA* 1989:2). They do not seem at all comfortable conceptualizing problem drinking without inferring genetic inheritance issues. Consider the type of evidence below which contradicts the idea of an inherited "at risk" nature of the children of problem drinkers.

Dr. Ernest Harburg, senior research scientist at the University of Michigan School of Public Health, compared the alcohol consumption habits of 390 couples with their children's habits 17 years later. As noted in Harburg (1991), it was found that children whose parents have drinking problems were no more likely to drink heavily as adults than were children of teetotalers. Among children of problem drinkers and children of nondrinkers, about 15 percent drank heavily (fifteen or more drinks a week for men, seven for women), while 85 percent drank moderately (three to fourteen drinks a week for men, three to six for women) or less. Harburg also found that among children of low-to-moderate drinkers, 26 percent drank heavily; 21 percent moderately; and 53 percent lightly (less than three drinks a week) or not at all (*Rockland Journal News,* 1991).

Another questionable example of this genetic risk factor is the oft-quoted notion that children of alcoholics (COAs) are four times more likely to develop alcoholism than children whose parents are not alcoholics. This statistic derives from the work of Goodwin and his associates (1973), who studied adopted children and compared their rates of later life alcoholism against the biological fathers' drinking history (while controlling for the drinking patterns of adoptive fathers). About 18 percent of sons of alcoholic biological parents became alcoholics, compared to 5 percent of sons of nonalcoholic parents. Fingarette (1988) analyzed this finding as follows:

> The hypothesis is that the difference between these groups is attributable to heredity. But to see the full picture, let's turn the numbers around: 82 percent of the sons who had an alcoholic parent—more than four out of five—did not become alcoholics. So if we generalize from Goodwin's results, we must say that about 80 percent of persons with an alcoholic parent will not become alcoholics . . . Even when parents or siblings are heavy drinkers, the fate of a particular person is crucially influenced by conduct, character, beliefs, and environment. (52–54)

This strikes us as incredibly good news. It shows the resilience of children in resisting later drinking problems despite parental patterns of alcohol abuse and alcohol dependence. It should also caution us to heed Mark Twain's warning about the improper use of statistics: "There are lies; there are damned lies; and there are statistics!" Yes, a ratio of 18 percent against 5 percent is a 4:1 ration but this does not really allow persons in the field to state that children of alcoholics are four times more likely to develop alcoholism than children of nonalcoholic parents. Nevertheless, many laypeople and alcoholism workers who do not read critical analyses of the research literature are not likely to know this. They cite the original statistic as if it were proven fact, in part because it appears consistent with their ingrained belief system. It thus becomes part of the cognitive dogma of their model.

Herbert Fingarette, in his controversial *Heavy Drinking: The Myth of Alcoholism as a Disease* (1988), discusses the idea that the public and scientists accept only limited parts of the disease concept of alcoholism:

> Few people (except those involved with alcoholics) can fully state this entire theory, and many people either do not believe every detail of the doctrine or hold some beliefs inconsistent with it. But versions of the classic disease concept remain a dominant theme in the public's thinking about alcohol abuse . . . And yet, *no* leading research authorities accept the classic disease concept. One researcher puts it quite baldly: "There is no adequate empirical substantiation for the basic tenets of the classic disease concept of alcoholism" (Marlatt 1983). Another expert, whose views are more conservative, dismisses the classic disease concept of alcoholism as "old and biased," a model whose propositions are "invalid." (Kissin 1983:3)

Pattison, Sobell, and Sobell (1977) help us to move toward new formulations by placing the original concepts in context:

> The field of alcoholism is changing rapidly. A scant quarter of a century ago alcohol problems were virtually neglected. At that time, except for a

> few professionals, the only concerned people were recovering alcoholics who heroically tried to help one another. When the first formal alcoholism programs did develop, there were few recorded clinical and experimental data. Since that time, the situation has dramatically changed . . . In 1950 there was a dearth of established clinical and scientific knowledge from which to design treatment programs. Most of the knowledge about alcoholism derived from the personal experiences of recovered alcoholics and rather perfunctory clinical observations. (1)

These researchers, in addition, point out that the disease theory which has begun to fill this knowledge void has nevertheless been effectively discredited by research evidence. They have discovered contravening evidence against six basic tenets of the disease model, which say:

1. There is a unitary phenomenon which can be identified as alcoholism.
2. Alcoholics and pre-alcoholics are essentially different from nonalcoholics.
3. Alcoholics may sometimes experience a seemingly irresistible physical craving for alcohol, or a strong psychological compulsion to drink.
4. Alcoholics gradually develop a process called "loss of control" over drinking, and possibly even an inability to stop drinking.
5. Alcoholism is a permanent and irreversible condition.
6. Alcoholism is a progressive disease which follows an inexorable development through a distinct series of phases.

(Adapted from Pattison and Kaufman 1982)

Peele (1985) similarly questions the continuing emphasis upon biomedical factors in addiction, and provides a list of types of social science studies that have actually refuted the disease theory. These are:

1. Laboratory studies showing that alcoholics' patterns of drinking do not conform to the loss-of-control model.
2. Clinical research demonstrating the efficacy of techniques aimed at moderating problem drinking and alcoholism.
3. Longitudinal studies both of the natural course of alcoholism and of outcomes for treated populations.
4. Cross-ethnic and cultural studies demonstrating that social and belief systems are a principal component in alcoholism.

(Adapted from Peele 1985:32–37)

Pattison and Kaufman (1982) called for a significant reformulation of the theory of alcoholism, and have proposed their own model, based upon the current scientific evidence. They call this updated model the "multivariate alcoholism syndrome." The model consists of eleven propositions and a number of corollaries for each proposition. For purposes of brevity we state only the main propositions, as follows.

The Multivariate Alcoholism Syndrome Model

1. Alcoholism dependence subsumes a variety of syndromes defined by drinking patterns and the adverse consequences of such drinking.
2. An individual's use of alcohol can be considered as a point on a continuum from nonuse, to nonproblem drinking, to various degrees of deleterious drinking.
3. The development of alcohol problems follows variable patterns over time.
4. Abstinence bears no necessary relation to rehabilitation.
5. Psychological dependence and physical dependence on alcohol are separate and not necessarily related phenomena.
6. Continued drinking of large doses of alcohol over an extended period of time is likely to initiate a process of physical dependence.
7. The population of individuals with alcohol problems is multivariate.
8. Alcohol problems are typically interrelated with other life problems, especially when alcohol dependence is long established.
9. Because of the documented strong relationship between drinking behavior and environmental influences, emphasis should be placed on treatment procedures that relate to the drinking environment of the person.
10. Treatment and rehabilitation services should be designed to provide for continuity of care over an extended period of time. This continuum of services should begin with effective identification, triage, and referral mechanisms, extend through acute and chronic phases of treatment, and provide follow-up care.
11. Evaluative studies of treatment of alcohol dependence must take into account the initial degree of disability, the potential for change, and an inventory of individual dysfunction in diverse life areas, in addition to drinking behavior. Assessment of improvement should include both drinking behavior and behavior in other areas of life function, consistent with the presenting problems. Degrees of improvement must also be recognized. Change in all areas of life function should be assessed on an individual basis. This necessitates using pretreatment and posttreatment comparison measures of treatment outcome.

(Adapted from Pattison and Kaufman 1982)

We refer the reader to the original writings for a more detailed exposition of this model, whose main purpose is to thrust the field forward and away from disproved ideas.

Dr. Jack H. Mendelson and Dr. Nancy K. Mello of Harvard Medical School are leading researchers in the field and the editors of the classic text *The Diagnosis and Treatment of Alcoholism* (1985). In the first chapter of that book they point out a number of the thorny issues involved in establishing diagnostic criteria for "alcoholism":

> The term "alcoholism" serves as a convenient shorthand for describing a series of complex behavior disorders which emerge as a concomitant of excessive or inappropriate use of alcohol by individuals with varying risk susceptibilities in heterogenous environmental situations. The nosological designation of "alcoholism" is no more precise than specifications of disorders such as arthritis, angina, or anemia . . . Inadequate definitions of alcoholism have often been cited as the primary reason for lack of success in developing adequate epidemiological, diagnostic, prognostic, and even prevention endeavors . . . In summary, professionals who have to make decisions about the presence or absence of alcohol abuse for their patient must make a series of complex judgments. These judgments involve behavioral and medical as well as social factors . . . Rigid diagnostic criteria for alcohol abuse are not possible or potentially beneficial for patients. (2–3)

There is no doubt that biological factors play both positive and negative roles in determining alcohol use and abuse. And there is no doubt that the search for further knowledge in this realm will help to illuminate the problem. But without devoting equal attention to psychological, interpersonal, and sociocultural factors, no understanding of drinking problems can be complete. The bias that has existed in the field—namely, that alcoholism is strictly a biomedical disease—may well have been necessary several decades ago in order to promote the establishment of treatment services for those with drinking problems. But the existence of treatment is now an established fact. It is time to move on. It is time to be informed by scientific study. Most importantly it is time for the fields of alcoholism, drug abuse, and mental health to share more than letters in the ADAMHA acronym. The future fate of mentally ill chemical abusers squarely rests upon our ability to bring the knowledge of the three fields into focus. This cannot be done until the alcoholism field reaches a level of maturity that takes it beyond the rigidities of the old disease conception of alcohol addiction. Focusing on a multivariate explanation will be necessary for the development of a more holistic, biopsychosocial model, which can take all etiological and developmental factors and their complicated interactions into account, without prejudice. The same focus and development would also be useful in the fields of substance abuse treatment and mental health treatment.

The alcohol treatment field must face the important questions raised about the relative efficacy of various treatment approaches to alcohol problems. The work of Saxe and his colleagues (1983) has pointed to the need for a thoughtful and tough-minded analysis of the effectiveness and costs of alcoholism treatment. In another, related study, Saxe, Dougherty, and Esty (1985) conclude:

> Alcoholism treatment has evolved steadily over the last thirty years. The last decade, in particular, has witnessed a dramatic increase in the availability of treatment as government, industry, and private insurers have made health resources available to treat alcoholism. Recent expansion of the alcoholism treatment system and increased use of public funds has, however, raised a series of important public policy questions about the efficacy and benefits of treatment. Unfortunately, evaluation of alcoholism treatment is relatively new, and neither the alcoholism problem nor evidence about treatment effects are clear cut. Because the effects of alcoholism are so diverse and the treatment multivariant, attributing effectiveness is extremely difficult . . . Perhaps most important from our perspective as researchers, we must develop currently lacking information about treatment effectiveness. Only with such information can reimbursement and treatment decisions be made with more confidence, and only then will we be able to develop a more effective treatment system. (529)

Evidently, there is some move toward the use and scrutiny of scientifically based treatment programs, as noted by NIAAA director Dr. Enoch Gordis in 1989:

> Our treatment research is now focusing on better ways to measure the outcome of different treatments, and on the whole typology or issue of matching a patient with a given treatment. The Institute's treatment research endeavors are intended to provide scientifically grounded and technically sound scrutiny of what does and does not work and for whom. (ADAMHA 1989:18)

It is certainly time to refute the probably exaggerated and, in some cases, patently false, unsubstantiated claims coming from treatment programs in the proprietary treatment sector. Emrick and Hansen (1983) mention one hospital-based program that claimed "for the patients that complete the program and continue in aftercare groups we have achieved a better than 90 percent recovery rate" (1078). This information appeared in a magazine advertisement for the program. What was not mentioned in the ad was that only 9.8 percent of the total number of patients actually attended the aftercare groups. Thus the real 90 percent figure pertained to those who had dropped out of care! Yet this same program had the gall to claim that

> the recognition of this treatment center, its goals, philosophy, and success have spread nationally and internationally. This has resulted in the creation of a division within a national corporation to further expand and develop additional treatment centers based on the same medical model of treatment

modality in different locations throughout the United States and abroad. (1078)

Emrick and Hansen (1983) comment: "Although this program has sparked corporate growth, it remains to be proven that the treatment offered is *exceptionally* effective" (1078). We would ask, to what extent was it effective at all? Relapse is the most common outcome of all treatment approaches in the addictions and since these corporations must certainly have known this, then it is no wonder that business flourished. That is, until recently, when managed care and insurance companies began challenging the assumptions underlying the unquestioning use of inpatient care and after having read the Saxe et al. (1983) report. We find it astounding that referral sources kept on using these programs despite a lack of evidence that they were doing the job for the clients. One can only wonder at the anecdotal stories of kickbacks and other incentives earned from referrals to these programs.

Finally, on the topic of treatment effectiveness we must raise the question why more alcoholism treatment programs in the United States have not used treatment methods supported by well-controlled studies but instead cling to methods that are unsupported by scientific evidence. In Table 2–1, the supported and the standard alcoholism treatment methods are delineated, based on Miller and Hester's (1986) exhaustive review of nine hundred studies.

In our clinical experience we have seen some programs begin to combine supported and standard modes of treatment. Controlled studies undertaken in future will help us to know if these new mixes are equally effective. In any event, some of the supported and the standard techniques are also used in drug abuse treatment and the treatment of mental illness. Miller and Hester's writings have, in effect, issued a challenge to the entire field. We have some serious doubts about how quickly the field can warm to

Table 2–1
Supported Versus Standard Alcoholism Treatment Methods

Treatment Methods Currently Supported by Controlled Outcome Research	*Treatment Methods Currently Employed as Standard Practice in Alcoholism Programs*
Aversion therapies	Alcoholics Anonymous
Behavioral self-control training	Alcoholism education
Community reinforcement approaches	Confrontation
Marital and family therapy	Disulfiram (Antabuse)
Social skills training	Group therapy
Stress management	Individual counseling

Source: Miller and Hester (1986), p. 162.

such heretical-sounding findings. Miller and Hester nevertheless offer us some prudent guidelines for use in designing future alcoholism treatment programs:

1. Treatment programs, both voluntary and involuntary, should comprise specific, effective modalities supported by current research. Consideration should be given to funding of programs so constituted.
2. The first interventions offered should be the least intensive and intrusive, with more heroic and expensive treatments employed only after others have failed.
3. As research warrants, clients should be matched to optimal interventions based on predictors of differential outcome.

(Adapted from Miller and Hester 1986:163)

Peele (1989) offers the following thoughtful and provocative analysis of the relevant issues:

> In the final analysis, what works in all these effective therapies is identical to what works for people who improve their lives without therapy: a strong desire to change; learning to accept and cope with negative feelings and experiences; development of enough life resources to facilitate change; improved work, personal, and family dealings; a changed view of the attractiveness of the addiction brought on by a combination of maturity, feedback from others, and negative associations with the addiction in terms of the person's larger values. The scientific research reinforces a very straightforward and logical view of how people quit drinking or otherwise eliminate addiction; that is, the science of addiction is a science of common sense and human coping. The best thing people can do to solve or prevent addiction is to learn to control their destinies, to find social and work rewards, and to minimize—or at least to bring within controllable limits—stress and fear, including their fear of the addiction. (202)

The field of alcoholism treatment and research is plagued by another problem: namely, a sexist bias that it has taken toward its research and programs. Simply stated, much of what is known and believed about alcoholism is based upon research dealing with male research subjects and male patients. One of the most formative texts in the field is Valliant's *The Natural History of Alcoholism* (1983). Both the core city and the college samples consisted of males. Yet a great many generalizations have been made from his work and that of other leading researchers and clinicians. Marian Sandmaier, author of *The Invisible Alcoholics: Women and Alcohol Abuse in America* (1980), states:

> Our culture's need to evade and deny the reality of alcoholic women is so powerful that it permeates the alcoholism field itself . . . Efforts of alcoholism programs to identify problem drinking women in the community are often lackadaisical or nonexistent, even as outreach programs for men are energetically pursued. As for alcoholism research, it barely acknowledges the presence of women: by 1970, only twenty-eight of the several hundred English-language alcoholism studies in existence, specially focused on the female sex. Meanwhile, alcoholic men, from skid row derelicts to corporation executives, have been exhaustively studied, with the resulting information used to design casefinding and treatment approaches for *all* alcoholics. So even when problem drinking women are "helped," their real issues and needs are often ignored. As women and as individuals, they still remain invisible. (xv)

This problem is echoed by Dr. Sharon Wilsnack (1982) of the University of North Dakota School of Medicine: "Until recently, women drinkers received little attention in the literature on alcohol problems. Most clinical and experimental research involved only men, with findings then often assumed to apply equally well to women" (718). Wilsnack also cautions us to carefully analyze any generalizations that may not be warranted or require further critical exploration, such as the issue of psychopathology in the alcoholic woman. The *DSM–IIIR* states:

> The natural history of alcoholism seems to be somewhat different in males and females . . . Females with alcohol dependence have been studied less extensively than males, but the evidence suggests that the course of the disorder is more variable in females. The onset often occurs later, and spontaneous remission is less frequent. Females with alcoholism are also more likely to have a history of mood disorder. (174)

Wilsnack comments:

> Many early clinical reports describe alcoholic women as more abnormal or pathological than alcoholic men. Data cited to support this belief have included alcoholic women's higher rate of marital instability, psychiatric treatment, suicide attempts, and marriage to alcoholic spouses. However, the interpretation of these data is unclear, as several reviews have noted. For example, the report of difference in suicide attempts may simply reflect the higher incidence of depressive disorders among women than men alcoholics. In any case, it is difficult to separate indicators of greater "pathology," which may have preceded the development of drinking problems, from the social consequences of drinking, which may be more severe for women than men. (720)

We have now seen that the alcoholism field has historically placed as much distance as it could between itself and the emerging mental health field. The same can be said for its separation and vice versa from the field of drug abuse treatment, as we will indicate further in the next section. The main reason for this is the alcoholism field's insistence on total abstinence from all mood-altering substances and the existence of one hundred thousand patients on methadone maintenance in the drug abuse treatment field. This, despite the fact that methadone treatment and the disease concept of alcoholism have much in common. The existence of the mentally ill chemical abuser forces the possibility of dialogue between all three fields, and this is emerging but in a painfully slow manner.

The Drug Abuse Treatment Movement

Chronology of the Drug Abuse Treatment Movement in the United States

1870: Morphine was used freely to treat wounded soldiers during the Civil War. Many continue use after the war has ended. Opium is legal as is cocaine (extract of coca) and they are used in hundreds of patent medicines which claim medicinal cures for countless human ailments. It is quite common to find many upstanding members of the community using such compounds. There are more women using opiates during this era than in modern times. Despite strong outcries against the "evils" of alcohol during this era in American history, no such hue and cry goes up warning of the dangers of these other substances.

1875: The city of San Francisco passes an ordinance prohibiting the smoking of opium, imposing heavy fines or imprisonment. This is a racist law aimed against Chinese-Americans. It mainly succeeds in driving opium smoking underground.

1883: Congress begins a series of raises on the tariff of imported opium.

1889: According to druggists and physicians, most users of opium are middle- and upper-class citizens.

1900: It is estimated that some one hundred thousand white, middle-class women are addicted to morphine.

1906: The Pure Food and Drug Act is passed. It requires that all medicines containing opiates and certain other drugs identify them on their labels and meet official standards of identification and purity.

1909: The importation of smoking opium is prohibited by federal law.

1914: The Harrison Narcotics Act is passed. It is seemingly a law to insure that sellers and dispensers of drugs such as opium and coca are licensed. In fact, due to some slippery language, law enforcement officials interpret it to mean that doctors cannot prescribe such drugs to addicts, as addiction is not officially a disease. In effect the act is a form of prohibition. Doctors are actually arrested and prosecuted; some are jailed. Physicians quickly learn to avoid the negative publicity. The mislabeling of drugs by the federal government has begun, as cocaine is clearly not a narcotic.

Estimates of the number of heroin addicts in the United States range from one hundred thousand to one million, but no one has any objective evidence. These are just guesses.

1918: A Special Commission on Investigation is appointed by the Secretary of the Treasury. It is found that there are equal numbers of drug-addicted men and women. By the late 1960s, the ratio of men to women will be about 5:1. That will change in the late 1980s, when more women will become addicted to crack/cocaine.

1923: The last of forty-four public maintenance clinics for heroin addicts is closed. After a brief period of public support for helping addicts, two Supreme Court rulings (1916 and 1919), which restricted physicians from issuing prescriptions for heroin to addicts, have led to public opposition to these clinics.

1924: Heroin, which is made from morphine, is also banned by law from any use, including medical usage. The U.S. Public Health Service, using reliable data for the first time, estimates that there are some 215,000 heroin addicts in the country.

1925: The Supreme Court declares drug addiction to be a medical, not criminal matter.

1930: Congress creates a separate Bureau of Narcotics in the Treasury Department.

1935: The U.S. Public Health Service opens a one-thousand bed hospital for narcotics addicts in Lexington, Kentucky. A few years later it will open a second in Fort Worth, Texas. These are the first federal efforts to assist drug addicts since the clinics of the early 1920s. The hospitals are originally referred to as "narcotic farms."

1937: The Marijuana Tax Act of 1937 is passed. It requires payment of a tax on all marijuana transactions. However, due to the prompting of Harry Anslinger, the first commissioner of narcotics, this is really an early effort to eliminate the importation and use of marijuana. Anslinger has his own scientifically unfounded ideas about marijuana and ignores research efforts by members of the American Medical Association who are studying the medicinal properties of cannabis.

1950: Mao Tse Tung Communists take over China. Notices are posted that anyone found possessing opium will be shot. After decades of opium addiction among countless numbers of Chinese (complicated and, some believe, caused by the British presence in China), there is a sudden cessation of the problem. The cost of getting high becomes too high.

1952: Dr. Maxwell Jones, a psychiatrist in England, describes his early efforts at establishing a "therapeutic community" (TC) for character-disordered individuals (Jones 1952). In some ways Jones's TC will provide a model for the United States, where TCs for heroin addicts will be established in the late 1950s.

1953: William Burroughs's book entitled *Junkie* popularizes the drug addict's image as a counterculture pop figure. "Junk," he writes, "is not a kick. It is a way of life."

1954: Aldous Huxley's *The Doors of Perception* describes his experiments with the drug, mescaline.

1955: In the first major treatise on heroin, Dr. Isadore Chein of New York University, documents the spread of heroin among black teenagers during the 1950s (Chein 1964). Monsignor William O'Brien, founder of Daytop Village, comments on how heroin addiction broke up the fighting street gangs of the 1950s.

1958: Synanon, the first residential therapeutic community in the United States, is begun in California by Charles (Chuck) Dederich. Dederich, who began his sobriety in AA, found the meetings too tame an environment for his form of confrontational therapy.

1961: The state of California begins a civil commitment program that provides for commitment of addicts in lieu of sentence or prosecution. Addicts are exposed to a form of confrontational therapy and three years of aftercare (parole). Results later show that addicts thus treated fare no differently than those who only "do time."

1962: In *Robinson v. California, 370 U.S. 660,* the U.S. Supreme Court states: "to be a confirmed drug addict is to be one of the walking dead." The Court, in addition, reiterates its support of drug addiction as a medical, not a criminal matter, stating: "We forget the teachings of the Eighth Amendment if we allow sickness to be made a crime and sick people to be punished for being sick. This age of enlightenment cannot tolerate such barbarous action."

Dr. Vincent Dole, a specialist in metabolic diseases, and Dr. Marie Nyswander, a psychiatrist, begin experimenting with a synthetic narcotic developed by the Germans in a search for a way to help heroin addicts. Their early work will lead to a collaboration between Rockefeller University and Beth Israel Medical Center that launches the Methadone Maintenance Treatment Program (MMTP). This approach to the treatment of opiate addiction rests on a metabolic deficiency theory.

1963: Daytop Lodge is established on Staten Island, New York, as a halfway house for addicts on probation. Several former addicts from Synanon in California will join the staff the next year, when Daytop Village will become the first major therapeutic, drug-free community on the East Coast.

1965: Congress passes the Drug Abuse Control Amendments of 1965. These laws bring barbiturates, amphetamines, and hallucinogens under federal control. The American Civil Liberties Union sues the state of California to have peyote excluded on the basis that it is used for religious rituals by some Native American tribes. The state supreme court two years later overrule the lower court ruling and permit its use for such purposes.

1966: David Solomon's book *LSD* presents a balanced look at the hallucinogen that got Timothy Leary booted out of Harvard. Leary and Alpert's early experimental efforts have by now turned into a siren call to "turn on, tune in, and drop out."

Congress passes the Narcotic Addict Rehabilitation Act of 1966 (NARA). The NIMH is made the primary federal agency involved with treatment and research in addiction. The act allows for the nonpunitive incarceration of addicts for purposes of treatment.

New York State, through its Narcotics Addiction Control Commission (NACC), embarks upon the civil commitment program (like the program California had begun in 1961) for the treatment of addiction. It has a mental health orientation and allows for commitment petitions to be submitted by family members. It is also genuinely committed to community aftercare. The program flounders, becomes the object of intense political criticism, and is ultimately denounced by its strongest backer, Governor Nelson Rockefeller, as a "$1.5 billion failure."

1967: The Addiction Services Agency (ASA) of New York City is created by Mayor John Lindsay. He brings Dr. Efren Ramirez, a psychiatrist who ran a modestly successful program in Rio Piedras, Puerto Rico, to New York City to act as ASA's first commissioner. Ramirez hires Dr. Mitchell Rosenthal, another psychiatrist, who ran a Synanon-like program at the Oak Knoll Naval Hospital in California, as his deputy commissioner for rehabilitation. Together they will create the Phoenix House therapeutic community program. While the state, through the NACC, is creating a civil commitment approach and will later support methadone treatment, ASA is fiercely committed to a drug-free treatment system. Phoenix House will become the largest TC program in the United States. ASA, at its height, in the early 1970s with a budget of over $100 million, will be out of business by the mid-1970s, a victim of many powerful and conflicting political forces.

1968: Heavy marijuana use is reported among American troops in Vietnam. The Army reacts with a strong anti-marijuana education campaign.

Daytop Village undergoes convulsive changes. A number of senior staff leave with two hundred residents. Within several years these people will be responsible for the founding of over thirty therapeutic communities for the treatment of addicts throughout the country (in, for instance, Rhode Island and Pennsylvania).

1969: The number of police officers assigned to the Narcotics Division in New York City is raised from 340 to 500. The number of arrests rises by 50 percent!

1970: The Food and Drug Administration (FDA) classifies methadone as an "experimental" and "investigational" substance for the treatment of heroin addiction. The New York Narcotic Addiction Control Commission (NACC, later renamed Drug Addiction Control Commission, DACC, and then Division of Substance Abuse Services, DSAS) provides the first large-scale funding for MMTP treatment.

Congress passes the Comprehensive Drug Abuse Prevention and Control Act (Public Law 91–513), which is also called the Controlled Substances Act. It charges a number of federal agencies—FDA, DEA, HEW, and the Department of Justice—with responsibility for the treatment and control of drug abuse. Under the act all controlled substances are placed in one of five schedules (the most dangerous in schedule I, the least in schedule V). The act imposes numerous controls on the manufacturing, obtaining, and selling of drugs. It is the first major revision of federal law since the passage of the Harrison Narcotics Act in 1914. There is a great deal of controversy over the schedule criteria. For example, marijuana is placed in schedule I along with heroin; Roche laboratories fights to keep Valium out of all the schedules (and it is finally placed in schedule IV). These judgments seem to be based more on politics and finance than science.

1971: How many heroin addicts are there? The Bureau of Narcotics and Dangerous Drugs estimates there are between 285,000 and 345,000 heroin addicts in the United States. The NIMH estimates 250,000. Whatever the actual figure, the public rates heroin addiction as the third most serious social problem facing the country.

The American media begins to cover stories of American troops in Vietnam smoking "OJs" (opium joints) and using heroin, which is plentiful and cheap. Most significantly, for the first time heroin is being used by whites, both in Southeast Asia and at home. Dr. Norman Zinberg (1971) of Harvard, states that the Army's anti-marijuana campaign was instrumental in soldiers' switching to heroin use once overseas.

The National Commission on Marijuana and Drug Abuse is officially established. President Nixon calls for the establishment of a special action office which will report directly to him on matters concerning drug abuse policy.

1972: The FDA, after reviewing extensive research, changes the status of methadone, from an "experimental" drug to an "approved" drug.

Congress passes the Drug Abuse Office and Treatment Act which establishes the Special Action Office for Drug Abuse Prevention (SAODAP). Dr. Jerome Jaffe will become its first director. SAODAP is charged with the responsibility of developing policies that coordinate the efforts of all of the various federal agencies that deal with treatment and prevention (but not law enforcement).

1973: The drug enforcement responsibilities of ten federal organizations are combined under the control of the newly formed Drug Enforcement Administration (DEA).

President Nixon announces that the United States has "turned the corner on the heroin problem."

The National Institute on Drug Abuse (NIDA) is established to coordinate and direct the federal government's drug abuse policy and activity in prevention, treatment, and rehabilitation.

1975: As many as sixty-one million prescriptions are written for Valium. This is the year in which Valium sales peak at a level that will make it the largest selling drug in the United States.

Dr. Lloyd Johnson and his colleagues at the Institute for Social Research, University of Michigan, with the support of the NIDA begin surveying drug use and related attitudes of American high school seniors. In addition to annual surveys, they will issue periodic detailed reports (such as the *National Trends in Drug Use and Related Factors Among American High School Students and Young Adults, 1975–1986,* published by the NIDA).

1976: Congress amends the Drug Abuse Act of 1972 and changes SAODAP to the Office of Drug Abuse Policy (ODAP) in the executive office of the president. This sets the stage for the coming "drug czars."

Avram Goldstein, Sol Snyder, and others publish articles detailing the discovery of opiate receptor sites in the human brain. Soon afterwards, endorphins and enkephalins—opiate-like peptides—will be identified as the "keys" that fit into the "locks" (receptor sites). Brain-related theories come into fashion to account for craving, habituation, dependence, withdrawal, and other phenomena related to opiate addiction.

1978: Nearly half (44 percent) of all admissions to drug abuse treatment centers are from minority groups. Heroin represents the primary drug of abuse: Blacks account for 43.6 percent of heroin admissions and Hispanics for 20 percent.

1979: The first cases of pediatric AIDS are encountered at the Albert Einstein College of Medicine in the Bronx, New York.

There are now three hundred TCs established across the country.

1980: There are now three thousand federally funded drug treatment programs in the United States serving some 207,946 clients in a one-year period. This degree of support is made possible by the public's belief that heroin use has been responsible for a rise in crime and violence in the inner cities.

1981: The Reagan administration allows the FDA to suspend a rule that would have required Valium to carry a warning indicating its addiction potential, its synergistic effects with other drugs, its potential for birth defects, and problems regarding usage for more than one month. This is just one of the many Patient Package Inserts (PPIs) that drug manufacturers do not want the public to receive (Bargman et al. 1982). In the previous year thirty-three million prescriptions for Valium were filled. Despite potent evidence of the drug's dangers, powerful efforts were made to keep this information away from the public.

The Omnibus Reconciliation Act establishes the block grant funding mechanism which will result in decreased public spending on drug abuse treatment in the 1980s. It also signals a lesser role for policy setting as well as reduced funding for the NIDA.

1982: There are now seventy-five thousand heroin addicts being maintained on methadone throughout the United States. In this year alone, 14,984 new clients enroll in MMTPs.

The Center for Disease Control (CDC) in Atlanta officially recognizes the Acquired Immune Deficiency Syndrome (AIDS).

The Director of the DEA now reports to the head of the FBI.

1985: Hanson et al. (1985), in their *Life with Heroin: Voices from the Inner City,* reveal the findings of the Heroin Life-Style Study undertaken with 124 men in the ghettos of three major U.S. cities. Written from the perspectives of these black male addicts, the findings reveal men who, despite regular heroin use, engage in many conventional activities and are able to control their heroin use. This life-style directly challenges the media's and the popular image of the heroin addict.

A total of 13,501 cocaine users are treated in hospital emergency rooms; of these 660 die.

1986: Congress passes the Antidrug Abuse Act of 1986 (Public Law 99–570). Among other things it provides for the forthcoming White House Conference for a Drug Free America. It also creates the Office of Substance Abuse Prevention (OSAP), as part of the Alcoholism, Drug Abuse, and Mental Health (ADAMHA) bureaucracy.

According to a survey of 245,000 prisoners in state penitentiaries undertaken by the U.S. Justice Department, drugs or alcohol are involved in two out of three violent crimes. Sixty-four percent of violent U.S. criminals say that either they or their victims—or both—were under the influence of drugs or alcohol at the time of the crime.

1988: The White House Conference for a Drug Free America issues its final report. It contains hundreds of recommendations. There is little federal money available to allow most of them to be followed through on, with the exception of law enforcement recommendations. Conspicuous by its absence are any recommendations dealing with the children of drug addicts. It also does nothing to support increased treatment services for addicts.

The Antidrug Abuse Act of 1988 significantly expands the scope and functions of OSAP. It now is responsible for the National Clearinghouse for Alcohol and Drug Information (NCADI) and the Regional Alcohol and Drug Awareness Resource (RADAR), and issues grants to community-based prevention programs. The act also establishes, under the Department of Housing and Urban Development (HUD), the Drug Information and Strategy Clearinghouse to provide housing officials, residents, and community leaders with assistance and information on drug abuse prevention and trafficking control techniques. In cities across the country, housing authorities begin evicting tenants who are convicted of drug trafficking.

According to the federal Bureau of Justice statistics, 2.3 million people are on probation (up 5 percent from 1987) and one million are in prisons and jails (up 4.3 percent from 1987). The Rand Corporation indicates that in the last decade the prison population has risen by 45 percent and the probation population by 75 percent. Experts estimate that 75 percent of the probation population is addicted to drugs or alcohol and very few are receiving treatment services. One hundred thousand of those arrested for violent crimes are adolescents.

Dr. Charles Shuster, director of NIDA, states that treatment is effective only for those who stay in treatment and that, unfortunately, only about 20 percent of those requiring help are in treatment programs. Some programs, like the TCs, lose from 50 to 60 percent of their residents in the first month of treatment. Self-help groups like Narcotics Anonymous lose 50 percent of their members in the first four months.

According to a survey conducted in five cities by the NIMH, almost one in three Americans will suffer from a mental or substance abuse disorder during their lifetimes, and more than 15 percent of these will experience such a problem during a typical month.

The bulk of available treatment involves some ten thousand drug and/or alcohol treatment programs; 75 percent of them are outpatient and 65 percent are supported by an estimated $1.3 billion in tax dollars. In 1988, 525,000 people are treated for drug dependency in these publicly funded programs. The National Association of State Drug and Alcohol Abuse director says sixty thousand people nationwide are on waiting lists for tax-supported facilities.

The ADAMHA estimates that drug abuse costs the nation $58.3 billion for legal expenditures, property destruction, lost productivity, morbidity, reduced productivity, and related costs.

A study of New York City police statistics reveals that crack addicts account for only 4 percent of felony violence. It seems that crack dealing is more closely associated with the spread of violence than its use.

1989: President Bush appoints William Bennett director of Drug Control Policy but he does not make this post part of the cabinet. Bennett will be replaced by Bob Martinez in early 1991. Martinez will be directly supportive of treatment efforts whereas Bennett is a strong advocate of law enforcement approaches to the drug problem.

Dr. Wendy Chavkin surveys seventy-eight drug treatment programs in New York City and finds the following in regard to pregnant women:

- Fifty-four percent of the programs refused service to pregnant addicted women.
- Sixty-seven percent denied treatment to pregnant addicts on Medicaid.
- Eighty-seven percent denied treatment to pregnant women addicted to crack.
- Fewer than 50 percent who accepted pregnant women made arrangements for prenatal care and only two provided child care.

The National Institute on Justice reports that in many U.S. cities, hard-core users of cocaine and heroin are now as likely to be women as men. Crack has served as the great "equalizer" and the fear of crashing on crack has led many users to heroin to counteract these effects.

The most comprehensive study of the effectiveness of drug abuse treatment is published by the Research Triangle Institute. Under the leadership of Dr. Robert Hubbard, a study is made of ten thousand addicts who underwent treatment in MMTPs, TCs, and outpatient modalities during 1979, 1980, and 1981. Its major finding is: treatment works (Hubbard 1989). Conspicuous by their absence are the private twenty-eight-day rehabilitation chemical dependency programs, which decline participation in the study. The report details the strengths and weaknesses of the modalities studied and provides encouragement for a beleaguered field. This research, funded by the NIDA, is also known as the *TOPS* (Treatment Outcome Perspective Study) project.

The NIDA's budget is $293 million, making it the largest institution devoted to drug abuse research in the world. The NIDA maintains the Drug Abuse Warning Network (DAWN), conducts the National Household Survey on Drug Abuse, the High School Senior Survey, the Community Epidemiology Work Group, and operates preclinical and clinical research divisions, among other activities.

The OSAP's budget is $69,853,000.

1990: There are now one hundred thousand heroin addicts being maintained on methadone throughout the United States. Thirty-five thousand of them are in the state of New York, while only ten to fifteen thousand are in drug-free treatment programs, both residential and outpatient in New York State.

By the end of the 1980s, 115,786 adults or adolescents in the United States have been diagnosed with AIDS, of whom 21 percent had the sole risk factor of injection drug use, and another 9 percent both injection drug use and another risk factor. Fifty-eight percent of pediatric AIDS cases are associated with injection drug use (Sorensen 1990). Syphilis is again on the rise, reaching its highest levels since 1949. The number of cases nationally rose 30 percent from 1985 to 1987. This is attributed to crack use and the sexual "marathons" and "freak shows" that accompany its use. Cases of pediatric syphilis are also on the rise.

The NIDA updates its estimate of the number of cocaine addicts from six hundred thousand to 1.7 million. Data from the annual high school survey conducted at the University of Michigan reveals a continuing downward trend in drug use; however, the survey does not include crack use nor count school dropouts. The New York State Division of Substance Abuse Services (DSAS) reports that the tremendous growth in crack and cocaine HcL, which it had reported from 1985 to 1989, has ceased.

The National Association for Perinatal Addiction Research and Education estimates that as many as 375,000 newborns per year may be affected by maternal drug abuse. Numbers like these are only "guess-timates."

Reports of child abuse and neglect have risen 147 percent in New York City in the past five years (650 percent in the last decade). Family violence has increased 400 percent in the last decade. The number of children in foster care has tripled. Most officials tie these increases to the spread of crack/cocaine.

A report issued by a panel of prominent medical and drug treatment experts, after a two-year study mandated by the Antidrug Abuse Act of 1986, specifies the following findings and recommendations:

- Treatment efforts have been allowed to erode during the last decade and should be greatly expanded.
- Sixty-seven thousand addicts are awaiting treatment; waiting lists must be ended.
- Treatment programs should do outreach to addicted pregnant women and young mothers.
- Clinical services must be restored to methadone programs.
- Community-based programs and treatment in jails must be expanded.
- Private treatment programs, often making extravagant claims for patient outcomes, are twice as expensive as public programs but "there was virtually no good evidence that the treatments were effective." On average these programs run at only 55 percent of their capacity.

In New York State, nearly one-fourth of black men aged 20–29 are under some sort of correctional supervision. According to the Correctional Association of New York and the New York State Coalition for Criminal Justice a great number of cases are directly attributable to the drug trade.

1991: The National Association of State Alcohol and Drug Abuse Directors estimates there are from six to ten million serious drug abusers but only 15 to 20 percent are receiving treatment.

The federal government proposes an $11.6 billion budget for combatting drug abuse (up 11 percent from the previous year). While this budget includes $100 million for expanding treatment centers, it asks the states to match the money at a time when they are in serious fiscal decline. The lion's share—70 percent of the federal budget—is reserved for police and military operations.

The Centers for Disease Control estimates that eighty thousand women in the United States may be infected with the AIDS virus. Estimates predict roughly 30 percent of their babies will contract the virus. IV drug abuse is the leading risk factor in the spread of the AIDS virus in women.

The New York State Division of Alcoholism and Alcohol Abuse and the Division of Substance Abuse Services are finally merged after years of internecine conflict. This leaves only two states that do not have merged agencies. Most states, however, have a single chemical dependency approach.

Summary. The drug treatment field is decidedly recent and relatively untested. Dr. Dan Waldorf, a research sociologist in San Francisco, wrote one of the early treatises on heroin addiction, after extensively interviewing over five hundred male and female addicts in New York State during the late 1960s. In his *Careers in Dope* (Waldorf 1973), he described the "state of the art" treatment practices used at that time:

> Only a small number of addicts in the United States become ex-addicts. As a nation we have given them little help. There has been very little serious treatment (and that only recently); there has been, instead, a heavy, moralistic attitude that has dictated incarceration and coercion. If anything, we have made it nearly impossible for the addict to survive the enforced imprisonment and coercive treatment programs we have erected to deal with the problem of addiction. (28)

Ten years later, under a contract with the NIDA, Dr. Robert Hubbard led a research team at the Research Triangle Institute in conducting a national study of treatment effectiveness. Known as TOPS (the Treatment Outcome Prospective Study), it studied ten thousand addicts who were treated during the period 1979–81. Clients participated in one of three modalities studied: drug-free therapeutic communities (TC), methadone maintenance (MMTP), and outpatient drug-free (OPDF) clinics. The majority of clients were under thirty years of age, were poor, 71 percent were male, only half had high school diplomas, and all three major races (ethnic groups) were represented. It has been the most ambitious undertaking of its kind to date. What did we learn from TOPS? The following are major findings of the TOPS study:

1. The most dramatic finding is that drug abuse treatment was notably effective in reducing drug abuse for up to five years after a single treatment exposure.

- The prevalence of regular heroin use for methadone clients in the first year after treatment (17 percent) was one-fourth of the pretreatment rate; the prevalence of regular cocaine use was cut in half; and regular, nonmedical psychotherapeutic use was cut by one-third.

- For residential clients, the posttreatment prevalence of regular heroin use (12 percent) was one-third of the pretreatment rate; regular use of cocaine declined by half, to 16 percent in the posttreatment period; and nonmedical psychotherapeutic drug use (9 percent) was one-fifth of the pretreatment rate.
- For outpatient drug-free clients, reductions in prevalence of regular use were one-half for heroin and nonmedical psychotherapeutic use, and one-third for cocaine.
- Except for therapeutic community (TC) clients living in-house, relatively little change in regular marijuana use or abuse of alcohol was found in any modality.
- Although relapse was not uncommon within five years after treatment, in any given year less than 20 percent of former clients in any modality were regular users of any drug other than marijuana or alcohol.

2. The three treatment modalities studied had more limited success in rebuilding the lives of drug abusers and reintegrating them into society. Evidence of positive changes in productivity in the posttreatment years was mixed.

- There were reductions in criminal activity and indicators of depression. The pretreatment proportions of clients involved in criminal activity and reporting suicidal tendencies were reduced by at least 50 percent after treatment in all modalities.
- There was little overall increase in employment.
- For the behaviors named above, "a pattern similar to that for drug abuse was evident: dramatic improvement during treatment, some deterioration immediately after leaving a program, and a leveling off in the years after treatment." (164–65)

3. The amount of time spent in a treatment program was the single most important factor contributing to the improvement seen after treatment. For example, TC clients who remained in treatment for more than one year were three times more likely to have full-time employment and not be engaged in crime. Similar findings were noted for the other two modalities.

4. Analyses of costs and benefits for all modalities revealed a "substantial return on investment" simply in terms of reducing crime. Treatment was far less expensive than incarceration.

5. Treatment substantially reduced the spread of the human immunodeficiency virus (HIV) and the spread of AIDS.

6. Drop-out rates were significant. Only 34.1 percent of MMTP clients, 13.4 percent of TC clients, and 6.6 percent of outpatient clients stayed in treatment at least one year. More than 80 percent of TC and outpatient drug-free clients were in treatment for less than six months.

- Across all three modalities heavy alcohol users were less likely to remain in treatment for lengthy stays than were abstainers or less frequent users.
- In general, younger clients stayed shorter periods of time in treatment (in particular, at TC and outpatient drug-free programs).
- Females stayed significantly longer in MMTP and OPDF but were likely to have shorter stays in TCs.
- Criminal justice system referrals stayed significantly longer in TC and OPDF programs than referrals from other sources. Criminal justice referrals stayed significantly shorter periods in MMTP; however, there are relatively few such referrals to MMTPs.

(Adapted from Hubbard 1989)

These are important findings. They spell out, for the period of time measured (1979–81) and the clients studied (primarily heroin users), the relative strengths and weaknesses of treatment efforts. It appears that treatment is like a great big upside-down triangle. Many clients enter the triangle at the top, only to have the retention rates dictated by a substantially high number of dropouts, so that only a small fraction remain to complete treatment in the case of TCs and OPDF programs and continue on in care at MMTPs. This is a revelation that makes many workers in the field uncomfortable and certainly contributes to staff burnout. We would guess that most treatment personnel are not familiar with these outcome studies and optimistically forge ahead without knowing what happens down the road. This may be a necessary self-deluding factor in keeping addiction treatment staff hardworking and optimistic in their outlook. Taking the opposite tact, Levy and Doering (1989) described the phenomenon of the "pseudoclient":

> The addiction treatment system, particularly the public sector, not-for-profit programs are straining under the weight of "pseudoclients" whose personal motivations, despite their often court-ordered presence in treatment, does not include a personal wish to be "rehabilitated." All programs including our own, have to make clear choices about handling "pseudoclients" or we risk exposing our staff to massive frustration and burnout. (30)

The problem of public perception is a different story altogether. The average citizen thinks you send someone to treatment and somehow magically all will be well. They merge the concept of enrolled in treatment with the idea of "cured"! Thus, many people in the treatment industry are leading the call for "treatment on demand." Dr. Herbert D. Kleber is deputy director for demand reeducation at the Office of National Drug Control Policy (formerly under Bennett, now Martinez). His rationale for President Bush's non-support of this concept was indicated in an Op-Ed contribution to the *New York Times*, as follows:

1. Many people who use drugs are not addicts and do not need treatment.
2. It is wrong to suggest that we know how to treat all addicts and simply need more money to do so.
3. Private treatment centers are, on average, only 55 percent full and can accommodate a good portion of the largest addict population: employed 18–40 year olds. Free, publicly funded facilities are filled to capacity.
4. We need to get more addicts to enter and remain in treatment. Addicts repeatedly and impulsively enter and drop out of programs. Programs seek to stop all drug use—however, clients often just want to reduce tolerance and thereby control their use.
5. Clients are often poorly matched to treatment programs. Evaluation and referral are the exception, not the rule.
6. Too many treatment dollars go toward expensive inpatient treatment when less expensive outpatient programs are often more suited to client needs.
7. We must solve the "NIMBY"—"Not in my back yard"—problem, which deters locating more new treatment centers. We must also find and train more needed staff.
8. The presence of waiting lists for public programs obscures the reality of the situation. In effect, while the need for treatment is high, the actual demand for it is low: "if tomorrow we were able to treat all current addicts, most of them would resist or avoid treatment."
9. Congress to date has not compelled the states to create plans that address these problems or funding distribution concerns.

(Adapted from Kleber, *New York Times* 26 Jan. 1990)

The TOPS data and Dr. Kleber's comments make a compelling case for a funding pattern based on demonstrated outcomes and certainly point to a need for serious efforts at change in order to achieve increased treatment efficacy. Treatment works when defined as follows: "Some treatment works for some people some of the time." Despite pleas from many quarters, the technology is overwhelmed by the politics of funding allocations. The attempt to define addict typologies has led to a debate that is as old as the field. Do we need "generic" treatments regardless of the drug of choice or should we foster "drug-specific" modalities such as methadone which only targets opiate addiction. Are the common denominators based on drug of choice or on even more powerful social forces such as race, socioeconomic status, job skills, gender, and the like? What is the meaning of "treatment on demand" in this broader context? Let us consider some differing views on the nature of drug addiction offered by a variety of experts in the field, quoted from a 1989 article in the *New York Times*.

Robert G. Newman, M.D., president of the Beth Israel Medical Center in New York City, which runs the country's largest methadone program:

> There's a fire going on right now killing people and our communities. Sure I agree we need evaluation. But what are we going to do immediately for hundreds of thousands who need help this minute? Waiting lists are grossly understated because many programs are so full they don't even bother keeping a list, and addicts, knowing this, don't even bother to apply.

Mitchell Rosenthal, M.D., president of Phoenix House:

> Waiting lists are soft. You've got one guy on four lists for two weeks and he's not waiting anymore anywhere. Addicts by nature call for help one moment and an hour later, they're far away, emotionally or geographically. It's a motivation built on sand. Treatment on demand? Sure, but we also need demanding treatment, which requires learning another mode of behavior so when life gets tough, they don't mindlessly go off and take drugs again.

Bob Gilhooly, director of substance abuse technical services for the Roanoke Valley Mental Health Services:

> I'm always suspicious of walk-ins. I could use fifty more residential beds tomorrow. But very few walk-ins want residential drug treatment. They're just looking to get detoxed for a couple days and go back out.

Salvatore di Menza, special assistant to the director of the National Institute on Drug Abuse (noting that for 1987 there was a "static" capacity of 338,365 treatment slots in the United States: 60 percent in private nonprofit centers, 25 percent in state and local centers, about 11 percent in private for-profit centers, and 3 percent in VA hospitals—with graduates, dropouts, and repeaters that means a "dynamic" capacity of about eight hundred thousand addicts per year):

> It may be more satisfying to think mainly of residential treatment programs because the addict is put away somewhere safe. But we're going to need a range of strategies. For many addicts, for instance, it's not rehabilitation; it's habilitation. They don't know how to read or look for work, let alone beat their addiction.

Daniel Patrick Moynihan, Democrat of New York and a member of the Senate Democratic Working Group on Substance Abuse (Moynihan 1989):

> This was and is a sweeping proposal (treatment on request). We understood this. And we had no illusion that large-scale treatment could be provided by existing therapies. A pharmacological block for cocaine will be indispensable. Until one appears, "treatment on request" must remain an aspiration rather than a program. I believe we understood that "methadone" clone for cocaine, while absolutely necessary, would not in itself be sufficient. Few cocaine addicts, it should be noted, use cocaine alone. For them overcoming addiction means swearing off alcohol, heroin, PCP, marijuana. Drug addiction is a chronic relapsing disease.

Charles B. Rangel, Democrat of New York, chairman of the House Select Committee on Narcotics (Rangel 90):

> Our drug problem nowadays is much broader than cocaine. But we do not seem to be tuned into the need to address it that way. We still lack a comprehensive plan. We need an approach that should look at the interconnected problems posed by drug use, rather than focusing on the "drug of the year." It is time for policy makers to acknowledge that all drug use is related, that users of one drug are willing, if not eager, to try others.

James K. Stewart, director of the National Institute on Justice (commenting on a 1989 study showing that women are now as likely as men to be hard core users of cocaine and heroin):

> This has challenged our notions about the drug abuse problem generally. We have always suspected that in terms of drug use, men tended to be the more hard core group. But now for the first time we are seeing a drug (crack/cocaine) catch on as a contagion.

Dr. Stanton Peele, social psychologist and author of numerous books on addiction including *The Meaning of Addiction* (1985):

> While some seem to be aided to recovery through treatment, we can never get enough people to accept therapy, cure enough people through therapy, and keep enough people from relapsing after therapy to change fundamentally our society-wide levels of addiction . . . More than anything, our failure at combatting addiction is due to our inability to prevent new addicts from being created.

George Beschner, M.S.W., former chief of the treatment services branch of the National Institute on Drug Abuse, and one of the editors of *Life with Heroin: Voices from the Inner City* (Hanson et al. 1985):

> To be successful, those providing treatment must have an understanding of the meaning heroin users attach to their life patterns. This includes not just the heroin experience itself, but also the social and cultural patterns which

> evolve around, and become integrated with the hustling, copping, and shooting of heroin. Their sexual behavior, social relationships, and ideas about themselves, as well as the communities they live in and the larger society, are all important intervention targets. This, of course constitutes a considerable challenge. It will require sensitivity, careful planning and the conviction that it is possible to help these men find alternative and rewarding lifestyles. (170)

Dr. Craig Reinarman, sociologist at University of California (Santa Cruz) and **Dr. Harry G. Levine,** sociologist at Queens College of the City University of New York, are authors of *Crack in Context: Politics and Media in the Making of a Drug Scare* (1989):

> Once in office, Reagan and his appointees attempted to restructure public policy according to a radically conservative ideology. Through the lens of this ideology, most social problems appeared to be simply the consequences of individual *moral choices*. Programs and research that had for many years been directed at the social and structural sources of social problems were systematically defunded in the federal budget and delegitimated in discourse . . . Drug problems fit neatly into this ideological agenda and allowed conservatives to engage in what might be called *sociological denial*. For the New Right, people did not abuse drugs because they were jobless or homeless, poor or depressed or alienated; they were jobless, homeless, poor, depressed, or alienated because they were weak, immoral, or foolish enough to use the wrong drugs. (560–61)

Dr. Phillipe Bourgois, assistant professor of anthropology at San Francisco State University and author of "In search of Horatio Alger: Culture and Ideology in the Crack Economy" (1989):

> In the day-to-day experience of the street-bound, inner-city resident, unemployment and personal anxiety over the inability to provide one's family with a minimal standard of living translate themselves into intra-community crime, intra-community drug abuse, and intra-community violence. The objective, structural desperation of a population lacking a viable economy and facing systematic barriers of discrimination and ideological marginalization becomes charged at the community level into self-destructive channels. (627–28)

Charles R. Schuster, Ph.D., director of the National Institute on Drug Abuse (ADAMHA 1989):

> Another major health problem NIDA must face is AIDS. About 30 percent of those recently diagnosed with the disease have been intravenous drug abusers. (17)

It is clear to us that controversy in a young field like this one is healthy when it stimulates dialogue and change. It can be pathological when public policy refuses to be informed by the voices of reason and science. Dr. Peele

(1985) reminds us: "Science cannot increase our understanding of ourselves and our world—nor can it show us the way to freedom—if it is held captive by our fears" (xii).

No clear thinking persons would be surprised by the role played by biology in addictive processes and behavior. However, it appears that NIDA, very much like the NIAAA, strongly favors the biomedical model of addiction. We quote from NIDA director Dr. Schuster (ADAMHA 1989):

> In 1958, when I began my career as a scientist studying the addictive disorders, drug abuse was seen as a problem of social deviants who were thought to lack willpower to control their drug taking. But since that time, the investigations of hundreds of researchers throughout the country have shown that drug addiction has a biological component . . . [and] we've learned that there is a specific receptor site in the brain where heroin exerts its addicting effects . . . NIDA's own Addiction Research Center identified a receptor believed to be the site of cocaine addiction. We've found one more reinforcement or "reward" pathways in the brain, where drugs of abuse act to cause the user to take a drug repeatedly. We haven't solved the puzzle yet, but each year new information is uncovered. By learning how drugs initiate the chemical reactions in the brain that ultimately produce compulsive drug-seeking behavior, we hope to be able to develop treatments to interfere with those processes so that the addictive cycle can be stopped. The biological evidence of a "reward" pathway suggests that drug craving may be linked to a common set of reactions in the brain. If we can learn how this pathway is turned on and off by one drug, we may be able to apply this knowledge to developing treatments for a host of drugs. (17)

In the drug abuse treatment field, as in the alcoholism treatment field, very little of actual treatment is medical in nature. Detoxification, prescribing of methadone, and medical complications are clearly the province of the physician. But in all other areas it is the substance abuse counselor who sometimes also receives input from mental health professionals, who carries the bulk of the work. Using primarily individual counseling, group counseling, and group education this army of counselors provides the primarily verbal "therapies" that constitute drug abuse treatment in America.

The search for the neurophysiological and neurochemical substrata of addictive behavior holds great promise—but it is as yet unrealized. To conceptualize discoveries in the biological arena as holding greater promise than clearer understanding of psychological, interpersonal, sociocultural, sociopolitical, economic, sex roles, and anthropological evidence is clearly a bias of major proportions. Sigmund Freud believed that it would ultimately be the hard sciences like biology and chemistry that would bear out his theories. We are still waiting for such evidence to be discovered. In fact, psychiatric and neurological discoveries seem to be taking us further and further away from psychoanalytic thinking. It is a mistake, in our view, to *medicalize* addictive behaviors. It would be just as grave an error to *psychologize* it as well. All evidence points to such behaviors as having multiple determinants, some of which are easier to control and change than others. A biopsychosocial holistic approach is better supported by the available evidence. And, again, we remind the reader: without the ability to *choose* to abstain from psychoactive substances, there can be no rehabilitation or recovery from addiction.

The closest thing to the medical model of drug addiction is the employment of methadone as a form of treatment. Based on a theory of metabolic change (Dole and Nyswander 1968; Dole 1980), the effectiveness of methadone maintenance treatment is posited as follows:

1. Prolonged use of heroin and other opiates may produce unspecified metabolic changes in the body of an addict and cause him/her to experience drug craving after detoxification is complete and there is no longer evidence of withdrawal.
2. With the discovery of opiate receptor sites and the endorphin and enkephalin neurotransmitters, speculation has moved toward the idea of a lock (receptor site) and a key (neurotransmitter). Naltrexone, a narcotic antagonist, can "fool" the receptor sites and keep real opiates from being absorbed. Methadone fills these same sites.
3. Sunderwirth (1985) maintains that "the concept of addiction as self-induced changes in neurotransmission that result in social problem behaviors is a sound definition of addiction."
4. Methadone can be administered in a "therapeutic range" between oversedation and withdrawal. It does this by binding to opiate receptor sites in the brain and requires a steady state of methadone brain levels. As Dole (1980) describes:

> Between the limits of narcosis and abstinence there is a functional zone. If the concentration of circulating methadone remains below the level that gives rise to narcotic effects but above the threshold for withdrawal symptoms, the subject will be both alert and comfortable . . . Moreover, the remarkable difference between methadone and heroin in continuous use provides a clue that I think is relevant to the fundamental problem: the nervous system responds mainly to changes in the concentration of neuroactive chemicals in the bloodstream and tends to lose its response when the concentration remains steady. Addicts seem to use drugs in ways that bring a sharp pulse of the substance to the brain, since it is the pulse that causes the "high." (Dole 1980)

As indicated above, the search for a methadone clone is under way to combat cocaine dependence. Such a mechanism would theoretically block pleasure sensation pathways, thus eliminating the feelings of elation induced by cocaine. However, when the success of the chemotherapeutic approach to addiction in the form of methadone maintenance is measured, one finds checkered results. Listed below are some of the strengths and weaknesses of emphasizing this biomedical approach to opiate addiction.

Strengths of the Methadone Maintenance Option:

1. It is the treatment of choice of the majority of opiate addicts enrolled in treatment. The ratio in New York State of methadone to drug-free clients is about 3.5 to 1.
2. It clearly interrupts the cycle of opiate addiction, and allows clients to move away from opiate use and the attendant life-style, which includes criminality.
3. It gives clients a chance to attend to previously neglected medical problems and dental problems.
4. It leads to stabilization of family life.
5. It is a powerful tool in the fight to stop the spread of AIDS and HIV infection.
6. Due to its powerful sedative nature, even when taken as prescribed, it has a calming and soothing effect on those emotional states most often experienced as uncomfortable by addicts (such as anger and rage, stress and dysphoria).
7. It offers addicts a "breather," during which some may elect to move on to a drug-free state.
8. Because MMTPs are outpatient programs, women are able to keep their children with them while in treatment

Weaknesses of the Methadone Maintenance Option:

1. The metabolic deficiency hypothesis has never been adequately explained or proven.
2. There are MMTP clients who use better quality heroin or "street methadone" to overwhelm the narcotic blockade and get high. No one is certain about the extent of this practice, called "double dosing."
3. The leading cause of failure and death of clients on MMTP has been alcohol abuse, although in 1987, AIDS became the leading cause of death among MMTP clients. Few methadone programs adequately address the problem drinking of their clients.
4. Methadone can only block the effects of opiates and not other drugs such as marijuana, cocaine, and alcohol. Studies have shown such drug use to be a serious problem for MMTP clients.

5. Cuts in funding have reduced many methadone clinics to little more than "turnstile" medication clinics. Little counseling or vocational training is made available. Studies have shown a significant need in the areas of education, vocational training, and job placement for MMTP as well as for drug-free clients.
6. Despite an unproven theory that encourages addicts to remain on methadone for a lifetime (due to the irrevocable metabolic change in their bodies), significant numbers have been able to go off the program and lead drug-free lives.
7. Women maintained on methadone who become pregnant will be at risk for relapse to heroin use if they stop taking methadone. Babies are often born addicted to methadone and suffer from neonatal abstinence (withdrawal) syndrome. Evidence has shown that women who supplement their clinic dose during pregnancy can have children with more prenatal and postnatal complications than women using heroin during pregnancy (Deren 1986).
8. Methadone treatment was oversold by politicians as a panacea for heroin addiction. It certainly does not justify such a description.

Given the realities of the methadone maintenance treatment experience, it is hard to understand the biomedical bias in addiction research (Bratter, Pennacchia, and Gauya 1985). There is no question that methadone maintenance represents a significant modality of treatment and should be supported so that it may add counseling, vocational, and educational services, and family-centered treatment to its strengths. However, it hardly provides us with the kind of encouragement that should make us optimistic about the efficacy of a methadone clone for cocaine dependence. It simply provides too narrow a model to greatly increase our understanding of this complicated multivariate phenomenon of addiction. As Peele (1985) reminds us: "Substance abuse exceeds biological predictability . . . Dependence is, after all, a characteristic of people and not of drugs" (23). The search to find the link between such discoveries as "reward" pathways and specific behavioral correlates continues. So too does the search for evidence for the operation of genetic influences in addictions other than alcohol dependence, and the search for biological markers for substance abuse. Eloquent theories all, but evidence is still lacking and the multivariate model still commands the logical scientific arena. These theories have yet to provide treatment personnel with practical tools.

One of the greatest unresolved problems in the field of drug abuse treatment is in fact the use of another drug, alcohol. One of the earliest reports of drinking among addicts came from Valliant (1966). He followed up on thirty addicts who had been abstinent from heroin for three years. He found that high school graduation, regular employment before addiction, and late onset of addiction were the best predictors of long abstinence. Most were found to be working and leading productive, happy lives but more than half were substituting other drugs, usually alcohol. The multitude of issues surrounding drinking among addicts has affected both drug-free and MMTP modalities.

Carroll et al. (1977) reviewed the entire literature on alcohol abuse among drug-dependent persons. They report:

> The literature review very clearly indicated that the majority of drug dependent persons abused alcohol before becoming addicted to other drugs such as heroin. A conservative estimate of this form of sequential multiple substance abuse would include 80 percent of all drug-dependent persons. The literature also indicated that substantial numbers of drug-dependent persons used alcohol as a substitute for their preferred drug(s) of abuse, as well as a means of boosting, balancing, counteracting, or sustaining the effects of the other drug(s). Based on the literature, this form of concurrent multiple substance abuse histories [accounts for] at least 30 percent of all drug dependent persons. (312)

Barr and Cohen (1979), in their study of the problem drinking drug addict published by NIDA, report:

> In viewing the person's total substance abuse history, problem drinking by drug addicts is the most common type of multiple substance abuse that has been identified in this sample. The findings show that problem drinking drug abusers are more deeply disturbed, and their disturbance can be traced to the earlier period of life. (44)

Kreek (1978) concluded: "Finally the single most common cause of serious medical complications in methadone maintenance patients during methadone treatment, during and following detoxification from methadone, is alcohol abuse."

The estimated usage of alcohol and other drugs by methadone patients in three MMTP clinics in New Jersey was reported by Levy (1977), as adapted in table 2–2.

The major issue is not that alcohol abuse and dependence exist among methadone clients and participants in drug-free programs. The greater problem is the lack of adequate response to this problem.

As noted in the *Proceedings of the Therapeutic Communities of America Planning Conference,* sponsored by NIDA in 1976:

> The therapeutic community concept and philosophy is not sufficient to understand and deal with alcohol problems. The large community and peer pressure are not effective in controlling drinking behavior. There is a need to utilize experts whose experience can be applied, in dealing with alcohol abuse problems. (105)

Table 2–2
Estimated Usage of Alcohol and Other Drugs by Methadone Patients in Three MMTP Clinics
(reported in percentages)

	Use Other Drugs	*Use Alcohol*	*Abuse alcohol*
Staff (n = 40)	47.5	60.25	36.25
Clients (n = 146)	41	56.8	39.2

Adapted from Levy (1977).

For many years the old-line TCs actually rewarded senior residents, reentry candidates, along with program graduates with "drinking privileges." This was known in the old days as "getting your wings." The idea always seemed counterproductive and confused: it rewarded people who had a history of serious drug abuse with yet another drug. Perhaps it helped to mask alcohol abuse among the staff, many of whom were self-medicating and sedating themselves with alcohol. This seems even odder when one considers that Synanon's founder, Chuck Dederick, came from a background in Alcoholics Anonymous. During our many years in the field there have been many rumors about prominent people in the TC movement with drinking problems—a number of them dying from liver disease. It is only in recent years that some of these programs have begun to discourage drinking, provide alcohol education, encourage clients to attend AA meetings, and in some cases actually conduct alcoholism counseling.

Methadone programs did even less for a long time. Since they were so focused on opiate abuse, they tended to ignore other forms of substance use and after all, alcohol is a legal, socially acceptable drug. While Dr. Levy was director of the Alcoholism Treatment program at Beth Israel Medical Center in New York City in the late 1970s, he worked closely with a number of methadone clinics. At one clinic which served three hundred clients, a fifteen-item alcoholism questionnaire was administered; the findings shocked the staff. Clients whom they never suspected of having drinking problems met the full-blown criteria for alcohol dependence. Some of the older clients who complained that their methadone wasn't "holding them" and asked to have their dosage raised were scrutinized, and as a result, heavy drinking was revealed. The liver was metabolizing the alcohol before the methadone and the brain wasn't receiving its "steady state" of methadone. They did not require more methadone—they needed treatment for their alcohol abuse and abstinence from alcohol.

At that same time, the fifty-bed alcohol detoxification unit of the Alcoholism Treatment program at Beth Israel began taking methadone patients (who had previously been detoxified from alcohol on the Drug Detox units). This was the first alcoholism treatment program in New York City to detoxify methadone patients from alcohol. The patients were grateful for the service. They received humane, polite treatment from the staff and for the first time, they were learning about the drug, alcohol, and the problems of alcohol abuse and rehabilitation. Getting them to follow-up on care for their alcohol dependence proved more difficult, however. Dr. Levy ended up recommending that the MMTP clinic staff needed to begin treating the problem (Levy 1982). Of course this meant the staff would now have to be educated about alcohol use and abuse; and many were pessimistic about their getting through to the clients about cutting back or stopping drinking. Years of systemic neglect had taken their toll. Another problem faced by MMTP clients was that they did not feel welcome at AA meetings because of the emphasis on being totally drug-free. Few alternatives had been developed. In the late 1980s, we finally heard about a methadone clinic in Baltimore that holds its own AA meetings. Chuck Eaton at Roosevelt Hospital's MMTP in New York City actually began alcoholism education and counseling right in the clinic around 1980. As far as we know he was the first to do so. Some things change very slowly.

In the TOPS project, fully 20 percent of clients across modalities had received treatment for alcohol-related problems prior to entering the programs under study. Heavy alcohol users in all three modalities were less likely to remain in treatment for lengthy stays than abstainers or less frequent users. This lack of commitment has been another contributing factor to the antipathy the alcoholism treatment field has felt toward the drug abuse treatment field. There remains much to be done to remedy this neglect and outright encouragement of alcohol abuse.

There is another parallel between the alcohol and drug fields: namely, their respective failure to provide quality care for female clients. While Dr. Levy was director of the Division of Drug Abuse he and Kathy Doyle were the first (see Levy and Doyle 1974) to formally document the sexist belief system and differential treatment of women in a major therapeutic community program. This study was followed by a similar documentation of problems faced by women in methadone maintenance treatment (Levy and Doyle 1976).

The problem originates from the fact that the early efforts to treat heroin addicts in the late 1950s and 1960s were conceived by men for the treatment of male addicts (who came to treatment in a ratio of four or five men to every woman in those days). The drug abuse treatment literature at that point had ignored the fate of female clients: Chambers and Inciardi (1972) observed that researchers had largely ignored or omitted female addicts from their analyses. The much heralded evaluation by Mandel (1973) of some nine drug abuse treatment programs across the nation was conspicuous by its failure in attending to sex differences between clients. Even the TOPS study (Hubbard et al. 1989), which had women accounting for some 29 percent of the ten thousand addicts studied, was able to draw very few conclusions about women. And, in commenting about future research, it did not draw attention to women's greatly increased number due to cocaine abuse.

Dr. Josette Mondanaro, a leading advocate of women's issues in treatment, states in her *Chemically Dependent Women* (1989):

> Programs admitted women as an afterthought, without regard for their particular needs. In fact, women were sometimes included primarily as objects onto which male clients could transfer their anger regarding mothers, wives, and girlfriends. Treatment designs included the breaking down of defenses through abrasive confrontational methods. Little thought or attention was paid to the fact that these techniques are countertherapeutic for most women and some men who are already extremely self-critical and have poorly developed boundaries.

Dr. Levy and Marie Broudy (1975) took a closer look at sex role differences in the therapeutic community:

> Most, if not all women entering the therapeutic community have had repeated negative experiences regarding their own femininity and concept of womanhood. For many, drug abuse represented a form of self-medication which temporarily assuaged negative self feelings. In addition, this self-medication also covered such physical problems as dysmenorrhea, amenorrhea, pelvic inflammatory disease, and other forms of body damage. Entry into a drug-free TC brings a woman face to face with her body symptoms and her psychic symptoms . . . Consider the biases practiced in the TC concerning: 1) job function assignments, 2) job training, 3) educational opportunities, 4) double standards concerning sexual morality, 5) different criteria for readiness for graduation, 6) the extending of privileges, 7) sexual voyeurism (the male practice of wanting to know all the intimate details of a female's sexual experiences), and 8) who gets pressured to learn to be a better parents. (293)

In their book *Children of Drug Abusers,* Dr. Levy and Eileen Rutter (1992) document many of the reasons why women do not come to or stay in drug abuse treatment, as follows:

1. No responsible relatives or others to care for their children if they enter residential treatment.
2. No responsible relatives or day care if they are to enter four- or five-day a week, day or evening hospital model programs.

3. No responsible relatives, evening care, or money for baby-sitters for evening outpatient programs.

4. Children's fathers are not available for sharing of child care responsibilities.

5. No car, rides, money, or reliable public transportation to get to treatment sessions on a regular basis (programs usually have rigid rules of attendance and are unsympathetic).

6. Many programs forbid bringing children, especially those that are highly active or otherwise require continuous supervision, to individual or group counseling sessions.

7. Husbands, boyfriends, or paramours refuse to allow "their woman" to enter a program especially if there are male counselors.

8. Many women fear that "exposure" to the authorities including treatment personnel will result in having their children taken from them. They fear urine analyses which might reveal continuing drug use.

9. Women often avoid programs with female counselors or women's groups because they would rather deal with males whom they perceive as easier to manipulate and "get one over on." They know that women are less likely to be sympathetic to such attempts to manipulate and can see through their defenses and excuses. These women are poorly socialized around having positive relationships with other women and have great difficulty overcoming the "street mentality."

10. Other women avoid programs with male counselors because they have been brutalized by men in the past—beaten, raped, molested, been victims of incest and otherwise abused and neglected. They may be particularly leary of male ex-addict or recovering counselors.

11. Many women avoid treatment because confronting the consequences of indiscriminate sexuality can induce powerful feelings of shame and guilt. Sexually transmitted diseases (STDs), HIV, AIDS, pelvic inflammatory disease (PID), ammenorrhea, dysmenorrhea, and the like are only part of the problem. Objectifying one's body into a vehicle for sex for drugs ("cocaine whoring") or money for drugs (prostitution, more common to heroin addiction) leads these women into feelings of a depraved humanity caused by participation in sexual "freak shows" (put on for men for money and/or drugs). These feelings can only be dealt with by skilled and sensitive counselors, who for the most part are sorely lacking in most drug abuse treatment programs.

12. Many women shun treatment for fear of having poor parenting revealed. As their children exhibit more problems than non-addicts', they are fearful of being judged by treatment, child care, or school personnel and tend to keep to themselves (thus leaving problems unsolved). This drives them deeper into drug abuse and depression.

13. Some women fear detection of child abuse and neglect. They are afraid of being reported to government authorities. They know that if such

action is taken and they drop out of treatment, their child(ren) can be placed in foster care.

(Adapted from Levy and Rutter 1992:98–99)

Levy and Rutter (1992) issue a call for psychodynamic, family-oriented treatment which places an emphasis on real life issues for women. They also describe treatment services for children who no longer live with their parent(s). The drug field, in failing to adequately help women, also fails the children of addicts. Efforts toward this type of clinical programming are only now receiving serious attention. Unfortunately, while women and their children have been deemed a priority, federal, state, and local government funds are dwindling for drug abuse treatment as a result of horrendous budget problems.

The drug abuse treatment field is young and cries out for the testing of new treatment approaches. MICAs will certainly require new approaches in a field with so limited a proven treatment technology. Dr. George Deleon, for many years the inhouse researcher at Phoenix House, points out:

> Recently, much attention has been paid to the MICA clients. These primary psychiatric patients with substance abuse difficulties have been excluded from TCs (and other drug abuse treatment modalities) because of the apparent unsuitability for this approach. Moreover, indications are that these same clients cannot be managed in existing mental health facilities. They appear to be the group that falls between the cracks of the two systems . . . Although few in number, plans are currently underway to evaluate the effectiveness of these adapted TCs for the MICA client. (Deleon 1989:186)

A Brief Review of Models

Attributing Responsibility for Problems and Solutions

Most of us have heard the expression "Perception is reality!" The frame of reference or perspective that one chooses to analyze a phenomenon is all-important because it can profoundly color one's interpretation of events and ideas. As we have seen in our brief review of the development of the three fields there is much controversy over two important issues: 1) the etiology (cause) of the problems we call addiction and mental illness; and 2) the most effective treatment strategies to be employed. Attribution of responsibility for problems and attribution of responsibility for improvement are not necessarily the same thing and can have very different consequences. Brickman et al. (1982) in "Models of Helping and Coping" provide important means of understanding the distinctions:

> By drawing a distinction between attribution of responsibility for a problem (who is to blame for a past event) and attribution of responsibility for

3
Clinical Issues

The Language of Diagnosis

Under ideal conditions, client diagnoses are determined over time with a good deal of data contributing to the process. This process of describing and labelling is influenced by many factors that may either add or detract from the ideal. Practicing clinicians need to sharpen their awareness and their skills in making diagnostic judgments. An unwritten maxim in medical circles is: "Treatment without diagnosis is malpractice!" This not only cautions the practitioner about legal concerns but also about the need for applying rational and appropriate treatment. A formal diagnosis is not always necessary to provide treatment, but it can help guide the selection of the most appropriate and hopefully also the most effective treatment.

Some of the factors that influence the labelling of client behavior are listed below:

1. training (or lack of training) of the clinician
2. clients' willingness/ability to cooperate with the clinician
3. intellectual model used regarding the target behaviors
4. relative urgency of making the judgment (owing to the severity of symptoms, acting out behavior, perceived danger, family pressures, and the like)
5. agency guidelines regarding acceptance criteria
6. biases and prejudices of the clinician
7. availability of treatment slot (triage)
8. compassion of the clinician
9. lack of treatment alternatives
10. family input and/or pressure
11. insurance reimbursement guidelines
12. clients' belligerence or menacing postures

Ever since Emil Kraepelin published his *Textbook of Psychiatry* in 1883, psychiatrists have sought to create a nomenclature which accurately describes mental disorders. We quote from the introduction to the *Diagnostic and Statistical Manual of Mental Disorders,* the third, revised edition, (*DSM–IIIR*), in which their attempts to define and classify mental disorders are described. Dr. Robert Spitzer, editor and chair of the work group to revise the *DSM–III,* and Dr. Janet Williams (1987), the text editor, comment as follows:

> *DSM–III* is only one still frame in the ongoing process of attempting to better understand mental disorders. *DSM–IIIR* represents another still frame. . . . (xvii)
>
> The impact of the *DSM–III* has been remarkable. Soon after its publication, it became widely accepted in the United States as the common language of mental health clinicians and researchers for communicating about the disorders for which they have professional responsibility. . . . (xviii)
>
> There is no assumption that each mental disorder is a discrete entity with sharp boundaries (discontinuity) between it and other mental disorders, or between it and no mental disorder. . . . (xxii)
>
> A common misconception is that a classification of mental disorders classifies people, when actually what are being classified are disorders that people have. For this reason, the text of *DSM–IIIR* (as did the *DSM–III*) avoids the use of such expressions as "a schizophrenic" or "an alcoholic" and instead uses the more accurate, but admittedly more cumbersome, "a person with Schizophrenia" or "a person with Alcohol Dependence." . . . (xxiii)
>
> Another misconception is that all people described as having the same mental disorder are alike in all important ways. Although all the people described as having the same mental disorder have at least the defining features of the disorder, they may well differ in other important respects that may affect clinical management and outcome. (xxiii)

With regard to this multiplicity, Schacht (1985) reminds us that

> by dividing a complex phenomenon into conceptually distinct but inclusive categories, we may succumb to an illusion of mastery, a false belief that complexity has yielded to simple, clear understanding. Such illusions of simplicity and mastery underlie dichotomization of science and politics in discussions of *DSM–III*. The *DSM–III* is both a tool for the production of scientific knowledge and an instrument of rhetoric, social organization, and power distribution. (520)

Thus, despite its popularity for clinical research and treatment and for third party payments purposes, the *DSM–IIIR* is a "work in progress." It is comparatively free of etiological bias when compared with earlier versions and far more descriptive in nature. It is only an incomplete map with much territory yet uncharted. But as much as it represents the ongoing search for clearer descriptions, it is also a tool for extending the power and influence of psychiatry over the arena of mental illness. In effect, the person who controls the diagnostic process can also attempt to control the marketplace.

That power and turf are never easily won nor shared among the various disciplines of the mental health profession is indicated in this case by the *DSM–IIIR*'s bias toward the medical model. In this model, human suffering is classified as diseases or disorders to be treated, primarily by physician psychiatrists. However, there are many who take strong exception to viewing human suffering as uniquely biogenic in nature (see Peele 1985; Peele 1989; Halleck 1971; Szasz 1961; Laing 1964; Marlatt and Gordon 1985; Orford 1985; Blane and Leonard 1987; and Fingarette 1988).

The *DSM–IV* is scheduled for release in 1993. For the first time, psychologists have been included on the task force charged with such an important mission as updating the "bible" of American psychiatry. The psychiatrists in power specifically avoided inclusion of psychologists until April 1991. There are numerous aspects of the *DSM–IIIR* that organized psychology finds worrisome: its medical emphasis apparently designed to maintain the medical monopoly on understanding and treating the mentally ill, its failure to duly note social and cultural forces in shaping human behavior, and its insensitivity to feminist issues. For example, debate rages over whether or not severe premenstrual syndrome should be included in the *DSM–IV* (DeAngelis 1991). It is important to keep these caveats in mind as we proceed in our review of the complex process of diagnosis of mental illness, including substance abuse.

The Binary Diagnosis

The client may present in crisis and the clinician has to make what is often referred to as a *binary diagnosis* (sometimes called the *presumptive diagnosis*). This is a strictly dichotomous decision—the client has *it* (that is, the specified condition—psychosis, drug addiction, and so forth) or not! Just as quickly, other mutually exclusive decisions must be made—admit or don't admit as well as treat or don't treat. There is usually little time for history taking: very simply, vital signs (both psychological and physical) are taken and the treat/don't treat decision is made. These decisions may not be made quickly for all patients, however. MICAs have been known to leave a facility because they had to wait too long to be seen: the ebb and flow of their mood and behavioral states (based on drug-related and psychological factors) make tolerating any delay impossible. Emergency room (ER) staff are the most practiced in doing binary diagnoses, which are part of the triage approach to emergency medicine.

Wolfe and Sorensen (1989) point out some of the factors that affect making clear diagnoses:

> When such people (MICAs) become acutely psychotic, suicidal, assaultive, or bizarre and are brought to a public hospital for assessment and care, a situation develops that is often problematic. Diagnosis is confounded by

> the coexistence of substance abuse and mental illness, and differential diagnosis of psychiatric co-morbidities is especially difficult. The patient's social context often precludes obtaining a coherent and informative history from a significant other. However, the patient's social context may contribute to dramatic signs of social deprivation ranging from poor nutrition and poor hygiene to the carrying of weapons for self protection. (169)

Pepper (1985) has described young adult MICAs as "attention seeking—help rejecting." Various authors have provided a composite portrait of the young adult MICA: They often present in psychiatric emergency settings in an acute state of crisis, but disdain the regular use of mental health services. They do not accept their identity as "mentally ill" and often pride themselves on an "identity of autonomy" (see Bender 1986; Lamb 1982; Segal et al. 1977; Sheets et al. 1982).

The practice of triage involves dividing the prospective patients into three groups: those with emergent symptoms who must be treated immediately; those whose symptoms appear minimally severe and can wait; and those with symptoms that are moderately severe, require immediate evaluation, and possibly treatment. The clinician facing this challenge must be able to think on his/her feet and respond quickly to crisis situations. Slaby et al. (1975) in the preface to their *Handbook of Psychiatric Emergencies* caution the emergency room psychiatrist:

> An ability to tolerate anxiety and ambiguity and to blend flexibility with firmness, as well as a readiness to tactfully contend with fear and anger, will stand the physician in good stead . . . Emergency room intervention may require careful listening and observation, as well as a certain degree of risk-taking and pragmatism. Emergency treatment can involve thinly veiled threats to one's self-esteem or personal safety; thus a diplomatic cautiousness tempered with courage will frequently be required.

Emergency rooms in large cities have become overcrowded, understaffed, and dangerous places in which to work. Increasingly, poor people are using emergency rooms as their primary medical care setting—the absence of medical insurance for 30 percent (some 34 million) of our national population, the soaring cost of medical and psychological care, and an absence of funds have jointly created this condition. Injuries, overdoses, or other health-related emergencies caused by smoking crack increased an astonishing ten times between 1985 and 1987, according to a survey by the National Institute on Drug Abuse. The crack/mental illness connection is aggravating an already tense situation. The very recent advent of smokable heroin mixed with crack and smokable amphetamines (even more closely associated with violent behavior than crack) is raising the situation to crisis proportions. Crack addicts exhaust the medical staff who must attend to them; and compassion quickly dissipates when clients return within a week in the same state.

Dr. Henry Pinsker (1983), of Beth Israel Medical Center in New York City, cautions us to look beyond the behavioral posturing of MICA clients that further complicates the diagnostic task:

> Many individuals who have addictive disorders display a behavioral style known as "street behavior". This style, often seen in jails, is characterized by self-centeredness, contempt for authority, exploitiveness, restlessness, and wariness. Much of their time is spent "hanging out," talking about drugs. Personal responsibility is denied and despite an air of toughness, there may be a thin-skinned quickness to take offense. An individual who has acquired this style may be interactive and approaching, even though there is a clear-cut schizophrenic disorder. (621)

A degrading and cynical term is sometimes applied to disheveled, intoxicated, poorer clients, many of them MICAs, whose appearance (and odor) offend ER staff: *SPOS* (pronounced *spoz*)—which stands for "subhuman piece of shit." These prospective patients are often evaluated last: they are, in effect, cast out of the formal triage procedure.

Crack/cocaine has had a powerful impact upon ER practice in the last several years. ER staff differentiate between the crack-abusing patients who are rude, mean, and, as one has termed them, "narcissistic dirtballs" and the "citizens" who do not use drugs. One ER chief physician who quit his position has been quoted as saying: "This place was turned into a zoo by crack and everything that goes along with it . . . Cocaine is the devil, the most savage drug that has ever come along." Another ER doctor has stated: "All we are doing is picking the bones . . . The work is postmortem. Many hospitals around the nation are being overwhelmed by drug-related emergencies and by AIDS."

But Zimberg (1982) alerts us to the limitations of binary diagnoses:

> Significant numbers of schizophrenics abuse alcohol and appear to be alcoholics when seen by mental health personnel. Conversely, alcoholics having alcoholic hallucinosis as a withdrawal manifestation are often admitted to psychiatric hospitals as schizophrenics. It is important to make these distinctions since the treatments appropriate for alcoholism, alcohol withdrawal syndrome, and schizophrenia are quite different. (41)

This brief examination of the binary diagnostic process provides an example of how the medical model has contributed to our understanding of the process of patient evaluation. The often frenzied atmosphere of the medical and psychiatric emergency room sometimes resembles a battle zone where lightning-quick decisions are routinely made. When more time and information are made available, more sophisticated and accurate diagnoses can be formulated. The field of psychology makes its own unique contributions to this process. There are several sources of information that contribute to the ultimate label or category chosen:

Psychiatric Model	*Psychological Model*
1. detailed client history	1. detailed client history
2. physical examination	2. psychological interview
3. laboratory tests	3. psychological tests
4. family history	4. family history

In the most sophisticated approach to client evaluation, a combination of these models is employed. It is interesting to note that many clinicians think of the medical approach as a strictly biological disease model. However, the final diagnosis does *not* have to presume the presence of an actual disease. For example, a single episode of severe intoxication could lead to a judgment of "gross intoxication with accompanying paranoid ideation" rather than a diagnosis of full-blown "paranoid schizophrenia" or "alcohol dependence." But in fact one can study the phenomena of symptomatology without feeling compelled to use a diagnostic category.

Persons (1986) makes a compelling case for studying psychological phenomena rather than psychiatric diagnoses. She lists six advantages to the study of symptoms over the study of diagnostic criteria (using the diagnostic category of schizophrenia as an example):

1. The use of diagnostic category design in a study of thought disorder results in the misclassification of subjects (not all schizophrenics have thought disorder and some patients with thought disorder are not schizophrenic).
2. The symptom approach studies important psychological phenomena that are ignored by diagnostic categories (that is, some verbalizations do not fit into any diagnostic category). Also, diagnostic labels do not specify what type of thought disorder is involved.
3. The study of symptoms contributes to the development of psychological theory, particularly the development of coherent, elaborate hypotheses linking clinical phenomena to underlying mechanisms.
4. The symptom approach permits the isolation of single elements of pathology for study.
5. The symptom approach recognizes the continuity of clinical phenomena and mechanisms with normal phenomena and mechanisms.
6. The study of symptoms contributes to the refinement of our systems of diagnostic classification.

(Adapted from Persons 1986:1252–60)

A number of commentators on the MICA client (such as the Group for the Advancement of Psychiatry 1986; Rounsanville et al. 1986; Pepper and Ryglewicz 1984) have pointed to severe limitations in the reliability of diagnostic categories, particularly when applied to young adult chronic patients (Ridgely et al. 1986). These limitations include the notoriously unreliable system of diagnosing personality disorders in the *DSM–III* (termed *axis II* disorders); confusion over the "primacy" of substance abuse disorders; and polysubstance abuse by clients. Consistent with the six suggestions of Persons (1986) listed above are the poignant observations made by Ridgely et al. (1986) concerning diversity among the chronic mentally ill young adults with substance abuse problems who, these researchers note, are "diagnostically heterogeneous. They meet criteria for a number of *DSM–III* diagnoses and have variable levels of functioning. [However, they] become difficult to place because of their levels of dysfunction" (58–59). Ridgely et al. (1986) also note:

> The concept of chronic mentally ill young adults fails to differentiate among psychotic and nonpsychotic patients, thus failing to differentiate the needs of individuals who fall into different diagnostic subgroups . . . Yet even though identification of diagnosis is important for some aspects of treatment planning, Adler and colleagues, like others in the field, focus on dysfunction and disproportionate impact on the service system in discussing chronic patients with non-psychotic psychiatric problems . . . Such focus on function and needs may prove to be more useful than diagnosis in planning for services and designing programs. (16–17)

In order for our attempts at clinical understanding to work as broadly and as deeply as possible, we must work both within and without the formal diagnostic framework defined by the *DSM–IIIR*. The points made by Persons regarding the study of symptomology are mostly germane to research. However, hands-on clinical practice within our mental health and substance abuse treatment networks compels us to use diagnostic categories for financial and administrative reasons, if not for actual clinical purposes. And by using such categories, psychologists and psychiatrists work side by side in an ofttimes uneasy relationship. Berg (1986), for example, elaborates:

> Over the years . . . clinical psychologists have found psychiatry's praise becoming increasingly fainter. Despite hopeful beginnings, the early promise of smooth collaborations between psychology and psychiatry has tempered as the relationship has stirred mutual disappointment and competition over professional turf. (52)

Among their interprofessional differences, Berg lists conflict over divergent professional identities, political conflict, economic rivalry, and identity conflict between the professions. He recommends that the dynamic of mental health professionals and the patient be viewed as a collaborative triad. Such a view can promote collegiality, consultation, better assessments, and more comprehensive treatment plans. The same recommendations could be made for collaboration between psychiatrists and clinical social workers. The two case illustrations at the close of chapter one suggest consequences which result from an absence of a cooperative attitude. Berg draws our attention to the dynamics of such cooperation:

> Just as the relationship between patient and examiner is a source of diagnostic information, the quality of the relationship between the professionals may in itself be of diagnostic significance. This relationship can reverberate to the tune of the patient's illness, because each professional is engaging in a triangular relationship with the patient and the other professional . . . Highly charged competitive striving may be provoked by a patient's seductive plea for rescue. (58)

Brown et al. (1989) summarize the single most important difference between a *stat* binary diagnosis and the process we will next consider, the differential diagnosis:

> Although there is pressure for swift evaluation for purposes of treatment planning or disposition, the complex needs for a dually disordered person cannot be served by a process that does not allow time for thorough assessment. If initial diagnosis of persons showing evidence of dual disorders is considered tentative, an initial period of treatment can be used as an opportunity for further evaluation and reexamination. Unfortunately, the separation of mental health and substance abuse treatment services tends to short-circuit this process. Mechanisms for joint evaluation and treatment planning need to be developed. (567)

The Differential Diagnosis

The same symptoms or behavioral clusters may have very different causes. Differentiating among the possible causes and isolating the one(s) that the symptoms most reliably and accurately describe define the art and science of good diagnostic practice. Let us consider an example of how this process might work. All of the conditions listed below would lead a prospective patient to present with anxiety:

- homosexual panic
- caffeinism
- cocaine abuse
- primary anxiety disorder

- hyperthyroidism
- alcohol withdrawal

How would you go about determining which of these conditions was the cause and then choose the appropriate treatment? This is referred to in mental health and medical circles as the process of *ruling out*. A hands-on medical examination, a good patient history (ideally with input from a responsible third party added to the patient's recollections), a urine analysis, a sensitive drawing out of the patient, laboratory tests, all would be important. As you went through these various procedures, you would systematically rule out each cause for which you could not find adequate evidence. You would use the evidence collected to differentiate between the probable causes, and finally arrive at a differential diagnosis that commends which course of therapeutic action is to be taken.

Here we must emphasize the following: *perception is reality*. What one perceives and how one interprets that information both are guided by orientation, training, and the use of appropriately objective methods of making such determinations. If everyone is a "dope fiend," or a "drunk," or a "crazy," or a "crack head," or an "hysteric," then one is employing a narrow perspective. This realization is especially important in considering the MICA client, who defies rigid classification and may, for example, suffer from a psychosis, a personality disorder, and also a substance abuse problem (of varying intensity). Way and McCormick (1990) in their review of the MICA literature summarize what we consider to be one of the most telling points concerning diagnosis:

> While treatment milieu may vary, a common lesson is shared in the literature: it is antithetical to effective treatment to presume the primacy of either psychiatric or substance abuse disorders. Practitioners need to recognize that issues surrounding mental illness and substance abuse must be equally recognized and treated and the unique needs and capabilities of MICA clients must be addressed and accommodated. That is, maximal treatment effectiveness results from simultaneous attention to both psychological disturbance and chemical use problems. (18)

Galanter et al. (1987), in their review of the literature on the *dual diagnosis* problem, comment:

> Diagnostically, the differentiation of general psychiatric and addictive syndromes can be difficult: [namely, separating] primary and secondary affective disorder from consequences of long-term substance abuse; cognitive sequelae of abuse from psychotic symptom pictures; antisocial personality disorder from behavior disorders due to abuse patterns; and self-medication patterns from primary general psychiatric syndromes. (1)

Lumping people into narrow categories is not only shortsighted, it may be dangerous. Even when we arrive at a clear diagnosis, in the case of MICAs in particular, the diagnosis does not necessarily commend a definitive or easy course of action to be taken. While conscious bias plays a role in how the client is perceived by the professional, one must also be on guard for those more subtle, unconscious biases which are based on earlier life experiences. Such biases can strongly color our ways of seeing and not seeing, having been formed by our prior experiences with authority figures, minorities, people whose sexual orientation differs from our own, people of the opposite sex, people who remind us of other people, and the like. Good clinical supervision (group and individual) is a helpful tool in uncovering and resolving such issues. The practitioner's own psychotherapy has long been recognized as an effective method as well.

The following features are those most commonly overlooked when trying to diagnose MICAs:

Neurological complications (often caused by alcohol or other drug use, history of head injury, brain lesions, or seizure disorders).

Family history (that might reveal factors such as prenatal complication, early childhood injuries or illness).

Learning disabilities of varying types and intensity

Presence/absence of substances (measured by Breathalyzer, or urine or blood sample).

Malnutrition due to poor diet and/or infrequent meals.

Physical conditions that cause psychological symptoms (such as hypoglycemia, hyperthyroidism, and allergic reactions to medication).

Mixing of one or more prescription medications with either over-the-counter or street drugs.

Manipulative patient behavior (which may include conning staff for money, drugs, a bed, food, and hiding from people in the street; threats of suicide or violence are known to deter or speed an admission).

Failure to take psychotropic medications or other medicines prescribed for illnesses or other medical conditions.

All of the above features tend to cloud the diagnostic picture. There are two types of basic errors in the art and science of diagnosis:

false positive: declaring the presence of a malady or disorder when it really is not there.

false negative: missing the presence of a malady or disorder when it really is there.

Sometimes staff will use a *therapeutic challenge* to aid in avoiding error. For example, if a comatose person is believed to have overdosed on a narcotic drug, the administration of Narcan (naloxone) will cause the person to awaken and speedily recover, if indeed this was a case of overdose. Thus, the giving of Narcan represents the therapeutic challenge. Similarly, a mixture of sugar and water would revive someone going into diabetic shock. The use of the procedure really depends on practical matters, such as the time available to observe the client, the ability to control contraband, the presence (or not) of reliable third-party information, and the severity of symptoms.

The ideal situation in which to establish a clear differential diagnosis would include the factors listed below:

- Controlled clinical environment
- Patient cooperation
- Family or significant other input
- Ability to prevent intake of substances not supplied and controlled by staff
- Opportunity to observe client over a significant period of time for any immediate toxic effects to have worn off (namely, 3 to 5 days for alcohol, 14 to 21 days for benzodiazepines, 10 to 14 days for cocaine, 5 to 7 days for heroin)
- Ability to ascertain effects of any medications being taken alone or in combination. In many cases, a total "drug holiday" is needed to determine baseline functioning and make a clear diagnosis
- Use of appropriate medical and psychological tests
- Establishment of rapport with client to obtain historical data
- Hands-on physical examination
- Securing of past psychological and medical records including previous treatment history

One can quickly see how the ideal diagnostic process, let us say, a month-long stay in an acute care facility, might significantly differ from the frenetic search for a binary diagnosis in an emergency situation. It is clear in working with MICAs that keeping the emphasis on the following will aid the diagnostic endeavor:

Hints for Diagnosing MICA Clients

- Keep it simple: Place the primary emphasis on an objective description and analysis of actual behavior.

- Determine alcohol and other drug-taking status. Don't trust intuition or client report. Use objective tests like urine analyses, blood levels, and Breathalyzers.
- Taking the time to elicit client cooperation through an empathetic and supportive posture is essential.
- Include the client's family wherever possible, at least for a preliminary assessment.
- Understand that the pre-abstinent client is not going to necessarily buy into a "cold turkey" approach to stopping illicit drug use. This possibility will often require a less rigid stance by clinical staff, and it applies primarily to those attempting to provide services on an outpatient basis. Just as clients often need to be weaned from medications prescribed by doctors, the same may be necessary with the MICA client's sense of survival needs surrounding alcohol and street drugs (self-prescribed medications).
- Understand that even small amounts of alcohol and street drugs have remarkably debilitating effects on MICAs. Their willingness and ability to be totally abstinent is often the reality basis for determining an inpatient versus outpatient approach.
- MICAs develop pathological patterns of ingesting their prescribed (and unprescribed) psychotropic medications. This must be taken into consideration as part of the substance abuse pattern.
- MICAs can't handle harsh confrontation; so keep in mind: "Don't kick in the door when a key will work!" MICAs have often been abused and neglected by their families of origin, many social service agencies, police, and others. They don't trust anyone! Verbal assaults bring out powerful, sometimes psychotic reactions.
- Survival needs come first! Food, clothing, shelter, personal hygiene, and a lot of TLC (tender loving care) can set the stage for establishing the communication necessary for proper diagnosis.

We have emphasized the importance of using objective analyses for determining client drug use. To assist you, as a guide in making these determinations, a schedule of the excretion rate for a variety of substances is provided as follows.

Alcohol: Decreases by .01 to .02 mg per deciliter per hour. That is equivalent to one glass of wine, one shot of liquor, or one can of beer.

Amphetamine: Excreted unchanged within 24 hours. Not readily detectable after 24 hours following a single dose.

Barbiturates: Excreted slowly, in general. Approximately 8% are excreted in the first 12 hours, 20% in 24 hours, and 35 to 65% in 48 hours. The long-acting barbiturate, phenobarbital, may be detected in urine in excess of four weeks after a single dose.

Cocaine: A single dose is excreted within 8 hours, depending on the level of dosage and purity. Cocaine metabolite is excreted in 24 to 48 hours.

Codeine: Excreted as free and conjugated codeine and, in part, methylated to morphine; 63 to 90% is excreted within 24 hours.

Dilaudid: Although traces may be found up to 48 hours, 90% is excreted within 24 hours.

Marijuana (THC):. Detectable from 3 to 10 days: 50% is excreted within 3 days, the other 50% is excreted within 7 days, following a single dose. It is detectable after 25 days or more in chronic, heavy users.

Methadone: Less than 10% is excreted unchanged; the remainder is metabolized by N–demethylation. Excretion is relatively rapid. Most of a single dose is excreted in 48 hours.

Morphine: Small amounts of free and larger amounts of conjugated morphine are excreted quickly: 90% is excreted within 24 hours, although traces may be found up to 48 hours.

PCP: Excreted within 24 hours following a single dose.

Quaalude:: Excreted almost totally metabolized within 24 hours. Not readily detectable after 24 hours following a single dose.

Quinine (often used as cut in heroin): Totally excreted in five days.

Talwin: Excreted within 24 hours following a single dose.

Valium: Serum half-life of 20 to 22 hours. Some Valium metabolites may be detected from 5 to 7 days after the initial dose.

(Source: Eastern Laboratories, Ltd.)

Understanding Organic Mental Syndromes and Disorders

According to the *DSM–IIIR,* the essential feature of all organic mental syndromes and disorders is: "A psychological or behavioral abnormality associated with transient or permanent dysfunction of the brain" (98). All psychological events correspond, in part, to some brain function. However, the primary factor in describing and diagnosing *organic mental* problems is the known or presumed presence of a physical central nervous system problem. If the cause is known or presumed, psychiatry refers to it as an *organic mental disorder.* When there is no reference to etiology (the cause of the condition), then it is referred to as an *organic mental syndrome.* Whether the cause is stated or not, the common denominator is the presence of brain dysfunction. The term *disorder* is used when an organic mental syndrome is associated with a specific cause (as, for example, a physical disorder or condition such as a brain tumor or multi-infarct cardiac problem).

The following lists indicate organic mental syndromes and organic mental disorders.

Organic mental syndromes:

Delirium

Dementia

Amnestic syndrome

Organic delusional syndrome

Organic hallucinosis

Organic mood syndrome

Organic anxiety syndrome

Organic personality syndrome

Intoxication

Withdrawal

Organic mental syndrome, not otherwise specified

Organic mental disorders:

Dementias arising in the senium and presenium (Aging process problems like Alzheimer's disease)

Psychoactive substance-induced organic mental disorders

Organic mental disorders associated with physical disorders and conditions (known as *axis III* disorders), or whose etiology is unknown

The process of assessment and evaluation leading to thorough diagnosis(es) must take these organic mental syndromes and disorders (OMSDs) into consideration for several reasons. The life circumstances of the MICA client often lead to the presence of OMSDs and can cloud the diagnostic picture. Safer (1987) reports that substance abusers, for example, are frequently misdiagnosed as schizophrenic, based on their substance-induced psychosis and psychosis-like hallucinatory behavior. One cannot hope to do a good differential diagnosis without first ruling out or including these categories. All too often workers in the fields of alcoholism treatment, substance abuse treatment, and the treatment of mental illness fail to recognize the significance of the presence of symptoms associated with OMSDs in evaluating MICA clients. Some of the presenting features of these syndromes and disorders are described as follows:

Delirium: reduced ability to maintain attention to external stimuli and to appropriately shift attention to new external stimuli; and disorganized thinking, as manifested by rambling, irrelevant, or incoherent speech. Also involves a reduced level of consciousness, sensory misperceptions, disturbance of sleep/wake cycle, and of reduced level of psychomotor activity.

Dementia: impairment in short- and long-term memory that is associated with impaired abstract thinking and judgment, and other disturbances of higher cortical functioning (such as, aphasia, apraxia, and agnosia).

Amnesia: impairment in short- and long-term memory that is attributed to a specific organic factor, not caused by active delirium or dementia.

Delusion: false personal belief based on distorted interpretation of reality. Does not change when person is provided proof to the contrary.

Hallucinations: seeing, hearing, smelling, or feeling stimuli that are not present and insisting upon the reality of the sensation.

Mood: prominent and persistent depressed, elevated, or expansive mood.

Anxiety: prominent, recurrent, panic attacks or generalized anxiety.

Personality syndrome: persistent personality disturbance causally linked to specific organic factor(s). May include effective instability, outbursts of anger and rage, poor social judgment, marked apathy and indifference, suspiciousness, or paranoid ideation.

Intoxication and withdrawal are also included in the *DSM–IIIR* under the heading of organic mental syndromes. However, these diagnoses are used only when the clinical picture does not correspond to any of the other specific organic mental syndromes as listed above. We are also cautioned that certain neurologic diseases may produce symptoms like intoxication; and physical disorders, like influenza, may mimic opioid withdrawal. Each intoxication and withdrawal syndrome is unique to the substance ingested. These are the only two kinds of syndromes to which etiology (cause) is specifically assigned (substance ingestion or reduction of use). The other syndromes are simply descriptive.

The *DSM–IIIR* also devotes a section to *psychoactive substance-induced organic mental disorders.* Remember, when we call something a "disorder," we mean that its symptoms are directly caused by the effects of various psychoactive substances. A listing of psychoactive substance-induced organic mental disorders follows:

- Alcohol intoxication
- Alcohol idiosyncratic intoxication
- Uncomplicated alcohol withdrawal
- Alcohol withdrawal delirium—formerly known as delirium tremens (DTs)
- Alcohol hallucinosis
- Alcohol amnestic disorder
- Dementia associated with alcoholism
- Amphetamine (or similarly acting sympathomimetic) intoxication
- Amphetamine (or similarly acting sympathomimetic) withdrawal
- Amphetamine (or similarly acting sympathomimetic) delirium
- Amphetamine (or similarly acting sympathomimetic) delusional disorder
- Caffeine intoxication
- Cannabis intoxication
- Cannabis delusional disorder
- Cocaine intoxication
- Cocaine withdrawal
- Cocaine delirium
- Cocaine delusional disorder
- Hallucinogen hallucinosis
- Hallucinogen delusional disorder
- Hallucinogen mood disorder
- Post-hallucinogen perception disorder
- Inhalant intoxication
- Nicotine withdrawal
- Opioid intoxication
- Opioid withdrawal
- Phencyclidine (PCP) (or similarly acting arylcyclohexylamine) intoxication
- Phencyclidine (PCP) (or similarly acting arylcyclohexylamine) delirium

- Phencyclidine (PCP) (or similarly acting arylcyclohexylamine) delusional disorder
- Phencyclidine (PCP) (or similarly acting arylcyclohexylamine) mood disorder
- Phencyclidine (PCP) (or similarly acting arylcyclohexylamine) organic mental disorder not otherwise specified
- Sedative, hypnotic, or anxiolytic intoxication
- Sedative, hypnotic, or anxiolytic uncomplicated withdrawal
- Sedative, hypnotic, or anxiolytic withdrawal delirium
- Sedative, hypnotic, or anxiolytic amnestic disorder
- Other or unspecified psychoactive substance-induced organic mental disorders (used to describe disorders induced by drugs other than those listed above) such as anticholinergic delirium and levo-dopa delusional disorder

The main point to keep in mind is that these psychoactive substance-induced organic mental disorders describe the direct acute and chronic effects of the various substances on the central nervous system. Some effects are acute: and, although they are sometimes quite intense, they are short-lived. Other effects are chronic and range from mild to severe in intensity: these are more persistent over time. Jamal's case, as described in the illustration below, indicates some of the complications that substance-induced organic mental disorders can present.

Case Illustration 11: Jamal

Jamal drank heavily on a daily basis for the last five years. When he spoke candidly about his experiences in Vietnam, it was clear that he had been suffering from posttraumatic stress disorder and that he was also an alcoholic. One night, after a particularly heavy drinking bout, Jamal found himself in a county psychiatric unit. He could not remember how or why he got there. The admitting psychiatrist had noted that the patient (Jamal) exhibited both dementia and delirium upon admission. The psychiatrist could not have known that amnesia was also playing a role at admission as Jamal was in a *blackout*—an alcohol-included amnestic syndrome. In addition he was suffering from hallucinosis, which is also caused by heavy drinking.

Despite the alcohol on his breath, he was sent to the inpatient psychiatric unit for evaluation. This hospital also had an inpatient alcoholism unit. Unfortunately, like so many publically funded hospitals, the psychiatric resident, not having been trained in the United States, was not culturally sensitive to the possibility of alcohol as the culprit in creating substance-induced organic mental dysfunction. She instead admitted Jamal under the diagnosis of schizophrenia, chronic undifferentiated type. Confused, and then angry, Jamal later insisted that he be transferred to the alcoholism unit, stating that he was not "crazy."

In the *DSM–IIIR* schema, these organic mental syndromes and disorders are distinguished from the psychoactive substance use disorders. In these diagnostic categories all pathological drug use exists under one of two headings: substance dependence (the more severe form of disturbance) or substance abuse (the residual category). Both abuse and dependence are conceptualized so that they refer to the "maladaptive behavior associated with more or less regular use of these substances." The specification of the psychoactive substances' negative influences on actual behavior leads to these diagnoses. According to the *DSM–IIIR:*

> The essential feature of this disorder (dependence) is a cluster of cognitive, behavioral, and physiologic symptoms that indicate that the person has impaired control of psychoactive substance use and continues use despite adverse consequences. (166)

Dependence has differing degrees of severity and differs from abuse mainly in the manifestation of tolerance and withdrawal syndromes (which differ from substance to substance). It is essential, however, that one keep in mind that even when substance use causes negative consequences, these effects must be weighed against what the client considers to be positive consequences. In the cognitive-behavioral model of addictive behavior, the paradigm is one of immediate gratification followed by delayed negative consequences (see Marlatt and Gordon 1985). Whether clients are trying to get high or self-medicate to ward off unpleasant affect states or other symptoms, they, like conventional drug abusers, are willing to trade one set of consequences for another. In the case of a person with schizophrenia, this could mean smoking some grass and stopping the voices, only to have this condition be followed by an acute psychotic state. Clinicians can only wonder at this type of behavior and thus identify it as yet another symptom of mental illness. Impaired judgment characterizes addiction and also mental illness. The combination of addiction and mental illness can explain the sometimes severely impaired judgment of the MICA client.

Dr. Lee Robins (1982) properly cautions us as to a remaining problem in the use of these diagnostic entities:

> Another difficulty that pertains to drug disorders is deciding when the intake of the drug is responsible for the behavioral difficulties. Arrests, traffic accidents, suicide, or death for unexplained reasons, in someone

> who has ingested drugs, may or may not be the result of the drug consumption. The persons who tend to have high arrest rates, high suicide rates, and high rates of impulsive behavior also tend to use drugs and alcohol heavily. Thus, the drug or alcohol use and the event may both be caused by some preexisting factors. (49–50)

Neurocognitive impairment can be caused by varieties of mental illness and substance abuse and by the coexistence of both problems. Meek et al. (1989) caution us regarding this often "unrecognized component of dual diagnosis," as follows:

> With the current emphasis on clients' displaying both substance abuse and psychiatric disorders, it is easy to forget that dual diagnosis may also include substance abusers with organic impairment. Deficits in neuropsychological functioning are far from uncommon among drug users, and may occur independently of other psychiatric disorders . . . Neuropsychological evaluation of substance abusers is fundamental to comprehensive treatment because patients may be limited in their capacity for education and adaptation. This has implications both for the overall design of a treatment program and for staff intervention with individual patients (e.g., noncompliance resulting from organic brain dysfunction may be misinterpreted as denial or resistance). With the increasing tendency to limit the length of inpatient programs, it is critical to determine a patient's capacity for treatment during the stages of detoxification and early recovery. (154–55)

In the sample drawn by Meek et al. (1989) of 34 drug abusers in a Veterans Administration hospital, 67 percent showed some type of performance difficulties upon admission. Only a few showed gross manifestations: most were more subtle. For example, the researchers point out that when chronic alcoholics have good verbal skills, such abilities may cause treatment staff to ignore cognitive impairment. The subjects' experiencing of these performance difficulties varied greatly. Meek et al. (1989) believe that their and other researchers' findings about neuropsychological functioning demonstrate a "compelling justification for the routine neurocognitive assessment of drug abusers" (158). They point out that even when the organic impairment is temporary, it has powerful effects on the patient's relative ability to benefit from treatment.

In our own clinical work we have encountered many clients who have learning disabilities and others who had suffered attitudinal impediments to learning. Ralph and Barr (1989) report that learning disabilities and attention deficit hyperactivity disorders are conditions frequently seen in chemically dependent adolescents. These disorders, they emphasize, "require careful evaluation, and differentiation from other psychiatric conditions" (214). In the absence of such evaluation, we can only wonder at the unmeasured and untreated neurocognitive impairment of the MICA population, as well as in all of the three fields.

There is clearly a relationship between educational level and addicted populations. In the Treatment Outcome Perspective Study (TOPS) conducted by Hubbard et al. (1989) of some 10,000 addicts in treatment, nearly half (47.6%) had not completed high school, and nearly three-quarters (73.8%) were both unemployed and not in school or in training at the time of intake. Arella et al. (1990) conducted a secondary analysis of the TOPS data and discovered that fewer than half of the clients (43.9%) reported receiving educational services (either on-site or by referral to community-based agencies) and substantially fewer (29.1%) reported receiving any vocational services within the first six months of treatment. Organic mental syndromes and disorders and other forms of neurocognitive impairment may be a major explanatory factor in the poor education and employment histories of substance abusers as well as be the major contributors to their overall, continuing maladaptive life-style.

The whole enterprise of diagnostics pivots on the ability to understand the various ways in which the ingestion of psychoactive substances affects human behavior. Some ostensibly puzzling features that should be noted during the diagnostic procedure of substance users are:

Substance use can masquerade as any number of non-substance-induced mental disorders and syndromes, primarily by its inducing of organic mental syndromes and disorders.

Substance use can mask other mental disorders and problems (thus causing temporary amelioration of unpleasant symptoms).

Substance use can trigger, in vulnerable individuals, mental disorder.

Neuropsychological impairment (such as temporal lobe seizure disorder) is often overlooked among substance abusers.

Differential diagnosis is most reliably achieved in a drug-free state. A period of abstinence allows the clinician to identify which symptoms are transient and which persistent.

Clients' failure to maintain abstinence clouds the clinical picture.

Rigid distinctions between substance dependence and abuse are not as important with MICA clients because small doses are often sufficient to trigger serious consequences.

Diagnosis requires objective indicators of substance use, such as drug toxicologies and breath analyses.

Diagnoses of both substance abuse and mental illness allow us to track clients into the proper treatment setting.

Clinicians must be alert to abusive patterns of psychotropic medication ingestion.

Clinicians must be aware of the destabilizing effects of alcohol, street drugs, prescription medications, and over-the-counter drugs that can interact with psychotropic medications, and they must screen for all of these.

Unsupervised withdrawal can lead to a host of problem behaviors and symptoms.

Clients often stop taking psychotropic medications on their own.

Clients maintained on methadone, who drink alcohol on a frequent and heavy basis, can destabilize their methadone medication. The liver metabolizes alcohol before methadone, thus reducing the steady state of the medication in the bloodstream and the central nervous system.

Clients who use drugs like cocaine, which can cause precipitous weight loss, may become *overmedicated*. Many psychiatrists will prescribe psychotropic dosage by body weight. Similar attention must be paid to patterns like frequent marijuana use and weight gain.

Clients may use caffeine (coffee, tea, soda, chocolate candies, etc.) which is a strong stimulant to the central nervous system when taken in high doses.

Clients may be abusing over-the-counter medications which have psychoactive ingredients.

Case Illustration 12: Juan

Juan has a long history of suffering from schizophrenia. He comes to the psychiatric day center on a regular basis. He is known to the staff to use cocaine on occasion. He is taking Prolixin on a continuous basis. One day Juan came in and suffered a psychotic *break*. During the previous week he had seemed his old self. Juan is known to the staff as a MICA client; and his case indicates several possibilities that can be weighed in understanding his sudden psychological decompensation as follows:

1. Patients suffering from psychoses are known to have "flare-ups"—that is, occasional breaks are part of the natural history of the disorder. Juan might have had a flare-up even if he were not using cocaine.
2. The ingestion of cocaine can cause behaviors that are problematic in their own right and can also worsen the clinical picture.
3. The ingestion of cocaine interacts with the Prolixin, causing a drug-to-drug interaction that can cause psychotic behavior. Conversely, the interaction may also stimulate momentary relief from some symptoms.

4. The Prolixin could have been destabilized by the cocaine so that it can no longer have a therapeutic effect.
5. Any client, like Juan, may have stopped taking his Prolixin or may not be taking it as prescribed.
6. Any client, in this case, Juan, may have suffered an unreported traumatic event that triggered a strong reaction.

Unquestionably, it is logically and scientifically invalid to classify all MICA clients in a single category. We are not comfortable with the term MICA simply because it implies a unitary phenomenon, when, in fact, it refers to extremely multivariate and complex manifestations. We must emphasize once again that *MICA* is used in this book merely as a convenient shorthand term. We need to remind the reader of this from time to time, to counter the criticism leveled by Ridgely et al. (1986) that current research is limited by imprecision in consensually validated terminology. The case illustration of Juan's decompensation indicates the complex nature of both diagnostic and descriptive explanations.

A final set of thoughts about the use/nonuse of certain diagnostic criteria. Each field is known for the labels it tends to use and also by those it chooses not to use. This accounts in part for the differing labels applied by each of the fields to the same client's symptomology. We summarize the features of general diagnostic practice in the three fields, as follows.

General Diagnostic Practices Within the Three Fields

Alcoholism Treatment Field:

1. Attempts to identify early, middle, and late stages of alcoholism by attending to drinking behavior, medical symptoms, and psychological signs.
2. The consequences of drinking rather than the causes of drinking are emphasized—alcohol drives behavior; the converse is not dealt with.
3. Even psychotic behavior is viewed primarily as an expression of pathological drinking.
4. Its single-minded intervention approach is based on complete abstinence from alcohol (and other mood-altering substances). In many cases, this directive may also include psychotropic medication.
5. Alcohol dependence is almost always the *primary* diagnosis.
6. Clients are viewed as suffering from a chronic, incurable disease. Even when one has been abstinent for years, one still has the "disease."
7. Treatment is dichotomized into one of only two outcomes: one is either

totally abstinent (this is judged as good), or else drinks some amount (this is judged as bad). Moderation of drinking is not viewed as a valid clinical goal.

8. The disease metaphor is so pervasive that family members are viewed as also suffering from the disease of *codependency* and children (including adult children) are labelled as children of alcoholics (COAs) or adult children of alcoholics (ACOAs). These people are said to suffer from the family disease of alcoholism.
9. The system does not easily allow for the teasing out of a differential diagnosis since alcoholism is almost always seen as primary. Alcoholism counseling studiously avoids dealing with premorbid or underlying conditions because this therapeutic work is believed to undermine sobriety. Clients are rarely referred for any type of psychotherapy. Many counselors do not even conceive of psychopathology when considering "drinking problems."
10. Little is done to diagnose neuropsychological impairment.

Drug Abuse Treatment Field:

1. Attempts to identify behavior as related to addiction. Drugs drive behavior; the converse is not dealt with.
2. Even psychosis is viewed as a consequence rather than a cause of addictive behavior.
3. Little interest is shown toward premorbid history—that is, events concerning the client's life experience before drugs or before mental illness (whichever came first).
4. In drug-free agencies, treatment outcome is dichotomized into total abstinence (except alcohol intake): this is judged as good. Any drug taking is bad. Few agencies allow for moderation of drug use as a valid treatment goal.
5. In methadone maintenance, abstinence from street opioids defines a good outcome. Little attention is paid to alcohol use at intake. Sometimes even drugs like marijuana and cocaine are ignored. Emphasis is instead placed on stopping opioid use.
6. Little attempt is made to establish differential diagnoses or to perceive mental illness and addictive behavior as equally important problems.
7. Agencies usually screen out mentally ill clients.

Mental Health Treatment Field:

1. Psychiatric and psychological assessments rarely utilize alcohol and other drug-taking inventories.
2. Even when alcohol and other drug use are considered, they are rarely

viewed as a primary disorder or cause of the aberrant behavior in question. Drug abuse is seen only as a symptom of an underlying pathology (whether biogenic or psychogenic in origin).

3. Substance use history is rarely considered in determining the emergence of a problem behavior and the possible interactions between the behavior and substance use.
4. Severely disturbed clients are not perceived as being able to negotiate a drug-related, street life-style (although many actually are).
5. Abuse of psychotropic medications is not considered as a possible vehicle for getting high.
6. Staff persons are not familiar with the means by which patients combine legitimate psychotropic medications with street drugs to get high and to control symptoms.
7. Staff rarely consider the specific relationship between the clients' drug(s) of choice and their symptoms.
8. Agencies usually deny service to serious drug abusers when they know of such abuse.
9. Because of a lack of emphasis on the effect of drug taking as a possible cause of symptoms, it is difficult to arrive at accurate differential diagnoses.

A holistic approach to the MICA patient and his/her unique needs is not commonly accepted. Richard N. Rosenthal, M.D., chief of the Division of Substance Abuse, Department of Psychiatry, at Beth Israel Medical Center in New York City for the past seven years, described this approach with us in an interview in 1991. It is achieved by focusing on differential diagnoses. Highly regarded as an expert clinician of the MICA population, Dr. Rosenthal shares his experiences of working with the MICAs served by the inpatient and outpatient facilities his division operates:

> We work from an integrative model that incorporates an awareness of psychological events, biogenetic dysregulation, target organ sensitivity, family influences, self-medication, and life style. Most clinicians are not comfortable with such a model. It's is a lot easier to come from one perspective than it is to combine perspectives. Anatomy alone is not destiny. Life style change, psychotherapy, and drug therapy can be effective. The most important idea is that of individual differences. We work very hard at trying to understand each patient as a unique individual. We studiously avoid reductionistic, lowest-common-denominator care. Among the most practical factors are things like social and vocational/educational functioning, and actual life functioning, with an eye on both functional impairment and productive levels of performance. We avoid slick high-tech talk and try to determine what people are capable of actually doing. This is as true for

patients with chronic psychoses as it is for those with personality disorders. Some have both disorders. Patients need support, structure, discipline, and *reparenting*.

Even when we arrive at a differential diagnosis, that doesn't always mean we know what to do. We are open to the idea that the pathological behavior we first observe may be a symptom or it may be an actual disorder. I consider the problem behavior to be organic until proven otherwise. Therefore, we do not medicate right away unless the patient is going into withdrawal or is dangerous to self or others. We do not want the patient's brain undergoing additional trauma due to withdrawal. Multiple traumas complicate the clinical picture and may even be etiologically linked to further dysfunction. The specific drug(s) that patients take determine when withdrawal will kick in and/or when we would reasonably expect substance-induced symptoms to remit. If psychotic or other symptoms persist beyond a time period during which withdrawal would occur or any residual effects from the particular drug might last, then we know it is not a toxic reaction but a symptom cluster or disorder in its own right. For example, if a patient smoked crack just prior to hospitalization for an acute psychotic state, we would expect him/her to be OK after three to five days. If symptoms persist, we are looking at something other than an acute organic state. It is very important to realize that most patients are polysubstance abusers. So if our crack smoker also drinks or takes Valium, we would need a full two weeks for all substance-induced toxic effects to clear. We use staff psychologists to do mental status examinations and call in neurological consults as needed. A history of seizures or delirium tremens are the best predictors for a reoccurence of this type of event.

In taking careful patient histories we have learned that the social service and clinical treatment systems that patients travel through are either comfortable or uncomfortable with their disorders. There are few comprehensive services for MICAs in New York City. We seek to make the *best fit* between patient and program. We look for the *hybrid* program that understand both mental illness and substance abuse.

Client Assessment

Some Problems with Assessment

Hayes et al. (1987), in "The treatment utility of assessment," make the following powerful points:

> Clinical assessment is an important and fertile area of psychology, and yet there is general agreement that it has not been in a state of continuous and healthy growth. One reason may be that clinical assessment has not yet proven its value in fostering favorable treatment outcomes. . . . Korchin defined clinical assessment as "the process by which clinicians gain understanding of the patient necessary for making informed decisions." Thus,

the "basic justification for assessment is that it provides information of value to the planning, execution, and evaluation of treatment." (963)

All three fields call for assessments that have real utility for treatment. Nevertheless, there is a relative absence of sound, empirical evidence showing that clinical assessments can adequately match clients and treatments. Pattison (1982), who favors a systems approach to alcoholism treatment, notes:

> In sum, the face validity of the matching concept appears sound. There are scattered empirical studies that support both the existence of social matching processes and the efficacy of treatment matching. From a clinical point of view, the value of matching is supported, but there is only modest research demonstration of the efficacy of matching in available rigorous studies. (1095)

Glaser et al. (1985), in their chapter on the use of differential therapy for alcoholism treatment, echo Pattison's conclusions:

> That simple objective criteria and client preferences, rather than judgment of highly trained clinicians, are relied upon in so important a matter as the assignment of clients to treatment may appear to some to be an unwelcome development. But the judgments and expertise of clinicians were utilized both in the overall design of the system and in the selection of criteria for assignment to treatment. Clinical judgment is also operative in the primary care, assessment, assignment, and intervention processes. Nevertheless, it must be emphasized that there exists no body of evidence proving that either the deployment of trained clinicians, or any other method utilized to date, results in highly effective treatment assignment. The criteria and goal statements of the system are capable of empirical validation and refinement. With the use of feedback data from outcome studies in the determination of future assignments, there is every likelihood that the system will increasingly direct its clients to those services they uniquely require. No method of dealing with clients could promise more. (446)

In commenting on the clinical assessment and diagnosis of addiction, Shaffer and Kaufman (1985) conclude:

> Is the assessment of addiction, with its state of pre-paradigm chaos and the attributional biases inherent in person perception still possible? Yes—it becomes a viable endeavor only when clinicians minimize the uncertainty often associated with the clinical assessment tasks by: (1) attending to and gathering explicit, observable, valid, and reliable information about drug use and its effects (i.e., physiological, psychological, behavioral, and sociological); and (2) testing relevant hypotheses within the clinical setting to

> ensure and confirm/disconfirm their observations, inferences, and assumptions. (246)

Hubbard et al. (1989), who, in the TOPS study, studied 10,000 addicts in treatment in the United States, observe in their chapter on strengthening drug abuse treatment:

> Even though concern for effective matching of types of clients and particular treatments has been expressed, there has been little direct research on the issue, particularly for publically funded programs. The appropriateness of any given type of treatment for a particular client depends on such factors as the effective match between client problems and the attributes of therapist, the goals and therapeutic approaches of particular treatment programs, and the provision of needed ancillary services that foster overall recovery. For example, drawing on the work of McLelland and others, Jaffe (1984) argues that some opioid clients, particularly those with severe psychological problems, do poorly in the confrontational environment of a therapeutic community and do better in methadone maintenance programs. Although the matching issue is a critical one, the question of what treatment works best for what type of client still needs adequate investigation. (175)

Wender and Klein (1981) comment on the two horns of the mental health dilemma when biopsychiatry and psychotherapy are the treatments in question:

> The response to treatment provides some partial data with regard to the correctness of the diagnosis. Rapid amelioration of a long-standing condition after drug administration would seem to confirm both the diagnosis that led to this prescription and the utility of the medication . . . If a patient has repeatedly failed to respond to biological treatments, however, it is certainly incumbent upon the doctor to review the entire situation for the possibility of misdiagnosis and mistreatment. Analogously, failure to respond to psychotherapy does not necessarily mean that one's problems are not psychological, since these failures may stem from differences in people's ability to change their entrenched ways, or possibly a mismatch between patient and therapist or therapy. (339)

The process of assessment usually plays a significant role in subsequent diagnostic labelling and treatment assignment. The process is a combination of science and art. Although as a science it is still in its infancy, as an art it is a well-established practice. Virtually all agencies working with MICA clients have some person assigned to such duties as *intake, screening, assessment, triage,* and so forth. For brevity, we will call all of these activities "assessment." For clarity it is important to state that the process of doing assessments usually results in a client's receiving a formal diagnosis. Formal diagnostics do not, however, have to be an essential component of conducting good assessments. In fact, diagnoses may be deferred until the staff gets familiar with the clients (that is, sees them in varying states of substance ingestion, ranging from intoxicated to drug-free). Instead, the clinician usually forms an initial *diagnostic impression*—that is, a hunch or best guess about the nature of a client's disorder. Such preliminary diagnoses are usually "quick and dirty" and have more to do with bureaucratic and economic necessities than anything else. In true emergencies the binary diagnostic process that we described earlier in this chapter is utilized.

Early assessment is the most crucial juncture in the sequence of clinical events; and it is also the one where the most errors (both false positives and false negatives) are made. In the case of the MICA patient, these errors result primarily from a failure to consider the two problems of mental illness and substance abuse as carrying equal weight in the assessment and diagnostic arena. Galanter (1989) speaks to this point in the New York State Task Force for Combined Psychiatric and Addictive Disorders (second annual report):

> The major problem in the provision of treatment programs to the MICA population is the entry point through which the patient is initially involved in treatment. Many of the MICA population has serious and ongoing medical problems which can seriously complicate the treatment of the patient through limitations on the use of medication and the types of interventions which can be deployed. Often symptoms on admissions are confusing and drug or alcohol use can compound or mask important issues in the successful treatment of the patient. In many instances, professionals who evaluate the patient at the time of intake are not familiar with the complex issues involved in taking an accurate history, nor [with] developing a successful and comprehensive treatment plan which addresses the complex treatment issues of the MICA population. The successful disposition of MICA patients throughout an uncoordinated system is also a problem. Separate screenings, admission criteria, and a lack of cooperation among the various agencies often means that an individual will only receive treatment for the most serious problems at the time of admission and, as the problems are addressed, underlying issues run the risk of being forgotten. (29)

At many levels, including the state agency level, coordination between the treatment fields is usually limited: for example, in the state of New York there are three separate and distinct state agencies: Office of Mental Health; Division of Alcoholism and Alcohol Abuse; and Division of Substance Abuse Services. But even in states where alcohol and other drugs are combined into a single agency, it is rare to find coordination between those agencies and the mental health agency (Thacker and Tremaine 1989; Ridgely et al. 1987).

The overwhelming perception in the field of mental health is that substance use and abuse are symptomatic expressions of underlying pathology. Whether the primary psychiatric problem is viewed as biogenic or psychogenic in origin, the person's substance abuse is thought to reflect this preexisting condition. Substance abuse treatment personnel, whether dealing with alcoholics or drug abusers, usually consider the substance(s) involved as the cause of the psychiatric problem. They usually screen out persons with serious mental disorders.

Can Substance Abuse Cause Mental Illness?

The relationship between mental illness and substance use/abuse/addiction is not well understood. In fact, the prevailing zeitgeist in the mental health field has not historically allowed for a serious consideration of the possibility that substance use may actually cause mental illness. The historical review in chapter two of the three fields indicated the relative youthfulness of the science of mental health/illness and addiction. All three fields are in a stage of evolution and development that have yet to delineate firmly with any degree of scientific certainty specific causes and specific solutions. Each field has its own profound problems to resolve. An even more difficult undertaking is bringing the fields into a common orbit around the MICA client.

There is, first of all, the problem of understanding the temporal relationship between mental illness and substance abuse. About this, Ridgely et al. (1986) note:

> While it may not be stated with assurance from the current evidence that the use/abuse of drugs "causes" mental illness, there is strong evidence of the relationship of the use/abuse of drugs and relapse and hospitalization. (35)

Breakey et al. (1974) report that twenty-four out of thirty-two schizophrenic patients who took drugs prior to the onset of psychiatric symptoms experienced these symptoms, on the average, four years earlier than those who did not use drugs. McLellan et al. (1979) studied fifty-one male veterans repeatedly admitted over a six-year period for substance abuse treatment: they found that nonnarcotic substance abusers were more likely than narcotic abusers to develop serious psychiatric problems across time (and hospitalizations). Narcotic abusers' psychopathology, however, remained stable. With regard to substance-induced organic mental disorders and syndromes, McLellan and his colleagues found the symptoms to be neither the result of acute toxic psychosis nor the residual from physical withdrawal. They speculate that repeated exposure to street drugs may have hastened the development of, and determined the nature of specific psychiatric disorders.

They suggest that *state dependent* learning and biochemical changes in the nervous system brought on by the prolonged use of substances may be the explanatory mechanisms for the emergence of the disorders.

There are a number of possible explanations for the interactions between substance abuse and mental illness. Well designed, controlled longitudinal studies will substantiate speculations about these explanations. In the meantime, we present some of the possibilities:

Biogenetic dysregulation: Certain persons are more likely to inherit a genetic predisposition to illness (such as schizophrenia and alcohol dependence). That is, their risk is statistically higher than the normal population. When this population uses drugs the dysregulation leads to serious problems and the emergence of the genetically "fated" illness. (Mechanisms of genetic transmission have yet to be discovered.)

State dependent learning: Repeated exposure to drugs "teaches" the brain to operate in certain discrete ways. Concomitant changes in brain chemistry can trigger problem symptoms—that is, long-term exposure to alcohol actually changes the permeability of brain cells. This explanation also posits that behaviors learned in a certain mental state are more likely to be repeated when one is again in that mental state.

Neurotransmitter deficiency: Persons with biologically depleted chemical message senders in the brain (such as dopamine) use street drugs and alcohol to *boost* these signals. This response appears to the clinician as *self-medication.* This explanation suggests the possibility of there being specific neurotransmitter irregularities for each type of chemical addiction.

Self-medication: Persons taking drugs to "medicate" painful affective states and other symptoms. This response can both disguise and exacerbate the mental problems. A client may be willing to trade delayed negative consequences for the immediate gratification of a substance-induced state. Thus drug usage causes self-induced changes in neurochemistry which can result in both relief and problems. Drugs become a maladaptive, overlearned coping mechanism.

Underlying psychopathology: Substance use and abuse is a symptom of an underlying psychogenically or biogenically determined mental illness. It is part and parcel of the pathological process. This is particularly true for personality disorders (PDs) such as antisocial PDs and borderline PDs.

Substance-induced organic mental syndromes and disorders: When this is the only cause, the symptoms will usually be transient, and disappear after residual withdrawal or toxic effects wear off. Alcohol is known to cause the greatest long-term damage both physically and psychologically while heroin causes little, if any, long-term damage. Examples include cocaine or amphetamine psychoses; PCP intoxication which can mirror psychoses; alcohol and other sedatives that cause depressive symptoms; "bad-trips" on hallucinogenic drugs like LSD; and intense affective states brought on by smoking marijuana. Most effects are acute; some are chronic in nature. MICAs sometimes have very powerful reactions to relatively small amounts of drugs.

Recreational drug use: Many MICAs, particularly young adults, want to "get high" and "party" just like so many other young adults in the American drug culture. Young adult chronic MICAs would rather identify with a youth drug culture than with chronic mental patients. They may be characterized by an active denial regarding both the severity of their drug problem and the coexistence of their mental illness.

One phenomenon that we find striking, based on our review of the literature, our own clinical experiences in the three fields, and the clinical experiences of many of our colleagues, is that the selection of the drug of choice is rarely random or arbitrary (see, for example, Jones 1973; McLellan et al. 1979; Lamb 1982; Rounsanville et al. 1982; Khantzian and Treece 1985). Many clients use multiple substances and many drug abusers use alcohol to "boost, balance, counteract, or sustain the effects of other drugs" (Carroll et al. 1977). MICAs, along with all people who take psychoactive substances, do so for specific reasons. Drawing upon the broader MICA literature and in particular the writings of Khantzian (1985), Milkman and Sunderwirth (1983), and Milkman and Shaffer (1988), the types of drug-taking patterns that often accompany certain mental states, and the motives for changing those states, are described as follows.

Opiates: The user seeks to control feelings of rage and aggression, and wants to feel "normal," calm, mellow, and soothed. Use leads to satiation and dulls any sensations of physical or psychic pain.

Alcohol: The user seeks to control feelings of anger and also to release these feelings. The user is seeking sedation and release from anxiety. Use leads to satiation and release of inhibitions, and allows for otherwise suppressed feelings of affection and sexuality.

Cocaine, amphetamines, caffeine, and other stimulants: Extroverts seek even greater stimulation but paradoxically may also feel calmer when taking stimulants. Those suffering depression seek relief from feelings of fatigue and depletion. Use leads to arousal and feelings of power which can overcome deep-seated feelings of powerlessness and fear.

LSD, mescaline, and other psychedelics; also marijuana and hashish: The user's main motive for use is to stimulate fantasy, to attempt to escape logical thought processes (straight thinking), and to indulge in "stoned" thinking (nonordinary reality). Fantasies often involve achievement of personal power and importance. Thoughts *feel* profound.

The leading spokesperson for the self-medication hypothesis of addictive disorders is Dr. Edward Khantzian, of the Harvard Medical School and Cambridge Hospital. We quote from his seminal article on this subject (Khantzian 1985):

> Recent clinical observations and psychiatric diagnostic findings of drug-dependent individuals suggest that they are predisposed to addiction because they suffer from painful affect states and related psychiatric disorders. The drugs that addicts select are not chosen randomly. Their drug of choice is the result of an interaction between the psychopharmacological action of the drug and the dominant painful feelings with which they struggle. Narcotic addicts prefer opiates because of their powerful muting action on the disorganizing and threatening affects of rage and aggression. Cocaine has its appeal because of its ability to relieve distress associated with depression, hypomania, and hyperactivity. (1259)

Dr. Khantzian, in a lecture given in March 1987 (attended by Dr. Levy), spoke of the addict's "core vulnerabilities" around both affect and life-style management. The vulnerabilities are the addict's need to:

- control painful affects (addicts have a "dread of distress")
- contain painful affects (problems with affect modulation)
- avoid both contact with affects and isolation from other people
- experience comfort within one's self (achieve an inner "glow")

Khantzian (1982) has also written about the interrelationships of psychopathology, psychodynamics, and alcoholism:

> Alcoholics seem to be constantly caught in an interpersonal and intrapsychic web in which they are unable to judge or measure adequately their actions and behaviors or to express, contain, or modulate their feelings. The use of alcohol becomes both an expression of these problems as well as an attempt to solve them. Rather than considering alcoholism as any one disorder, the condition of alcoholism and the problems that alcoholics display might more usefully be considered a spectrum disorder in which at one pole of the problem behavior disturbances are paramount, and at the other pole affect disturbances loom large . . . It is little wonder then that debate continues [about] whether psychopathology causes alcoholism or alcoholism causes psychopathology. Both are true. (593–94)

Hanson et al. (1985) in *Life with Heroin* quote a number of inner city heroin addicts as they attempt to describe the heroin high (89–90):

> Rather than taking off, you feel deeply implanted. Rather than going on a trip, it [heroin] brings you back home. You don't go out like a jet or a rocket, you accommodate yourself to this world.
>
> —Addict named *Jim*

> It is a highly personal experience. You feel like you are deep inside yourself.
>
> —Addict named *Nathan*

> It [heroin] gives me the feeling that I don't have a care in the world.
>
> —Addict named *Zulu*

> I feel like I'm floating, like being in the womb.
>
> —Addict named *Larry*

> Getting high is the *norm* for me . . . I just get *normal.*
>
> —Addict named *Ace*

> If you have heroin you're going to do everything on a smooth basis.
>
> —Addict named *Hollywood*

Cocaine (like all drugs) is also chosen for *its* particular effects on the user. Spotts and Shontz (1980), using the representative case method, help us to understand cocaine use in relation to life themes, in the case of *Arky L.*:

Life Themes. Arky L. is a warm-hearted and congenial loner who has made his living as thief, burglar, and armed robber since he was thirteen years of age. His life expresses six major themes:

- I am alone, an alien in a world I can't understand or find my place in.
- I don't understand this world because it's so indifferent to me.
- I need love, affection, and care like a child—
- but I don't want to be dependent upon anyone ever again.
- I have a lot of explosive energy that must be released somehow—
- yet sometimes I want to give up and quit trying.

Cocaine Use in Relation to Life Themes. Arky is an intermittent, low-dosage, intravenous cocaine user. He prefers cocaine to a variety of substances that he uses, because it

- makes him feel powerful and independent instead of dependent and ineffectual;
- increases his sexual performance, reassuring him of his potency and masculinity;
- temporarily frees him from the anger he feels toward an indifferent world;
- provides a rare sense of well-being, euphoria, and freedom from discouragement; and
- helps him shake off loneliness and eases the attainment of closeness with others.

Spotts and Shontz (1980):3–4

Ridgely et al. (1986), in speaking about the work of Lamb (1982), state:

> Lamb has proposed that self-medication with illicit drugs relates to the problem that chronic mentally ill young adults have with accepting the label of "mentally ill." Rather than joining an "army of misfits" by becoming willing recipients of mental health services, they prefer to medicate themselves. This provides not only some relief from symptoms, but the added benefits of retaining control over their own lives and gaining acceptance in the young drug subculture. (36)

Drug taking, including alcohol use, is purposive. Specific drugs are taken separately or together to achieve specific effects. Dr. Rosenthal, of Beth Israel Medical Center's Division of Substance Abuse in New York City told us about the "downtown high" sought by some more seriously disturbed MICA clients. They are looking for the "cocktail effect"—that is, just about any change of mental state that any drug can stimulate. Others have referred to this pattern of drug ingestion as the "garbage head" phenomenon—taking whatever is available just to get some kind of "buzz." We believe that even this type of drug taking makes sense when you consider that it is being sought by a disordered mind and by someone in great psychic pain. Many clients have talked to us about taking drugs to "just get over," or to survive another day or night in a hostile world.

Nonpsychotic MICA clients have always been in the three systems. It is the failure to perceive and diagnose that obscures our recognition of them. This point needs to be driven home to clinicians and administrators in all three fields. Most alcohol and drug treatment agencies can tolerate the MICA with personality disorders (PDs). They are not nearly as accepting or understanding of those with psychoses and major mood disorders. The mental health agencies are more accepting of those with major mental disorders and are less comfortable with the personality disorders—particularly borderline PDs and antisocial PDs because of the attending acting out tendencies and street behavior. All three systems fail the seriously chronic mentally ill client. As long as this remains true, jails and prisons rather than hospitals and treatment programs will be the only "clinical intervention" available to them (Torrey 1988).

Individual Differences

Stigma—it's an ugly word. It is defined in the *American Heritage Dictionary of the English Language* (1978) as "a mark or token of infamy, disgrace, and reproach." In our culture substance abusers and the mentally ill have been stigmatized for several centuries. The MICA client suffers from *double jeopardy* in the matter of stigmata. Each group also suffers from the stereotyping that contributes to this stigmatizing.

Stereotypes are cognitive frameworks that consist of knowledge and beliefs about certain social groups. Stereotypes operate when it is suggested that all members of a given social group possess certain traits or characteristics. Stereotypes exert very powerful influences on the way we process information. Dividio, Evans, and Tyler (1986) demonstrated, for example, that information that is relevant to a certain stereotype is processed more quickly than information that is not related to it. Stereotypes also determine which information we pay attention to and how well we remember (or forget) it. Generally, people pay attention to information that is consistent with a stereotype and they are more inclined to remember such information. Once a stereotype is adopted by a person, it is hard to change.

How does this process work in labelling and stereotyping the mentally ill? Let us consider one well-documented example. Hollingshead and Redlich (1958) and Meyers and Bean (1968), in the famous New Haven studies, suggested that not only is psychological disturbance a social phenomenon but it is closely related to social class. The New Haven studies showed that when people from lower socioeconomic levels suffered from behavior disturbances, they were more likely than middle-class people to be placed in state mental hospitals. Poor people could not afford private outpatient care and tended to manifest their unhappiness in aggressive and rebellious problems. Middle-class people demonstrated a different "style" of behavior disturbance: they were more likely to withdraw and show signs of self-deprecation. So the middle-class people were labelled neurotic and the lower socioeconomic status people were more often labelled psychotic. Interestingly, the poor people considered the behavior disturbances as legitimate expressions of personal frustration while the middle-class mental health professionals considered the same problem to be bizarre and placed them in the "sick" role.

Braginsky et al. (1969) summarize these findings by observing that socioeconomic differences can determine who is considered to be suffering from severe mental disorders and, therefore, can also determine the individual's chances for improvement. Snowden and Cheung (1990), upon examining more contemporary statistics, discovered that this general trend continues:

> National data on psychiatric hospitalization point to marked ethnic-related differences. Blacks and Native Americans are considerably more likely than Whites to be hospitalized; Blacks are more likely than Whites to be admitted as schizophrenic and less likely to be diagnosed as having an affective disorder; Asian-Americans/Pacific Islanders are less likely than Whites to be admitted, but remain for a lengthier stay, at least in state and county mental hospitals. These differences are clear-cut but they ignore a major source of care: psychiatric hospitalization in placements other than psychiatric units and hospitals. Explanations for observed minority-White differences in hospitalization can be evaluated only partially or not at all. Such explanations include ethnic-related differences in socioeconomic standing and in the prevalence of major psychopathology; differential stigma, or capacity to tolerate or support a dysfunctional significant other; access and use of alternative services; and bias in the behavior of gatekeepers, especially practitioners assigning diagnostic labels and making involuntary commitment decisions. More research is needed to help explain these striking differences in utilization. (347)

Another example of a stereotype that is harmful to quality work with MICA clients is the notion that people need to use drugs in large doses or on a frequent basis to be harmed by them. Pepper and Ryglewicz (1984) warn us:

> We can no longer base an assessment of whether a patient is significantly affected by alcohol or drug use on our usual standards for "moderate" or "excessive use." A quantity of alcohol or marijuana that is "not that much" in terms of current social norms for the average young adult may be "too much" for a person with underlying pathology or an unknown chemical vulnerability, with or without a prior psychiatric history.

Juxtaposed to the dehumanizing practices of stereotyping and stigmatization is the doctrine of individual differences. In our graduate school training, this important doctrine was taught as if it were sacrosanct. After studying various perspectives and techniques we were constantly reminded of the uniqueness of the individual. We were also taught that the "map is not the territory" and that, at best, our language and our methods could only approximate the reality of the client in our attempts to communicate effectively with them. We were taught to "tune in" on the client, to try to see the world as he or she sees it without our having too many preconceived notions or a need to fit the client to a theoretical stance. Carl Rogers was held up as a model for how to really listen to and hear clients and achieve an "empathic attunement" with them.

In his *A Way of Being* (1980), Rogers speaks to us about listening:

> When I say I enjoy hearing someone, I mean, of course, hearing deeply. I mean that I hear the words, the thoughts, the feeling tones, and personal meaning, even the meaning that is below the conscious intent of the speaker. Sometimes, too, in a message which superficially is not very important, I hear a deep human cry that lies buried and unknown below the surface of the person . . . So I have learned to ask myself, can I hear the sounds and sense the shape of this other person's inner world? Can I resonate to what he is saying so deeply that I sense the meanings he is afraid of yet would like to communicate, as well as those he knows? (8)

Rollo May cautions us to try to understand clients through the meanings they ascribe to events. He asks us to understand their *being* in the world, not view them as merely a cluster of symptoms and behaviors. By attending to the clients with maximum empathy, we will be open to hearing everything they are saying and help them not to fear telling us what we need to know to help. May (1961) asks, "What are the essential characteristics that constitute this patient as an existing person, that constitute this self as a self?" (74).

When we are free as clinicians to really hear our clients, then the process of conducting a useful assessment can begin. We are less likely to miss things and more likely to ask the right questions. The first step is to evaluate our own belief systems regarding mental illness and substance abuse. Only then can we really remove the stigma too often associated with being mentally ill or drug addicted or substance abusing. To be there for the MICA client necessitates the equal removal of punitive and harshly judgmental attitudes about drugs and mental disorders. These are sick people who desperately need our compassion and understanding. It is ironic that many clinicians can have this deeply felt empathy for clients with so many categories of mental disorders and then act as if people suffering from substance-induced organic mental syndromes and disorders and from psychoactive substance abuse disorders were not worthy of the same care and respect. We share a case illustration of Dr. Levy's that plunges right into the heart of this attitudinal and emotional morass.

Case Illustration 13: Daniel

Daniel had first been diagnosed as suffering from schizophrenia at age nineteen. He has been hospitalized for psychotic episodes on two different occasions. He responded well to Thorazine, delusions and hallucinations going into remission each time. Dr. Levy met him when Daniel was age twenty-seven. He was living at home with his mother, who also was suffering from schizophrenia. Both were functional enough to live in the community and share an apartment. They were recipients of various social support services as well as mental health services. He was quite articulate and enjoyed his therapy sessions. He even exhibited a fair amount of insight about his illness and his general life-style. Daniel, tall and handsome, constantly wavered about the possibility of joining the work force. Due to his medication, he was functioning quite well. However, he would really rather "hang out" and smoke marijuana with his friends. The problem was that he could not handle even small amounts of cannabis. He suffered an exquisite sensitivity to certain substances. The marijuana destabilized the Thorazine in ways that were unclear. Within several hours of smoking marijuana, Daniel would go into violent rages, usually breaking things and punching holes in walls and doors. The episode that precipitated his next hospitalization was a similar scenario but this time when he became violent, he beat up his mother, who had to be admitted to the intensive care unit for her medical injuries. This occurred despite Dr. Levy's attempts to instruct Daniel on the dangers of smoking pot. His rationalization was that he didn't always get violent and he just wanted to be like other young people. He entered a hospital day program after an inpatient stay of over a month.

What feelings, thoughts, and fantasies does this case illustration evoke in you? Take an inventory of what you are thinking and feeling. Does Daniel frighten you? Are you angry at him for beating up his own mother, who is also mentally ill? Would you be willing to work with him? How would you help him stop smoking pot? How would you motivate him to get even a part-time job? How would you do an assessment with a client like Daniel?

The choice is yours. Every time you do an assessment with a client, you are free to see each of them as an individual or you can see each as products of a "cookie cutter." Most addiction treatment programs and far too many mental health agencies see their clients from the cookie cutter perspective (Levy 1974a). They level the uniqueness and fail to sharpen the individual differences. Everyone gets homogenized into the stereotypes: "schizophrenics," "crazies," "dirtbags," "dope fiends," "drunks," "street people," "homeless," and "MICAs." Every one of these terms communicates some limited degree of knowledge, an attitude, and a lot of gross generalizations. We came across a definition of the MICA by Arthur Sauter, Ph.D., which unfortunately was untitled and undated but we share it here with you:

> Mentally ill chemical abuser: A person with a family, a personal history, a life style, thoughts and feelings, a value system, needs and wants; whose life is at times seriously distressed by an assortment of symptoms . . . from both chemical abuse and mental illness!

In the section on differential diagnosis, we provide you with some hints on diagnosing MICA clients. Next, we list some of the major issues you must address to conduct a good initial assessment with the MICA client.

Setting the stage: Take nothing for granted! Clients are not used to being heard or treated with respect. Be supportive and patient. The social and clinical systems they travel in breed a sort of institutional paranoia. Find out how they got to your agency and what their current needs are. You might begin with the following:

Ask them what they would like to be called.

Would they like to hang up their coat?

Offer them a seat.

Would they like a cup of coffee or a cold drink?

Do they need to use the facilities?

Where did they sleep last night?

When was the last time they ate?

How are they feeling right now?

Tell them who you are and how you might be able to help. Allow them to become oriented to you and your setting. Listen carefully to what they have to say. Be friendly!

Dealing with intoxication: Dealing with intoxicated clients can range from being difficult to impossible. Exactly what you do will involve three factors: 1) agency policy; 2) your own tolerance for intoxicated behavior; and 3) the actual services you offer. Assuming the client can communicate and understand, you may wish to do the following:

Offer them a place and some time to sober up (which may or may not occur quickly).

Assess for medical crisis.

Let them know that you are not afraid and that you expect them to behave in a civil manner.

Use humor.

Don't play into their fears and delusions. Try not to use threats or threatening language.

Let them know that you will not leave them and that they are going to be OK.

Don't call security unless you really need them. When security arrives, try to keep them in the background. Let them know that you and they (not security) can "work it out."

Do not go into a room alone with them. Arrange a staff buddy system for such an occurrence.

Ask them: What did they take? When? How much? Ever use this drug before?

If possible, get a urine, blood, or breath specimen.

Getting the information: Avoid *why?* questions—they often sound accusative and hostile! Instead ask how, when, where, and what? Do not preach or seek to indoctrinate. Let them tell you in their own words what is happening to them. Keep in mind the following:

Remember, they know more about themselves than anyone else.

Since they may be in a toxic state (suffering from drug-induced organic mental syndrome or disorder), it is very important to get a current substance use history.

They will not tell you they are drinking or drugging if they detect a judgmental or punitive attitude on your part.

You can help elicit the information by saying things like: "Sometimes drugs make people feel the way you do right now," or "I can better help you if you tell me what you took."

Blood or urine analyses are the most objective way of knowing what substance(s) have been taken. The sooner you get them, the better. (Some drugs metabolize quickly.) You will need to win their confidence if you are going to take an *observed* specimen. Random, unannounced, and observed specimens are the least likely to be adulterated.

In addition to the current drug taking, the history should ideally go all the way back to the first use. This probing may have to wait until the client can tolerate a lengthier interview.

We cannot overemphasize the important role that an accurate substance use history, taken together with personal, family medical, and psychological history can play. There is always "life before drugs," no matter how young the drug user began. Getting an idea of how a person functioned prior to drug use is vital to the process of understanding the role that drugs now play in this person's life and in arriving at an accurate diagnostic picture. It exercises a pivotal role in assigning the client to the correct modality of care. For example, if you can establish that a person has a history of mental disorder that predates substance abuse, that is a very different clinical picture from a person with no such history but who presents as mentally ill only when using drugs. The first type of client would need a MICA program while the second would need a substance abuse program. You cannot make an accurate assessment without this information. If you track clients into an agency in which they cannot identify with other clients, they are quite likely to leave *AMA* (against medical advice) and you, not the client, would be to blame.

Another important fact to keep in mind is that after one conducts an initial assessment and formulates working clinical impressions, this is not the end of the assessment process. Observation of and interaction with the client will reveal additional information, and diagnoses and treatment plans should be amended accordingly. Family members, employers, medical and psychological records, neuro-psychological data, and ongoing urine and blood analyses all can contribute vital additional material which should be factored into the ongoing assessment and will contribute ultimately to a fully informed differential diagnosis.

A second important reason for taking careful and complete histories is to avoid "cookie cutter" or "least common denominator" treatment assignments. Remember, different people use different drugs to achieve different effects. Clients do not start off with the same abilities and strengths. We need to look at their actual coping abilities and skills and decide which programs will enhance and supplement their strengths as well as deal adequately with their deficits. Despite the rhetoric in all three fields, treatment plans are rarely individualized. This is owing to a failure to really attend to individual differences and to the finiteness of the services we have to offer. We must move further and further away from the cookie cutter approach. In chapter two we reviewed the relative merits of current models. It is time for new models and new programs.

We end this section with a few simple thoughts about a practical model for assessment of the MICA client:

- It is time for a complete rethinking of previously accepted models, philosophies, and orientations.
- Each treatment system must weed out what is not shown to be useful.
- Each treatment system must make the effort to identify what does work and preserve and strengthen these aspects.
- An inventory of unsolved practical and theoretical problems and issues must be identified.

- Communication, both clinical and political, must be encouraged between systems. In some cases, it will have to be imposed by "power politics."
- Where possible, systems must actually be combined. If alcohol and other drug problems are not forms of mental disorders, how did they get into the *DSM–IIIR?* MICA clients are not new: they have been traveling throughout the systems under different names. In the end, the denial of the mental health problems of all substance abusers is as harmful as the denial of substance abuse problems among all of the mentally ill.
- The alcoholism treatment field must understand the limits as well as the strengths of its folk origins and now also incorporate the psychosocial and cultural influences on drinking behaviors. These, in addition, must be integrated with the biomedical model. The field must work more closely with mental health practitioners. There is a need for more than gratuitous training on mental health issues.
- The drug abuse treatment field must understand its tendency to isolate itself from mental health practitioners and move toward integration. There must be a professionalization of the staff who are currently not prepared to deal with serious mental disorders.
- The mental health treatment field must do more than token in-service training on substance abuse. They must stop trivializing the progress and accomplishments of the other two fields.
- Recommendations abound both for training and treatment issued (see, for example, Ridgely et al. 1987; Torrey 1988; Brown et al. 1989; Galanter 1989). Most go unfulfilled, falling on deaf ears and economic hard times. Real change is needed.

Abstinence and Relapse

In their foreword to *Relapse Prevention,* Marlett and Gordon (1985) say:

> It is virtually a truism to note that addictive disorders are characterized by disturbingly high rates of relapse following initial treatment success. Yet it has been only in the past decade that investigators have directly addressed the problems of facilitating maintenance of treatment-produced change. Primarily under the impact of social-learning theory, it has increasingly come to be realized that effective therapeutic interventions must distinguish between the initial induction of behavior change and its maintenance over time, and accommodate both components if lasting personal change is to result. (ix)

Relapse: A Common Problem

We need to remind you of the power and accuracy of this statement. Relapse is the most common outcome of all treatment experiences, regardless of modality. Here are the hard facts:

- Half the people who attend 12-step meetings like Alcoholics Anonymous (AA) or Narcotics Anonymous (NA) are gone after four months. According to Trice (1983), those who affiliate with AA usually have had experience with small groups, share these emotions easily, and enjoy the casual, give-and-take of the meetings. There are few controlled studies of AA. Baekland et al. (1975) estimate that the success rate in AA approximates 34 percent, which is not nearly as high as popular statements suggest. According to Peele (1985, 145), "the only controlled comparison of AA with other treatments reported the highest dropout and relapse rate for those randomly assigned to AA (Brandsma et al. 1980)."
- The two Rand studies (Armor, Polich, and Stambul 1976; and Polich, Armor, and Braiker 1981), in a follow-up of alcoholics treated in 6 federally funded programs, showed that at eighteen months: 22 percent were drinking normally and only 24 percent were abstaining; and at the end of four years of follow-up, 40 percent reported drinking with no problems. The alcoholism treatment field has simply ignored these studies because they challenge doctrinaire thinking. Peele (1985) comments: "Thus the ultimate significance of the reports rests in the cultural response to them rather than [in] their actual findings" (36).
- Longitudinal data collected by Valliant (1983) showed that those alcoholics who were exposed to medical treatment and to AA fared no better than untreated alcoholics.
- Eighty percent of the alcoholics and drug addicts in this country go untreated by choice.
- There is no evidence which demonstrates that any modality of care for alcoholism is more effective than any other type of care (Saxe et al. 1983). In 1990, it was noted that private treatment centers were only 55 percent full.
- Miller and Hester (1986) reviewed 900 studies in the alcoholism treatment literature. It was discovered that the treatment approaches most clearly supported as effective are rarely practiced in the United States.
- Robins, in summarizing the Epidemiological Catchment Areas study funded by ADAMHA (see ADAMHA 1989), reported that of the substance abusers studied, 81 percent believed they should be strong

enough to handle it alone; 77 percent believed they will recover without care; and 49 percent sought care only because of family pressure (13).

- Califano (1982), in a report to the governor of New York State concluded: "Unfortunately for most addicts, the dream of lifelong abstinence from all narcotics is just that. The number of addicts who kick the heroin habit for good without turning to another narcotic or alcohol is exceedingly small, perhaps 10 percent of those who enter a treatment program" (30).
- Hubbard et al. (1989) reported good outcomes for heroin addicts who remain in treatment. Treatment was less effective in reducing use of marijuana and alcohol. Dropout rates are significant: only 34.1 percent of MMTP clients, 13.4 percent of TC clients, and 6.6 percent of outpatient, drug-free clinic clients stayed in treatment at least one year. More than 80 percent of TC and outpatient clients were in treatment for less than six months.

Ask your friends who have tried to give up smoking and they will tell you the same thing that Mark Twain did: "Stopping is easy. I've done it dozens of times." Staying stopped is the key. This process is what we now call *relapse prevention*. It is important to stress that relapsing is a process over time and not a static event. Whether the theorist/clinician comes from a disease model like Gorski and Miller (1982) and Daley (1987) or a cognitive-behavioral model like Marlatt and Gordon (1985) and McAuliffe and Ch'ien (1986), all are agreed on this important point about relapse being a process. Relapse, it seems, is a natural part of addictive behaviors and fits into the natural course of events when one attempts to stop using substances (and halt other compulsive behaviors as well). How people think about the relapses they have experienced has a lot to do with the indoctrination they may have received about the process. Katz and Liu (1991) in reporting on the work of Chiauzzi (1989) give us some insight on this important issue in their book, *The Codependency Conspiracy:*

> When researchers ask a group of ninety relapsed alcoholics to describe what they had to do to recover, 34 percent said that they just had to attend AA meetings. Indeed, on average they had attended 586 AA or NA meetings apiece! Yet they kept relapsing. One reason, concluded the researchers, was that their recovery goals were too narrow. They did not consider self-awareness to be an important goal, for example. Nor did they associate recovery with success in relationships, or with acquiring coping skills or a sense of purpose in life. In short, they failed to repair the underlying causes of their addiction and left themselves open to relapse. (157–58)

Chiauzzi (1989), in addition, identified five basic character traits that seem to enhance continuing addictive behavior and inhibit the recovery process:

1) compulsiveness; 2) dependency; 3) passive-aggressive tendencies; 4) narcissism; and 5) anti-social tendencies.

Mescavage (1989) helps us to understand the roots of controversy and failed inter-field communication. He argues that alcoholism in the mentally ill is coexisting, not a secondary aspect. In so saying, he attacks the mental health movement in a manner which further fuels the antagonism between the fields:

> The idea that alcoholism is a symptom of a more basic underlying problem is the hallmark of what can be called the "Mental Health Approach" to alcoholism. Milam, in discussing this approach, offers that the causative agent is thought to be deeper neurotic process, a "personality inadequacy or character defect." . . . Except among analysts, the usefulness of the mental health approach to treating alcoholism has been seriously questioned. Milam, in reviewing the clinical literature of the efficacy of this model, concludes: "It is a matter of record that the vast majority of alcoholics who have recovered, have done so outside of, and in spite of, the mental health movement rather than within its boundaries. Without exception, each author (who has surveyed the literature), in turn has been forced to the same reluctant conclusion, that no acceptable evidence has been reported that would warrant the assumption of psychological causation of alcoholism or that persons with any psychological characteristics are more likely to become alcoholics than persons with other psychological characteristics." (20–21)

By detaching alcoholism from psychology, such views project a deterministic, mechanistic, and probabilistic view of human behavior that leaves little room for the creative work of relapse prevention. The all-important point about viewing mental illness and alcoholism as equally important and worthy of conjoint treatment is lost in the vicious and intellectually impotent assault on the entire mental health field, with special invective reserved for the analysts. Good work in relapse prevention views the client as capable of understanding the nature of his/her addictive behavior, capable of being trained in the necessary skills, and capable of making life-style changes. It involves clients' taking a proactive and self-responsible stance rather than viewing themselves as the passive victims of events beyond their control.

Gottheil and Waxman (1982) suggest a more integrative, practical approach to the coexistence of mental illness and substance abuse:

> The patient should have a primary therapist who can employ those treatment techniques that are commonly helpful across these conditions, is capable of assessing and evaluating the specific, special treatment needs of particular patients, and is prepared to request, discuss, and incorporate consultant recommendations in fashioning an appropriate treatment plan. (643)

In order to experience relapse, a client has to have a conscious intent to abstain or otherwise change his/her use of a substance. Thus a clear goal is stated and one mobilizes behaviors to achieve it. A person with a clear goal of continuing the use of drugs as in the past cannot relapse since there is no intention of changing. Whether one formally enrolls in a treatment program or not, a similar process seems to be involved in achieving success with the new goal (Shaffer and Jones 1989: Peele 1989). This includes a seriousness of purpose about the goal, making a major life-style change, removing oneself from other compulsive drug users, and developing personal coping strategies, a personal support system, and a belief in one's ability to achieve the goal. The last point, alluding to a belief in one's ability to master that which is important to them, is called *self-efficacy* (Bandura 1977). In relapse prevention work "a feeling of confidence in one's abilities to cope effectively with a high-risk situation is associated with an increased perception of self-efficacy, a kind of 'I know I can handle it' feeling" (Marlatt and Gordon 1985:40).

Relapse Prevention and the MICA Client

There are two goals in relapse prevention. The first is the successful anticipation and prevention of a momentary lapse (smoking one cigarette, drinking a single beer, doing a line of cocaine). The second is to prevent a lapse from turning into a full-blown relapse involving binge behavior and a renunciation of the original goal. When addiction treatment outcomes are dichotomized into abstinence (which is always good and desirable) and any drug use (which is bad and undesirable), a problem occurs. If drug use is viewed as a loss of control, then what is abstinence? Surely, it is a form of self-control. Drug users and abusers without accompanying major mental disorders do modify drug use in ways other than total abstinence. There is a whole range of behaviors possible between total abstinence and complete abandon (see Pattison and Kaufman 1982).

Telling seriously disturbed MICA clients, "Don't drink and go to meetings," is not a suggestion which they can easily follow. Harshly confronting them in encounter groups is counterproductive. Psychoeducational group education is a start, but certainly by itself, is insufficient for leading to a firm commitment to abstinence. You also can't tell the clients: "Don't take any mood-altering substances," without risking their going off their needed psychotropic medications. (There are already enough issues centered around medication compliance.) Their cognitive and emotional impairment can make it difficult for them to aspire to a demanding goal like total abstinence. Osher and Kofoed (1989) state:

> Abstinence is not the end of substance abuse treatment for the duallydiagnosed patient . . . Lapses or "slips" are to be anticipated. The patient's

> cognitive and affective responses to these lapses may determine the degree to which the patient will return to his former behavior. Both the clinician's and the patient's anticipated responses to lapses should be discussed before they occur. Relapse can be a learned experience. The discovery and rapid arrest of initial lapses may help in the prevention of latter ones. (1027)

Ridgely et al. (1987) quotes from Harrison et al. (1985) who address the need to set realistic goals for MICA clients:

> For many of the dual patients, "recovery" must be defined with cautious realism in view of their limitations. Some cannot be expected to achieve optimum recovery goals: permanent abstinence from alcohol and other drugs, a future free of psychiatric hospitalization, a return to the work force, and stable interpersonal relationships. Rather, recovery for some patients must be measured in terms of less frequent and less destructive encounters with chemicals, increased intervals of abstinence and satisfying sobriety, compliance with medication maintenance and fewer hospitalizations, less injurious behavior, and increased social responsibility and self-esteem. (24)

We agree that goals must be realistic but fear that for too many clinicians in the mental health field, the idea of chronic mental illness spells disaster for the client's future. By this we mean that the staff have given up seeing the client's potential. A kind of institutional myopia sets in after a few years of working with "chronics" in which staff members overfocus on the pathology and don't see the healthier possibilities. Too often staff are merely babysitting chronic clients. They simply don't believe such clients are capable of real change. They often fail to set limits on patients around issues like substance use and either ignore it or try to transfer the client into the substance abuse treatment system, thereby abdicating responsibility for having to attend to such issues. For these staff, many of whom have long since "burned-out" (see Freudenberger and Richelson 1980), the idea of doing relapse prevention work seems fruitless.

What must be struck is a balance between emotional/cognitive deficits and strengths. Unless staff are willing to work patiently and enthusiastically with clients, then the whole affair becomes a self-fulfilling prophesy. We realize that there are dedicated hardworking clinicians in the mental health field but it is also true that most shun working with severely mentally ill clients, including MICAs. The vast majority are not well-trained in issues of substance abuse. The shame is that if they took the time to learn about substance abuse, they might be able to effectively intervene with drug misuse and lessen client suffering (from the toxic effects of the drugs which they take). When this is done right, both client and staff member benefit from the experience.

Substance abuse follows multivariate patterns. There is little evidence that supports the idea that addictive behavior follows a lock-step pattern. Substance abuse has multiple determinants and multiple consequences. Relapse prevention with MICA clients must communicate a number of important facts. Your role in this communication process can be defined as follows.

1. As with any other clients, help the MICA client to make an honest appraisal of the actual consequences of his or her substance use. In order to do this you need to:

   - be a good listener
   - be willing to learn rather than indoctrinate
   - let the client be both teacher and learner
   - let the client know it's safe to be honest about substance use—you need to be supportive, understanding, and nonjudgmental
   - not equate any substance use with "failure."

2. Help the client to understand how the use of substances can trigger both pleasant and unpleasant experiences. Remember, people use drugs for a reason! Help the client to understand the cost/benefit ratio of continuing substance use.
3. Don't lie! Scare tactics are counterproductive. When the terrible consequences don't materialize, you will lose your credibility with the client. Most clients do engage in periods of controlled (nonharmful) use and will use this fact to rationalize and justify continuing use (despite negative consequences which do occur at other times).
4. Accept reduced and nonharmful use as legitimate short-term goals. Understand that the client's cognitive and emotional deficits may make compliance with total abstinence problematic. They may reject total abstinence in an outright fashion. You will then have to work within more limited goals or refer to another clinician who can. This accommodation is unique to outpatient work. Inpatient facilities can more closely monitor and supervise the client.
5. Help the clients understand that at least part of their mental illness is owing to problems with neurochemistry. Teach them that adding exogenous (external) drugs like alcohol, marijuana, cocaine, or heroin to their endogenous (internal) brain chemistry, which is already out of balance, causes "double trouble." Because minute quantities of drugs can have powerful effects in the human brain, they need to know that due to their mental illness, they have a unique sensitivity to these drugs. Also teach them about the destabilizing effects which alcohol and street drugs can have on psychotropic medications.

6. Teaching and practicing coping skills must be accompanied by "self-efficacy ratings." That is, even after skills acquisition lessons and rehearsals, clients may still not feel that the coping mechanisms will work in the real world. Ask them: "Do you think this will work when you are outside the program?" If they respond negatively, allow more practice; and you may then wish to accompany them into real world settings to actually try out the skills.
7. Do not generalize. Treat each of the clients as unique. Learn the overt and covert antecedents (triggers) that are likely to trigger *their* use of substances. Do not rely on overly broad slogans like "people, places, and things trigger lapses and relapses." Find out which ones are high risk situations for them. Tailor prevention strategies to the specific trigger.
8. Teach them that lapses and relapses are a *mistake*. Nothing more and nothing less. Remember, relapse prevention places the responsibility on the individual—it is self-help. When people are practicing new skills, they are most likely to make more mistakes at the beginning. They need to know that you and they can go on, even after a series of mistakes. Each mistake carries with it the possibility of new learning.
9. Teach them that relapse is common but not inevitable.
10. A lapse or relapse does not mean that all good things have been lost. When people count "clean" time and then relapse, they have a tendency to negate everything that occurred and go back to "day one." Help them to understand that each day is a mixture of positive and negative events. MICAs can be pretty hard on themselves. Don't join in by dichotomizing relapse outcomes into all-or-none thinking.
11. MICA clients have value systems. They feel guilty when they make mistakes. Don't attribute relapses to forces beyond their control. Validate their feelings and help them learn and rehearse skills to prevent mistakes from occurring in the future. If forces beyond their control are totally responsible for their mental illness and their substance abuse, then you cannot do relapse prevention. Instead, teach them that some things are under their control, and focus on those.
12. Avoid concepts like "one drink, one drunk" unless this has really been the client's own pattern. You will be telling them there is no such thing as a lapse and encouraging uncontrolled use (bingeing). *Loss of control* has little scientific support. The best way to prove this to yourself is to take good relapse histories. Remember, even MICAs have periods of controlled use. The distinction between lapses and relapses is a real, not just semantic, one.
13. Relapse prevention is a set of learning tasks in which clinician and client play the role of both teacher and student. Help clients to *restructure*

their erroneous beliefs about substances through honest dialogue. Substitution by some cognitive dogma rarely works because this tends to externalize responsibility for both the problem and its solution.

14. If you plan on including 12-step meetings of groups like AA or NA, you will need to make sure of the following:

    - that they will not tell clients on psychotropic medications to rid themselves of all mood-altering substances;
    - that they are "double trouble" groups, who understand and respect the dual problems of mental illness and substance abuse;
    - that, in the case of traditional AA meetings, they do not reject other types of substance abusers; and
    - that if clients select sponsors, they are willing to work with and not against therapists and case managers.

The authors work from the compensatory model (see chapter two). In this model, clients are not responsible for the origins of their problems but are responsible for working with them in the here and now. Whether problems stem from poor parenting or errant brain chemistry or both, clients are encouraged to work toward their own highest level of functioning today. We are not as interested in any "chicken and egg" etiological controversy as we are in empowering clients to seize control of their own lives. Relapse prevention done from this perspective allows clients to become agents of their own change.

Overreliance on staff diminishes the client's role. More seriously disturbed clients will not do as well but they still deserve a real opportunity to try to master what they can. Allow dependency where real attempts at independent behavior have been tried and did not work out. Maimonides said: "Give a person a fish and he eats today. Teach a person to fish and he eats for a lifetime!" Working from this model allows a more holistic, cooperative, and optimistic stance on the part of the clinician. It also tends to remove rigid barriers and distinctions between staff and clients. It helps clients to develop as much of a self as they possibly can. Wonderfully, it tends to use the same effect on the clinician. Gordon (1981), in writing about the paradigm of holistic medicine, states:

> Though none would deny the occasional necessity for swift and authoritative medical or surgical intervention, the emphasis in holistic medicine is on helping people to understand and to help themselves, on education and self-care rather than treatment and dependence. Holistic practitioners tend to believe that each person is his or her own best source of care, that their job is to share rather than withhold or mystify their knowledge, to become resources rather than authorities . . . Holistic medicine transforms its prac-

> titioners as well as its patients . . . Many have learned to be less dogmatic with and more generous to their patients, to regard their own consultations as opportunities to learn about their own shortcomings as well as their patient's illnesses. (21, 26)

This is the spirit in which we believe the best care can be given to all MICA and other clients with any maladies. It is also the best way in which to make use of the art and science of relapse prevention strategies.

Psychotropic Medications

In *Mood, Mind and Medicine,* Wender and Klein (1981) note:

> The role of biological factors in both normal and abnormal psychological functioning has been comparatively neglected, not only because of genuine scientific disagreement and pendulum-like swings from one intellectual pole to another, but also because of the hopelessness that has been associated with the idea that behavior may have biological roots. This position is as difficult to accept now as was Freud's assertion, at the beginning of this century, that feelings, values, and intellectual outpourings were the result of unconscious forces beyond the control of conscious will. We think that an assertion of the importance of biological factors in thinking and feelings is as important as an assertion of the importance of unconscious factors. [Footnote to this sentence reads as follows] Freud usually argued that the discomfort produced by his discussions of the unconscious was further evidence supporting his assertion. This is clearly a "catch-22," no-fail method of proof. In contrast, we believe that the evidence for the role of biological factors in mental illness is no stronger if the reader rejects it. Such fairness undoubtedly represents scientific progress. (16)

Graedon (1980), in *The People's Pharmacy–2,* says this about the use of medications for treating the mentally ill:

> The care and feeding of the psyche is a difficult task. It requires people who care and are willing to spend the time to look for the reasons behind the pain and suffering and then help the victim to do something to create meaningful change. Dignity and a sense of self-worth are essential to mental health. If you load someone up on tranquilizers and push him or her back into the same maelstrom of society, you haven't accomplished a damn thing. Drugs can be useful but only if they are used as tools in a total treatment program. When they are the only response to psychological problems they can become a terrible trap. (424)

Zweben and Smith (1989), in *Considerations in Using Psychotropic Medication with Dual Diagnosis Patients in Recovery,* add the following:

> Recovering chemically dependent patients differ from those with psychiatric difficulties alone in several significant ways. Their specific drug use history makes the use of certain medications highly problematic because of the potential for abuse of the prescribed drug or for precipitating relapse to the primary drug of abuse. They also have complex feelings and attitudes toward medications that need to be understood and addressed. Recovery is often defined as living a comfortable and responsible life style without the use of psychoactive drugs; yet some medical conditions require their use. Certain support systems may generate conflict about using medications in ways that undermine treatment. A patient may see the use of prescribed medication as yet another sign of defectiveness or as a sign of failure because "I can't do it myself." All these factors need to be taken into account by both the prescribing physician and nonphysician therapist involved in the patient's treatment. (222)

Writers like Levy (1983), Graedon (1980), Wolfe et al. (1980), and Griffith (1987) all have emphasized the taking of medications as a shared responsibility between doctor, patient, and pharmacist. Levy (1983) describes the ideal approach to drug therapy as one in which:

1. The doctor is clear and explicit in advising the patient about the drugs to be used: their intended benefits, known side effects, dosage instructions, and so on.
2. The pharmacist assists and reinforces the directions given by the doctor and answers any questions the patient has.
3. The patient has used both consultants and clearly understands the intentions of the therapy and what to do if problems arise.

(Levy 1983:186)

The prescription and use of psychotropic medications for the relief of a variety of symptoms, syndromes, and disorders of mental functioning in the MICA client are far more complicated. There are several reasons for this:

> The client's condition may make clear understanding and responsible behavior around medication compliance difficult to accomplish.
>
> The client may be seeking to manipulate in order to get drugs.
>
> The client may use prescription medications (usually in combination with street drugs and alcohol) to get high or otherwise exercise control over his or her "self-medication."
>
> Prescribing doctors may not be sufficiently acquainted with the client's drug history or the effects of various drug-to-drug interactions.

Zweben and Smith (1989) raise the issue of patient compliance with prescribed medications. MICA clients may "operate on the assumption that if one is good, three are better, and escalate the dose of prescribed medication." Conflicting messages between mental health and substance abuse staff confuse clients, who tend to see things in an all-or-none manner, which leads clients to either reject or accept the need for medication as part of their recovery plan (Wallace 1985). Zweben and Smith (1989) also mention control issues:

> Some patients have a high resistance to surrendering control over their drugs to the physician. For example, one patient refused to get rid of his small stash of opioids "so I can never be in unbearable pain and have a physician refuse me relief." Although his stance grew out of remote events in his medical history, his intense need for control were by far the more salient feature. (222)

Salzman et al. (1973), like Zweben and Smith, describe some of the medication and other problems that arise from working with one type of MICA client: patients with paranoid schizophrenia and opiate abuse enrolled in a methadone maintenance program. Problems include: 1) the patient sees the clinic rules as an attempt at control and tries to manipulate them, usually raging against the staff and threatening lawsuits; 2) the patient is in denial as to the morbid preoccupation with the methadone medication; 3) in an attempt to deny the importance of his or her need for methadone, the patient will ask for reductions in dosage, sometimes below therapeutic levels; and 4) the patient will denigrate both the medication and the staff.

Many observers of the MICA young adult patient have commented on their misuse of medication and substance abuse. Young adult MICAs often demand treatment and then refuse it. One such observation is their tendency to discontinue neuroleptic medication at will (see Bachrach 1982; Lamb 1982; Pepper et al. 1981; Pepper and Ryglewicz 1984; Schwartz and Goldfinger 1981; Egri and Caton 1982). Another of their tendencies is to destabilize neuroleptics with cannabis or antidepressants with alcohol.

Not a great deal is known about the drug-to-drug interactions when psychotropic medication and street drugs are mixed. Stimulants have been found to worsen active psychosis in schizophrenic patients (Richard et al. 1985); and stimulant use has worsened psychosis even in the presence of neuroleptic medication (Janowsky and Davis 1976). Earlier, we cited several cases involving the destabilization of neuroleptics by crack/cocaine and marijuana. There exist other isolated studies but the literature speaks with the greatest degree of knowledge about the interactions between alcohol and psychotropics, some of which are as follows:

Psychotropic Drugs and Alcohol

- Drug interactions in the alcoholic with permanent physiologic impairment differ from those in the occasional drinker. This is due mainly to changes in hepatic (liver) functioning.
- Acute ingestion of alcohol can impair hepatic extraction of tricyclic antidepressants, increase the amount reaching target tissue, and cause drug toxicity including increased sedation.
- Alcohol consumption with its attendant fluid load and diuretic effect can alter renal absorption of Lithium and cause fluctuating serum levels.
- Alcohol/drug interactions may be:

  additive: separate effects of the drugs summate when taken together
  synergistic: one drug potentiates the other with the overall response being more powerful than either one alone
  antagonistic: one drug neutralizes the effect of the other
- When alcohol is combined with other sedatives (that is, barbiturates or tranquilizers) cross-tolerance may be established.
- Persons on Mao inhibitors who drink will have more intense, longer lasting effects. If the alcohol contains tyramine (as found in red wine or dark beer), it can trigger a hypertensive crisis including acute headaches and elevated blood pressure.
- Chlorpromazine inhibits alcohol dehydrogenase and also directly potentiates the CNS depressant effects of alcohol.

(Adapted from Weller and Preskorn 1984:301–9)

Since MICAs also suffer from a variety of medical conditions and disorders, it is important for clients and the prescribing physicians to know how any medications used to manage these problems might interact with psychotropic medications. For example, clients taking phenothiazine and nonphenothiazine antipsychotic drugs must take care when using: anticholinergics, anticonvulsants, antidepressants, antihistamines, high blood pressure drugs, muscle relaxants, narcotics, sleeping pills, and tranquilizers because antipsychotic drugs are central nervous system (CNS) depressants. When combined with the drugs listed above, the antipsychotic drugs become interacting depressants. Antipsychotics and anticholinergics may cause excessive anticholinergic side-effects such as blurred vision, dry mouth, constipation, heart palpitations, slurred speech, difficulty in urination, stomach irritation, and possible toxic psychosis (the symptoms bring agitation, disorientation, and delirium). For further information we suggest books like Harkness (1984), *Drug Interactions Handbook,* from which was drawn much of the foregoing information about psychotropic drugs' interactions with other medications (292–94).

Hubbard et al. (1989) report that traditional opiate treatment programs, even when relatively successful in helping clients renounce opiate use, were far less successful in leading to diminished use of alcohol or cannabis. The researchers also report that, across modalities, one-fifth of clients had received treatment for alcohol-related problems and one-fourth for mental health or emotional problems. Also across the three modalities, 14 to 25 percent of clients had felt depressed, 23 to 34 percent had thought about suicide, and 6 to 14 percent had attempted suicide. Symptoms of depression were more common among younger and female clients. Three to five years after treatment 10 to 20 percent still reported suicidal indicators. DeLeon (1989) reports that most clients entering TCs received dual or multiple diagnoses that included drug dependence plus one other *axis I* or *axis II* diagnosis. The most frequent accompanying diagnoses were anxiety, phobic disorders, and antisocial personality disorder. We can only speculate on how many of these clients, many of whom fit the description of the young adult chronic mentally ill patient, primarily but not exclusively without psychoses, could have benefitted from the administration of psychotropic medications. Certainly anxiety and phobic disorders should be evaluated for drug therapy (Zweben 1986; Zweben and Smith 1989). How many continued drinking and using marijuana as a form of self-medication after "successfully" completing treatment? According to empirical and anecdotal evidence, far too many!

We have already mentioned that MICA clients must be on the lookout for certain problems when attending 12-step self-help (in actuality, these are mutual help) groups. For alcoholics and drug addicts who do not require medication for either physical or mental illness, the admonition to avoid all mood-altering substances is a reachable goal. For the MICA on psychotropic medications, this same advice could spell disaster. Despite the publication by AA of the pamphlet entitled *The AA Member—Medications and Other Drugs: Report from a Group of Physicians in AA* (Alcoholics Anonymous 1984), there are still many individual AA and NA members who adhere to the more conservative admonition and make the meetings an uncomfortable setting for MICAs. They are also uncomfortable with some of the behaviors exhibited by MICA clients. Many individual AA meetings, particularly those with long-term older members, do not react well to "qualifications" (substance abusers' stories) about drugs other than alcohol. Thus, if your clients are to attend 12-step meetings, they should, with your help, choose groups that are accepting of MICAs (sometimes called double trouble groups).

The famous author William Styron (*The Confessions of Nat Turner, Sophie's Choice*) has written a powerful and moving account of his own struggle with suicidal depression. Suffering from the ravages of both depression and years of heavy drinking, Styron (1990) reminds us of the human dignity and of the possibility for recovery of a mentally ill chemical abuser:

> For those who have dwelt in depression's dark wood, and known its inexplicable agony, their return from the abyss is not unlike the ascent of the poet, trudging upward and upward out of hell's black depths and at last emerging into what he saw as "the shining world." There, whoever has been restored to health has almost always been restored to the capacity for serenity and joy, and this may be indemnity enough for having endured the despair beyond despair. (From *Darkness Visible: A Memoir of Madness*, 84)

4
Models and Recommendations

It's More Than Just Semantic Differences

There are no true MICA models of treatment. There is only good treatment. Any one of the three systems is capable of delivering good treatment. Our review of the efforts to date leaves us with two inescapable conclusions. The first is that "there is nothing new under the sun." The principles and practices which have defined quality care have not changed because of the advent of the MICA clients. The best efforts to date appear to be those based on sound and solid, fundamental clinical and administrative practices. Our second conclusion is that agencies providing these types of care are all too rare. While some MICA programs are sprouting up here and there, the vast majority of mental health and substance abuse agencies are stuck in a time warp and refuse to change.

At first glance, the MICA literature seems to suggest a tower of Babel in which the citizens all speak different languages. But their linguistic usage addresses deeply felt emotions that solidify cognitive dogma. We have spoken with countless professionals and clients whose first question is rarely: "What do you know?" followed by, "How do you know this?" and "How credible is the source?" and "How was this conclusion reached?" Instead almost everywhere our readings, our interviews, and our clinical and administrative experiences took us, we encountered the provocative question: "What do you believe?" Sometimes the use of the word *believe* implied a distinction between empirically and intuitively derived knowledge. Far more often it was more like entering a great cathedral and being challenged by the religious leader about whether we were indeed believers in the "one and true" faith. On far too many occasions, this was a withering experience. We found we were seen as outlanders and nonbelievers and were therefore perceived as being just plain wrong in our views if we questioned any of the biases of the three fields, or worse yet, demanded evidence for the claims that people made.

At times our ideas were rejected our of hand by substance abuse treatment personnel who wanted to see us as mental health professionals and not as addiction professionals. In effect, we were told that our holistic views were radical and they were fearful of us. We found that their definition of mental illness did not consider those characterological distortions which the *DSM–IIIR* labels personality disorders to be "real" mental illness. The addiction programs consider real mental illness to be *axis I* disorders (they used terms like *truly* and *really* crazy). And they characteristically refused services to the more severely ill clients. How had they detached the addictive behavior from the abusers' personal psychology? We found that pointing out logical inconsistencies did not help. Neither did quoting from scientific studies. These folks had made their minds up long ago. They were informed by personal suffering and the transformation of recovery. And they had learned to rely on their peers-in-recovery. They and not the professionals were their comrades-in-arms.

We also discovered that many professionals in the field of substance abuse were avoiding and ignoring entire bodies of literature—namely, the ones that were not in accord with the cherished views of the agencies they worked for. We talked with too many professionals who had quit their jobs in disgust over the anti-intellectual bias they encountered. One clinical psychologist we spoke to received his doctorate from a prestigious graduate training program, was state licensed, and had completed his postdoctoral analytic training certificate. He had worked in substance abuse for five years. He finally quit when his clinical recommendations for medication evaluation, suicide watches, and individual therapy fell repeatedly on deaf ears in the well-known residential drug-free therapeutic community where he had been employed. Materials given to paraprofessional counselors to read were "stupid, simple," watered-down versions of important and complex ideas about addiction and other aspects of human behavior. Several clinical social workers we interviewed left their methadone maintenance agencies when the administration would not support a suggested requirement for weekly group and individual counseling for all clients with alcohol, cocaine, and marijuana problems. Their requests to institute a MICA group were also turned down.

Language usages reinforce bias: wealthy and middle-class people who misuse drugs suffer from the disease of "chemical dependency" and are called "drug dependent" and "alcoholics," while poor people engaging in the same behaviors are "substance abusers," and are often referred to as "drug addicts," "gutter hypes," "dope fiends," thirsty "crack heads," "winos," and "drunks."

When conversing with many mental health professionals, we found their knowledge of addictive behaviors to be quite limited and doctrinaire. They also seemed closed off to consideration of such ideas as spirituality and religion as part of treatment and recovery. They did not support client participation in mutual support groups or family-oriented programs. Their views of addiction were characteristically riddled with fear and stereotypes adopted from the media and not from real addicts and real addiction treatment experiences. For example, they rarely understood the distinction between the confrontation of client behavior on the one hand and the use of harsh encounter group confrontational tactics on the other. So the word *confrontation* became a trigger for rejecting any form of group counseling. Sadly, by overemphasizing intrapsychic dynamics they were not only out of step with addictive behaviors but also with a host of other stultifying life problems like broken families, AIDS, domicile issues, poverty, nutrition, friendship, and street violence. We were told, on too many occasions, of agency policies that penalized seriously mentally ill clients for drinking and drugging. One such practice—suspending clients from the programs, led them to be permanently lost to contact. This practice is tantamount to setting up the client to self-destruct. These mental health agencies were as guilty as the more rigid substance abuse treatment agencies. Neither was willing to work with realities of the MICA client.

We also found that some agencies just hired a "lone ranger" substance abuse specialist. No one else on staff got training in substance abuse issues or was asked to examine and change his or her unsympathetic attitudes toward substance abusers. Just as so many agencies in all three fields simply refer the more disturbed clients to the psychiatrist, these mental health agencies referred the MICAs to the substance abuse specialist. We are certain that the majority of such lone ranger efforts were doomed from their inception.

The basic nature of this profound communication problem is due in great measure to a lack of "translators"—that is, reasonable people trying to understand complex phenomena. Most staffs refuse to even enter into a dialogue. As indicated in chapter one, the three fields are deeply entrenched and rarely look over the rim of their bunkers.

There are sound recommendations for improving care for MICA clients and for the agencies and staffs that work with them. Many have been voiced since the mid-to-late 1980s. Most have never been implemented. Nor is this likely to happen any time soon. Some of the early experiments with providing good treatment have also dissipated, victim to economic hard times, shortsighted funding configurations, and government apathy. Most notable among the published recommendations are the following authors, listed chronologically:

Ridgely, M.S.; Goldman, H.H.; and Talbott, J.A. 1986. *Chronic mentally ill young adults with substance abuse problems: A review of relevant literature and creation of a research agenda*. Baltimore: University of Maryland School of Medicine.

Ridgely, M.S.; Osher, F.C.; and Talbott, J.A. 1987. *Chronic mentally ill young adults with substance abuse problems: Treatment and training issues*. Baltimore: University of Maryland School of Medicine.

Torrey, E.F. 1988. *Nowhere to go: The tragic odyssey of the homeless mentally ill*. New York: Harper & Row.

Brown, V.B.; Ridgely, M.S.; Pepper, B.; Levine, I.S.; and Ryglewicz, H. 1989. The dual crisis: Mental illness and substance abuse: Present and future directions. *American Psychologist* 44 (3):565–69.

Galanter, M. 1989. *Task force on combined psychiatric and addictive disorders: Recommendations for program development, policy, and regulations, staff de-*

velopment and training, and data collection. Albany: New York State Office of Mental Health.

Way, B.B., and McCormick, L.L. 1990. *The mentally ill chemical abusing population: A review of the literature.* Albany: Bureau of Evaluation and Services Research, New York State Office Mental Health.

Torrey, E.F.; Flynn, L.; Wolfe, S.; and Erdman, K. 1990. *Care of the seriously mentally ill.* Washington, D.C.: National Alliance for the Mentally Ill and the Public Citizen Health Research Group.

Here are some quotes from these various publications, all of which indicate problems involved in providing services to the MICA population. Brown et al. (1989) note:

> Expanded efforts to provide quality care for dually diagnosed patients are difficult to implement . . . Congress mandated statewide mental health planning as a response to fragmented and inadequate mental health services for severely mentally ill persons. In the planning, particular attention must be paid to the large segment of the severely mentally ill population suffering from concurrent drug and alcohol abuse problems.

Nevertheless, Torrey et al. (1990) conclude:

> Services for individuals with serious mental illness in the United States are a disaster by any measure used. The abandonment of the public sector by mental health professionals whose training was supported by public funds and the failure of publically funded mental health centers are shameful chapters in the history of contemporary American psychiatry.

Divisiveness among the treatment fields is described by Way and McCormick (1990) as follows:

> Currently, rigid boundaries surround the administrative divisions of mental health, alcoholism, and substance abuse agencies, with the "system" separating rather than working to integrate their agencies. Such segregation results in disjointed and, therefore, ineffective treatment systems. Each division has its own treatment philosophies and funding streams which often lead to territorial battles for clients: "many treatment systems are intimidated by the prospect of losing their clientele to a new system of service delivery."

No field accepts responsibility for the MICA client, as Ridgely et al. (1986) explain:

> There is no consensus among clinicians about the proper place for the chronic mentally ill, either within the psychiatric service system or within society. Because they are "system misfits" whose needs are out of tune with existing services they may prove to be intolerable to an already overloaded

> service system . . . The "system" of community treatment, resulting from the policy and practice of deinstitutionalization, is not working well for a number of chronic young adult patients. The limitations of traditional treatments have been repeatedly reported and significant numbers of chronic mentally ill young adults have "voted with their feet," refusing to use community agencies that are not appropriate to their needs and/or fail to attract and engage them in treatment.

In addition, Ridgely et al. (1987) say:

> It is necessary to focus not only on developing "technology" but also on the reasons why we do not already incorporate what we know into our programs, whether these be attitudinal (the stigma against young patients as difficult patients), a result of inertia of the mental health and substance abuse systems of care, or the negative consequences for going beyond the boundaries of one's system. In fact, it is germane to question whether the focus of new programming will be on the most sensible approach to the problem, or on the more political question of what the existing order will permit.

And Galanter (1989), in a New York State task force report, concludes:

> Two cultures have emerged in the mental hygiene field, one that addresses general psychiatry and the other that addresses addictive problems. Each group has developed its respective modalities, training programs, and treatment settings. These cultures have grown apart in their philosophical orientations, as well as in the practicalities of how patients are cared for. It has become clear to the Task Force that the current situation cannot continue if dually-diagnosed patients are to be treated adequately.

Some Early Attempts at Rectifying the Situation

As we have indicated, there is no shortage of recommendations for improving the services delivery system to MICA clients. Drawing upon the multiple sources we have reviewed, we have compiled the major recommendations for improvement of services to MICA clients and the components necessary for the realization of each.

Establish a research agenda:

- develop operational definitions that will allow for intelligent dialogue within and between fields and disciplines
- conduct longitudinal studies with matched control and comparison groups
- examine existing data bases for utility in learning about subgroups of MICA clients

- develop data bases unique to MICA populations
- develop interagency client tracking systems
- evaluate current efforts to serve MICA clients
- translate findings from "researchese" into a language comprehensible to the line staff (and use only credible, empirically sound studies)
- share research funds across disciplines and specialties
- study the interactions between psychotropic medications and alcohol and other drugs
- increase funding for research projects which examine the causes and treatment of serious mental disorders
- conduct studies to find out where the majority of the people who were deinstitutionalized currently are located and reach out to them

Establish a training agenda:

- establish training programs for each field to learn about the work of the other fields
- bring together workers from the various fields for training (cross-training)
- do cross-disciplinary training
- teach all clinical staff how to do behavioral assessments and mental status examinations
- provide special training for clinical supervisors
- teach staff how to set realistic goals for clients, themselves, and their agencies
- provide comprehensive training around relapse prevention
- provide educational forums for family of clients
- have workers actually visit each others' programs
- encourage clinicians to expose themselves to nontraditional modalities such as mutual help, advocacy, and family support groups
- develop training agendas that can be conceived and delivered by teams from the various fields and disciplines
- include consumers in training programs
- promote continuing in-service and other training on a regular basis for all disciplines
- provide training that draws upon the research as well as the clinical literature, taking care not to promote ideas which have been discredited by valid research

Establish innovations in treatment settings:

- establish the helping of the seriously ill MICA client as the number one priority in the field
- encourage hybrid programs among existing treatment agencies
- use cross-training to launch "cross-treatment"
- help agencies to share staff by allocating assignments on a part-time basis
- include past and current substance use history in all assessments
- develop qualified interagency provider agreements which enable rather than inhibit cross-referrals of clients
- develop consumer mutual help groups
- develop family-oriented treatment
- engage the services of psychopharmacologists to run medication management programs
- develop aggressive outreach and engagement programs
- develop permeable boundaries with more flexible client "readiness" criteria (that is, the traditionally rigid rules about client abstinence)
- use multitrack approaches, which combine formal treatment, and vocational, educational, housing, and skills-in-daily-living issues
- provide objective alcohol and other drug education for clients
- combine case managers and counselors/therapists into teams
- do all of the above in the spirit and reality of dealing with mental health and substance abuse issues simultaneously!

Address policy issues at all levels of government and programming:

- change leadership of state agencies which refuse to cooperate; mandate their cooperation
- establish joint policymaking and planning at the state, county, and municipal levels
- fix responsibility for the seriously mentally ill at the state and local levels
- increase awareness of the cost-effectiveness of cross-training and cross-treating; funding streams should understand and encourage this practice
- establish cooperation at the federal level through federal agencies such as the NIMH, NIDA, and NIAAA as role models to the states
- insist, when determining credentialing and licensure at the state level, that criteria reflect contemporary needs for well-trained professionals

which include both mental health and substance abuse knowledge and skills

- link continued funding to demonstrated effectiveness
- develop legislation with teeth and funds, which is needed to insure treatment of the seriously mentally ill
- prohibit policy-making which only supports one point of view, such as deinstitutionalization
- provide emergency funds needed now to help the homeless mentally ill
- review laws that do not permit helping those mentally ill people who cannot or will not help themselves
- distribute funds more equitably: in the case of New York State, for example, three-quarters of the mental health budget still goes to state mental hospitals when funds are desperately needed for community support programs
- develop ways to bring mental health professionals' service to the seriously mentally ill
- appoint consumers and family members to policy-making bodies

Innovative Programs

In addition to recommendations for improvement of services to MICA clients, we provide nine examples of innovative programs which have been developed for the MICAs' special needs.

A Community Mental Health Center. From 1975 to 1977, Dr. Levy was director of research and evaluation at the Community Center for Mental Health in Dumont, New Jersey. In chapter one we described his study of staff diagnostic practices regarding substance abuse (see also Levy 1975). A group of young chronic MICA clients hung on the periphery of the clinical services offered at the center—namely, a day program and individual psychotherapy—and felt estranged from the older chronic clients. Dr. Levy began working with these clients in a group. The only other staff member who was willing to join in was a young entry-level mental health aide. Diagnoses included bipolar disorder, depression, schizophrenia, schizoaffective disorder, and a variety of personality disorders. Alcohol and drug use ran the gamut from periodic to chronic usage and from few negative consequences to many.

Dr. Levy recalls:

> We did confront client behavior but not with loud voices or curses or insults. Mostly we engaged in plain talk, free of therapeutic jargon and hostility. We confronted self-destructive behavior, the breaking of center

rules, and harassment of older, more disturbed clients. The main message we gave out was: "We like you but we don't like some of the things you do." For the most part, the clients began to comply with the rules and expectations laid out by the group. We got group members involved in talking with and caring about each other. These clients responded well to a mixture of behavioral confrontation and genuine acceptance. We did alcohol and drug education right in the group and followed it up with individual teaching sessions. Clients respond to what is offered to them and to staff caring. We used the drug TC concept of "responsible concern." That is, you literally use your ability to respond and show your concern for your peers by pointing to their mistakes. This runs counter to the ethos of the street, where you never "pull anyone's covers" (tell on them).

A turning point in the group's development came just three weeks after its inception. A group member, a twenty-seven-year-old male suffering from major depression, posttraumatic stress disorder, and alcohol dependence, committed suicide. Although he was not well known by the others, they took the death very hard. We were doing bereavement counseling both in and out of the group and did so in concert with the clients' own individual therapists. It brought everyone (including my co-leader and I) much closer to each other and opened the door for a deeper sharing and addressing of problem behaviors. It was simultaneously the most difficult and the most rewarding clinical work. It was enervating and humbling at the same time. The clients needed so much that on some days it felt like our personal wells were running dry. We tried to draw other therapists from the center into the group experience, but to a man and to a woman, they refused. That's how powerful the fear and the aversion was toward the young adult chronic mentally ill chemical abuser in a traditional mental health center.

A Comprehensive Alcoholism Treatment Program. From 1977 to 1982, Dr. Levy was program director of the Alcoholism Treatment Program (ATP) at Beth Israel Medical Center in New York City. The program was part of the department of psychiatry unlike many other hospital-based alcoholism treatment programs which operate out of the department of medicine. This is a very important distinction. Dr. Henry Pinsker, associate director of the Department of Psychiatry, also acted as medical director of the ATP. The program was comprehensive: it included a fifty-bed detoxification unit, a forty-four-bed co-ed halfway house, and an outpatient clinic (serving four hundred patients per month). The program's first director was a psychiatrist (Dr. Bernard Bihari), the second a social worker (Olive Jacob, MSW), and the third, Dr. Levy, is a psychologist. The staff consisted of an internist, two part-time psychiatrists (one in the clinic and one running the detox unit), nurses, social workers, alcoholism counselors, vocational rehabilitation counselors, and so forth. As you can see, this is a staffing complement not unlike a mental health agency's. The program was licensed and funded by the state alcohol agency. The target clients were poor alcoholics living in the surrounding catchment area.

Dr. Levy recalls:

> Rather than exclude mentally ill patients with serious *axis I* diagnoses or personality disordered individuals (*axis II*), we included them. Alcoholism programs without such a professional staff commonly reject such clients. One of the social workers, Lee Shomstein, is still employed at Beth Israel, still working with MICA clients in the Division of Substance Abuse's outpatient clinic. So is Dr. Robert Halem, who worked in the ATP outpatient clinic. Shomstein for many years ran a group of older male MICAs with major mental disorders. Many of the social work and counseling staff routinely provided individual services to MICA clients and, as you might expect, a number of MICA clients made use of the day program (with its part-time physician and two nurses) as well as mental health services. When a client was referred to Dr. Halem, the counselor often sat in on the session. Medications were ordered by the psychiatrist but monitored by both staff members. By treating both disorders—the alcohol dependence and the mental illness—at the same time, the ATP was able to attract and maintain a large MICA clientele. Dr. Pinsker, along with other department members, provided inservice training to the staff on mental health issues. Staff also attended psychiatry grand rounds. The only clients who were not served were those whose behavior could not conform to clinic rules. Although we encouraged abstinence, we did not terminate clients for failure to comply.

The main point we wish to make in citing this program is that when staff have basic training, ongoing inservice training, a good skills mix, and a "can-do" approach, then MICA clients are well served.

Three Methadone Maintenance Treatment Programs (MMTPs). In the early 1980s funding was allocated by the New York State Division of Substance Abuse Services (DSAS) that established what became known as the methadone maintenance model project. State and federal regulations dealt mainly with the control and dispensing of methadone. Regulations regarding counseling and ancillary services (such as, vocational, education, medical, and dental) were far less stringent. For example, individual counseling was to take place only once a month and no group therapy was called for. The new mandate called for intensification of services.

We are aware of the efforts of two DSAS-approved methadone programs that took advantage of the new funds—the Lower East Side Service Center (LESSC) and Greenwich House Counseling Center. Jackie Cohen worked for the LESSC. Rather than the usual "turnstile," medication-only program that many MMTPs had degenerated into, these two programs provided much more. The staffing complements were doubled in both agencies with more clinical social workers added. There was team building and the assignment of specific tasks. Jackie Cohen's caseload was reduced and she was made the agency group worker, an innovation in methadone maintenance treatment. She ran a detox group, an alcohol group, a woman's group, and a pill group. Counseling contacts, both group and individual, were increased to several times weekly. Group participation was mandatory. Social work staff began to combine classical drug counseling with individual psychotherapy. Clients came and participated. Those clients who failed to attend were terminated from the program and were referred to less demanding methadone programs. MICA clients were simply integrated into all service components. The program addressed the use of alcohol, marijuana, cocaine, and pills (usually tranquilizers).

The LESSC began a workshop project, which was a component of their mental health clinic, a mini–day treatment center for psychiatric clients. Staffed by Cohen and a psychiatric nurse/social worker, it served mostly clients who suffered from schizophrenia and abuse of drugs, particularly opiates. Clients' behavior, attendance, and abstinence improved. Clients learned to take their medication (methadone) responsibly and abstain from other drug use (except other medications). This is another demonstration that clients respond to what is offered, particularly when staff have a positive attitude toward the clients.

The Greenwich House Counseling Center in New York City has been in operation for several decades. Thirteen years ago its staff began a mini–day treatment center and did group work with MICAs long before that client description evolved. Jackie Cohen did her first graduate social work placement there in 1978–79. Almost all staff were social workers with several recovering people also on staff. They did standard outpatient psychotherapy with substance abusers, which is a truly innovative approach even now. This exemplary agency has demonstrated that providing good care for all clients could be done under one roof.

In addition, VanEtten Hospital in the Bronx has a methadone program which for many years has also provided a sophisticated clinical day treatment program for their more severely mentally ill substance abusers. They also believe that substance abusers could benefit from such services. Clients attend these service components on a regular basis and do much more than simply stop using drugs.

A State Psychiatric Center. The authors met with Kathleen Sciacca, the former director of Alcohol/Substance Abuse Programs for Community Services, at Harlem Valley (New York) Psychiatric Center. For the past seven years Ms. Sciacca has been developing clinical programs for MICA clients and training programs for staff. In 1984, she began developing new initiatives in the treatment of chronic patients with alcohol and substance use problems (see Sciacca 1987). Active users of drugs within the state-run psychiatric care system were in active "denial," not ready, willing, or interested in substance abuse treatment. Brown et al. (1989) describe Sciacca's approach as follows:

> In an educational framework the client does not have to recognize or publicly acknowledge alcohol or drug use as a problem in his or her particular case, nor does the group leader have to assume the role of expert in this area. Groups devoted to discussion of educational materials (written and video materials) and of group members' experience can begin wherever the client is and gradually work toward a more treatment-oriented and abstinence-directed approach. This allows the client to feel her or his way into a recognition of the impact of drug and alcohol use on daily functioning and a commitment to, or at least a trial of, abstinence based on increased knowledge and understanding. At the same time, it allows the staff of the treatment program to address the issues of substance use or abuse without taking a more confrontational line than the client can tolerate. To engage pre-abstinent clients and involve them in the ongoing process of treatment, it is necessary to modify traditional treatment approaches. (567–68)

Sciacca elaborated on her approach for us, noting that clients were not spontaneously willing to attend AA or NA groups so speakers were brought into the psychiatric facility. Clients found the meetings highly engaging and some began to attend community-based, 12-step meetings. Clients attended substance abuse groups twice a week (each lasting forty-five minutes) with optimal group size being about eight. Staff began to use a brief substance abuse screening questionnaire, which helped them to begin considering the impact of alcohol and other drugs on client functioning. Clinicians were thus enabled to combine their clinical intuition and other skills with the substance abuse issue. Sciacca stressed reality-based treatment with respect for the fragility of the client's illness. Total abstinence is not demanded and small gains, like hearing fewer voices, are considered valuable.

A Drug-Free Treatment Residence. Harbor House is a drug-free residential treatment program for homeless substance abusers who are also mentally ill. It is apparently the very first such program to "treat the dually diagnosed within a drug-free therapeutic community and to integrate treatment teams of mental health, substance abuse, educational, vocational, and housing professions." According to its first annual report on their federally funded New Leaf Work Experience Project (Sturz 1991), 55 percent of all the participants served from February 1990 to March 1991 (the program also serves substance abusers who are not MICAs) had been hospitalized for psychiatric illness, with 63 percent of the 24 MICA clients having a primary diagnosis of schizophrenia and 17 percent having a personality disorder. The criteria for participation in Harbor House are: a) homelessness; b) history of chronic substance abuse; c) history of mental disorders with at least two prior hospitalizations for psychiatric problems and a substantial functional deficit caused by that disorder; and d) an ability to relate to others. This is very different from a program like, for example, Eagleville Hospital (Eagleville, Pennsylvania), which will not admit a MICA client with a serious or unstable psychiatric condition (see Wallen and Weiner 1989). At Harbor House, a past history of suicidal behavior, violence, or criminal involvement is not in itself grounds for exclusion. While the program calls itself "drug-free," some clients are maintained on prescribed psychotropic medication.

Some of the hallmarks of the Harbor House program are:

- integration of ex-addict paraprofessional staff with mental health professionals
- use of modified TC confrontational techniques in order to express respect for clients' fragility
- residents are under the care of a psychiatrist
- residents, when indicated, are maintained on psychotropic medications
- use of a well-structured environment that is both challenging and supportive
- inclusion of a strong educational and vocational component
- inclusion of higher functioning, seriously mentally ill clients
- emphasis on provision of both transitional and permanent housing when the residential phase is concluded

In its first annual report of the New Leaf Project, despite a small sample size in that pilot year, Sturz (1991) concludes:

> Our most suggestive finding, one with national implications, is that even the most severely dysfunctional of the homeless and employed—mentally ill chemical abusers—can be successfully trained for employment and for independent living at the highest level of which each is capable. (87)

A Program for MICA Women and Their Children. In *Children of Drug Abusers,* Levy and Rutter (1992) describe a truly innovative program that they encountered in the fall of 1987. In the heart of one of America's worst ghettos—the South Bronx—they discovered a beacon of light. Under the leadership of Dr. Carolyn Goodman, clinical psychologist and psychoanalyst, the PACE (Parent and Children Education) program was developed as an empowerment model. The program's clients were poor minority women, most of whom were patients at the Bronx Psychiatric Center, and almost all of whom were also substance abusers. Clients were divided between an entry group and a core group. The core group program met for five hours per day, four days per week. The major program components were: 1) parent competency training; 2) therapy group; 3) social and/or recreational activities; and 4) individual sessions that focus on special needs. Between the PACE staff and community resources clients received such services as individual, group, and couples counseling; psychiatric services, including medication; social services; educational and vocational services; and client advocacy.

MICA women want to be drug free and want to be effective parents. The PACE program realized that they must provide care for both mother and child(ren) if the mental illness and substance problems were to be successfully addressed. The hallmarks of the PACE program were:

- families remain united
- experiential, hands-on parent/child workshops (with videotape feedback)
- regular parent/teacher conferences
- dance therapy (providing reaching out, touching, joy, and closeness)
- educational workshops (health care, family planning, nutrition, home management, etc.)
- parent education group discussions (providing cognitive method of teaching parenting skills)
- informal gathering of mothers each morning (establishing friendships, and planning sharing of babysitting and home visits)
- three nursery rooms, each with its own classroom teacher and helpers
- Bank Street College of Education basic curriculum modified for special needs
- collaborative efforts of mothers and teachers
- evaluation of developmental status of each child at six-month intervals

Dr. Goodman believes that the key to the program is the quality of the staff. The key to staff success involves:

- multidisciplinary teams with social workers, teachers, family workers, dance therapist, part-time psychiatrist, and undergraduate students
- ongoing staff training (videos, case conferences, field trips)
- regular clinical supervision (senior staff in tandem with less experienced staff)
- viable system of backup supports
- task-oriented "T" (training) groups

A Private Psychiatric Hospital Program. The Dual Diagnosis Unit at Holliswood Hospital, which opened in 1986 in Queens, New York, typifies the "marriage" that is taking place between private acute-care psychiatric hospitals and 12-step-oriented chemical dependency model programs. In these programs, chemical dependencies—on alcohol and other drugs of abuse—are viewed as addictive diseases (Attia 1988; Progress 1991). Following the medical model, the various mental disorders are likewise considered part of a disease process. Holliswood Hospital is managed by the same organization, The Mediplex Group, that manages Arms Acres and Conifer Park, both "free-standing," private, for-profit chemical dependency programs located in New York State.

For those clients with the proper insurance coverage or other means of payment, Holliswood's Dual Diagnosis unit offers "highly individualized, inpatient treatment and after care planning, with the Unit's dozen or so professionals—psychiatrists, psychologists, social workers, alcoholism and substance abuse counselors, recreational therapists, and nurses—working closely together as part of its team concept approach" (Progress 1991:1). According to its medical director, Dr. A. Lawrence Rubin:

> The unit was developed for individuals whose drug abuse was the predominant and presenting problem, but for whom psychiatric pathology precluded treatment in standard drug rehabilitation centers. These people generally were drug dependent and often had the secondary characteristics of chronic drug abusers which include broken marriages and failed jobs. They were most strongly responsive to the message of fellowship and spirituality offered by the 12-step model, which became the core of the psychotherapeutic program. Often the people referred to this unit who had been identified as addicts were found to have undetected severe psychiatric illnesses while patients previously treated for mental illness were discovered to have previously unknown drug addiction. (*Progress* 1991:2)

And according to Patricia Rose Attia (1988), program director of the unit

> For dual diagnosis treatment to be successful,, the staff must challenge one another and integrate the 12-step models into the treatment of every patient . . . Recovery from addiction is a lifelong process, and self-help meetings must be a part of that process . . . It is not uncommon for a dually diagnosed patient to have a continuing care plan, including self-help meetings, individual psychotherapy, group therapy, psychopharmacological treatment, and continuing care groups. Patients who have not accepted their two illnesses usually choose to focus on half of their recovery, inevitably resulting in a relapse of both illnesses. (61–62)

A Voluntary (Not-for-Profit) Hospital Dual Diagnosis Unit. In the last chapter, in the section on organic mental syndromes and disorders, you met

Dr. Richard N. Rosenthal, psychiatrist and chief of the Division of Substance Abuse at Beth Israel Medical Center in New York City. The division operates an inpatient psychiatric unit for mentally ill chemical abusers and an outpatient program for substance abusers in which MICA clients participate. The inpatient unit began in 1979 under the direction of Dr. Charles Baron (currently at Elmhurst Hospital in Queens, New York).

Beth Israel Medical Center (BIMC) began treating addicts in its Morris J. Bernstein Institute in the 1960s. BIMC pioneered hospital-based detoxification for alcohol and other drugs, the development of a large methadone maintenance treatment system, a comprehensive alcoholism treatment program (mentioned earlier in this section), and the inpatient program for MICAs. The alcoholism treatment program, originally targeted at poor people living on the Lower East Side, is gone, having been replaced by the Stuyvesant Square Chemical Dependency Program (typical of the 12-step model). However, poor street MICA clients can still get excellent care in the detoxification and the inpatient psychiatric unit run by Dr. Rosenthal. Those who do not have Medicaid are helped to become "Medicaid eligible." The inpatient unit also accepts commercial carrier insurance.

The inpatient unit is most highly regarded for its excellent diagnostic work and quality care for MICA clients. Toxic drug effects, symptoms of detoxification, and attendant psychological and other symptomatology are patiently tracked over time. Urine screens and drug histories reveal when acute and residual toxic effects should subside. "I consider it to be organic until proven otherwise," says Dr. Rosenthal. Pathological behaviors that linger and persist give evidence which makes for a careful differential diagnosis. Patients whose problem behavior subsides and is shown to have been the result of drug toxicity are referred to substance abuse programs. For those with persistent mental disorders, programs must be found which will care for both the mental illness and the substance abuse. Twelve-step meetings are held on the unit but speakers are oriented by Dr. Rosenthal—"Doctor Rick"—himself to make sure that they understand the significance of the dual diagnosis. He lets them know that he is grateful for their participation and help and that they need to understand that the MICA client is not just like any other alcoholic. In so doing, he hopes to remove the stigma of both mental illness and substance abuse. A double trouble group has recently been instituted on the unit.

In describing his staff, Dr. Rosenthal says: "They are good people who often work outside their job descriptions." Since there are few comprehensive services for MICAs in New York City, the staff strive very hard to find the "best fit" referrals for continuing care. This is an important practical issue. Talbott and colleagues and the Group for Advancement of Psychiatry (1986) have conceptualized intersystem difficulties as a problem of "interactive fit" between client, caregiver, and system of care and between mental health and substance abuse care systems (see Ridgely et al. 1987). The common denominator for treatment planning is the patients' social and vocational functioning. The therapeutic goal is to bring them to their highest level of such functioning. The staff searches for hybrid programs to continue care for both the mental illness and the substance abuse disorder. Dr. Rosenthal says some of the old-line addiction programs are beginning to take clients on psychotropic medication but for the most part they remain "very choosy." This means that a depressed patient who responds to his/her medication is acceptable. But atypical depression (failure to respond to medication) is not acceptable. They also tend to want only those clients whose psychosis-induced problem behaviors like hallucinations and delusions are "completely in remission" or otherwise controlled by medication. The mental health agencies are slowly beginning to develop hybrid programs but recent state and city funding cuts have seen innovative programs closing across the city as staff lines are cut.

An Outpatient Cocaine Treatment Program. In mid-1986 George R. Doering, Jr., executive director of Youth Counseling Services, Town of Ramapo (Rockland County, New York) and Dr. Levy began the Rockland County Crack/Cocaine Program (CCP). The premise of the program was that a staff of well-trained and highly experienced mental health professionals could deliver quality care to cocaine abusers by attending to their addictive behavior, their psychopathology, and their life-styles. Clinical supervision of staff has been the mainstay of the delivery of quality mental health care since the beginnings of psychotherapy. Therefore, at this program, each of the six counseling staff received one hour a week of individual supervision with Dr. Levy and all met together for group supervision once a week for ninety minutes. Dr. Levy also met for supervision with Mr. Doering several hours each week. The clinical program, which consisted of individual and group counseling and group education, was delivered in the evening hours. All of the staff had full-time jobs elsewhere in Rockland County. They were truly a interdisciplinary and multimodality group of people. They included: 1) director of quality assurance for a county community mental health agency, who was also a registered nurse and certified alcoholism counselor (CAC); 2) director of a day hospital program for substance abusers who also had his CAC; 3) a certified social worker who worked in a methadone maintenance program; 4) a certified social worker who worked in adult and child protective services and was pursuing her CAC; 5) an activities therapist from an inpatient psychiatric unit, also a CAC and pursuing a masters degree in social work; and 6) a certified social worker who worked in an outpatient mental health clinic. Staff included men and women, recovering people, and bicultural and bilingual people.

As Dr. Levy recalls:

> All of the clients we saw had personality disorders, many quite severe. Quite a few also suffered from mood disorders. We reached out to mental health agencies which worked with clients diagnosed as schizophrenic but they were unresponsive. Only one attempt was made to have a case manager escort a client to our program. So we began to concentrate our learning and supervision around clinical work with personality disorders. We are indebted to Dr. Bruce Lowenstein, a clinical psychologist, who provided neuropsychological testing and staff training during this period of time and three years later took over as clinical supervisor. Although the clients clearly fitted the criteria for *MICA,* we never used that term. Diagnosis was often helpful but the clinical course was primarily determined by the clients' own choices. Our orientation was drug-free and we used drug toxicologies to monitor drug use (only 10 to 15 percent of urine tests were "dirty" throughout the first three years). The main thrust of our work was relapse prevention. We made distinctions between lapses and full-blown relapses. We viewed addiction as both maladaptive behavior and adjuncts to psychological defenses. Clients were encouraged to attend 12-step meetings but attendance was not mandatory. We worked with the ebb and flow of clients' lives and tried to understand their struggles. The staff began spontaneously making home visits. A woman's group was started at the very beginning of the program. We helped them deal with family and child problems. I trained five probation officers and together with them ran a pre-treatment group at the county probation department. The CCP staff utilized a mix of psychotherapy and drug counseling techniques. We used both cognitive-behavioral and supportive-expressive treatment techniques. I met periodically with clients and their counselors together. Inservice training and supervision were ongoing.

There are many other efforts too numerous to mention here. We chose the ones we felt are representative of attempts to break some new ground and demonstrate what can be done when people decide to "just do it!" We applaud the efforts of individual agencies around the nation who have begun to realize that things really get going for MICA clients at the grass roots program level. For example, in 1988 Jackie Cohen attended a MICA conference and was exposed to some very sound treatment efforts being run in small agencies by conscientious clinicians in California, Maine, Pennsylvania, and Virginia. Here we list some other types of efforts that are being applied to MICA populations:

- Outreach workers give sandwiches and beverages to homeless MICAs living in the streets and hope over a period of days or weeks to establish contact and bring them in for social and clinical services
- Outreach workers comb shelters for the homeless seeking to bring needed services to clients
- Mental health workers try to bring clients in jails and prisons some small modicum of clinical programming

- Self-help and volunteer groups do outreach work in many settings (for example AA and NA around the nation, GROW groups in Illinois)
- Family groups like the National Association for the Mentally Ill (NAMI) provide education and peer support for parents of MICAs
- In some settings, workers from a mental health agency may spend some time in an addiction treatment setting and vice versa providing educational or therapy services
- Some municipal social service agencies operate vans that bring homeless street people to shelters and other services
- ADAMHA agencies, like the NIDA, NIAAA, and NIMH are beginning to fund MICA projects (for example, Harbor House described above is a recipient of a $4 million NIDA grant)
- Some mental health agencies are designating "substance abuse specialists"
- Case managers may bring MICAs to 12-step and other mutual support meetings in the community
- Some mental health and substance abuse programs are hosting double trouble 12-step meetings
- Some transitional housing programs are insisting that residents attend their mental health and substance treatment programs
- Funds being scarce, some agencies are actually trading training services

Contemplating the Future

And so the authors' journey winds down to the end of the road. This book has been a labor of joy and a difficult task. So much has been written in any one field and we have attempted to survey and summarize all three. We leave it to your tender mercies to judge the relative merits of our efforts. One of our favorite books is *If You Meet the Buddha on the Road, Kill Him!* by Dr. Sheldon B. Koop (1972). The book is about the pilgrimage of the psychotherapy patient and also about the transformations that the therapist goes through (the patient envisions the therapist as a guru). At this point we wish to share some of Koop's writings with you. We think that they are informative in contemplating our future role in working with all patients including the MICA client, whose story we have tried to tell in human terms.

> In every age, men have set out on pilgrimages, on spiritual journeys, on personal quests. Driven by pain, drawn by longing, lifted by hope, singly and in groups they come in search of relief, enlightenment, peace, power, joy, or they know not what. Wishing to learn, and confusing being taught with learning, they often seek out healers, and guides, spiritual teachers

> whose disciples they would become. The emotionally troubled man (and woman) of today, the contemporary pilgrim, wants to be the disciple of the psychotherapist. If he does seek the guidance of such a contemporary guru, he will find himself beginning on a latter-day spiritual pilgrimage of his own. . . . (3)
>
> The pilgrim, whether psychotherapy patient or earlier wayfarer, is at war with himself, in a struggle with his own nature. All of the truly important battles are waged within the self. . . . (7)
>
> Some men undertake their pilgrimages in solitude, others in the company of other seekers. Even those who set out alone may find helpful companions who join them along the way. But for most of us, at the troubled time at which we set out on the search for the meaning of our lives, it seems wise to turn to a helper, a healer, or a guide who can show us the way (or at least can turn us away from the dead-end paths we usually walk) . . . Such a spiritual guide is sometimes called a guru. This special sort of teacher helps others through the rites of initiation and transition by seeming to introduce his disciples to the new experience of higher levels of spiritual understanding. In reality, what he offers them is guidance toward accepting their imperfect, finite existence in an ambiguous and ultimately unmanageable world . . . Even the contemporary Western guru, the psychotherapist, can only be of help to that extent to which he is a fellow pilgrim. . . . (11)
>
> The truth does *not* make people free. Facts do *not* change attitudes. If the guru is dogmatic, all that he evokes in his pilgrim's disciples is their stubbornly resistant insistence on clinging to those unfortunate beliefs that at least provide the security of known misery, rather than openness to the risk of the unknown or the untried. . . . (13)
>
> What the guru knows that the seeker does not is that *we are all pilgrims*. There is no master, and there is no student . . . The teaching mission of the guru is an attempt to free his followers from him. His metaphors and parables make it necessary for the pilgrims who would be disciples to turn to their own imaginations in the search for meaning in their lives. The guru instructs the pilgrims in the tradition of breaking with tradition, in losing themselves so that they may find themselves. (19)

The more we read, the more people we spoke with, the more clients we treated, and the more questions we asked, the more overwhelming the problem seemed. So many views and so little real wisdom. It finally has occurred to us that the search—the creation of the dialogue itself—is the road truly less traveled. And so we wrote this book as our own attempt to further stimulate the dialogue. Part intellectual exercise and part catharsis, we have struggled to find a common ground with all the people we met. It is a damned difficult task. We meet a lot of rigid gurus in our travels. Some, jealously guarding their "own" work, were not willing to share. A few generously shared their experience and their knowledge with us. Each one left us with something valuable—a piece of their own passion and belief—to use to stimulate our own cognitive and spiritual growth. It really is as Burglass and Shaffer stated in 1981:

> Thus, the various discipline-specific ideas and theories can neither disprove nor invalidate one another. These perspectives simply coexist; each has its loyal adherents; each pursues its particular version of truth about the addiction in its own way. (xxii)

This circumstance applies equally to the ideas, theories, and clinical practices in the mental health field.

Our last task is a listing of those recommendations that we perceive as necessary and helpful. First, we make some general recommendations, followed by several specific to each of the three fields. Like the recommendations already listed above, we can't be sure that anyone is really listening. Many of those were made four and five years ago and still go unheeded. A few modest efforts have been actualized. Thus, in the earnest hope that the dialogue can continue and individual MICA clients will be helped, we offer them to you.

General Recommendations

A Holistic View. In order to work successfully with the mentally ill chemical abuser we need to see him or her as a total and unique person. We must provide "health for the whole person." Hastings et al. (1980), in the preface to their book by that title, spell out a holistic approach:

> First, such an approach involves expanding our focus to include the many personal, familial, social, and environmental factors that promote health, prevent illness, and encourage healing. Second, a holistic approach views the patient as an individual person, not as a symptom-bearing organism. This attitude emphasizes the self-responsibility of the person for his or her health and the importance of mobilizing the person's own health capacities, rather than treating illness only from the outside. Third, the holistic approach tries to make wise use of the many diagnostic, treatment, and health modalities that are available in addition to the standard materia medica—including alternative medical and healing systems as well as psychological techniques and physical modalities. (xi)

Dr. Michael Smith has been using acupuncture and herbal teas with severely addicted clients at Lincoln Hospital in the Bronx for the past decade with great success. Dr. Steven Kipnis, medical director of both the Blaisdale Alcoholism Treatment Center at Rockland Psychiatric Center and the Recovery Center of Nyack Hospital in Rockland County, New York, recently completed the acupuncture training program taught by Dr. Smith and his staff. He told us:

> Acupuncture relaxes the patient to the point where he or she is much more receptive to other treatment inputs such as counseling, self-help groups, and the like. I have seen it used effectively with mentally ill drug addicts and alcoholics. Acupuncture, as a treatment technique in addiction medicine, is now well documented in modern thinking, based on its successful use for centuries and its recent applications in detoxification, crisis management, and ongoing recovery. Western medicine may remain skeptical but seeing the rapid and effective results makes one a believer rather quickly. Seeing is believing.

The alcoholism field speaks of the disease of alcoholism as having three components: physical, psychological, and spiritual. This is the beginning of a holistic view. When the sociocultural and psychological aspects are emphasized *equally* with the physical and the spiritual, then a more realistic holistic view will have been achieved. When the substance abuse field embraces the full range of psychological functioning, it too will have come close to a real holistic model. The mental health field needs to place the psychological and the biological components in equal perspective and also include the sociocultural and spiritual aspects of life before they can become more attuned to a holistic approach. Using this approach would be best suited to caring for the MICA client, who Dr. Arthur Sauter describes as follows: "A person with a family, a personal history, a lifestyle, thoughts and feelings, a value system, needs and wants; whose life is at times seriously distressed by an assortment of symptoms from both chemical abuse and mental illness." Taking a more unidimensional approach at first blush is easier, but given the high relapse rate of addictive behaviors, and the acute and chronic effects of mental illness, the clinician ultimately benefits from the multidimensional perspective contained in a holistic model. In order for any model to be comprehensive it must be humanistic. That which reduces, mechanizes, and oversimplifies does not help. When we take a holistic approach, we need not fear complexity. The holistic approach allows us to build real teams, trade real knowledge, and be empowered as people and as clinicians.

Attributes That Work. Lisbeth B. Schorr reviewed educational and social welfare services for children and their families in the United States. The results of her compelling analysis are reported in *Within Our Reach: Breaking the Cycle of Disadvantage* (Schorr 1988). Her description of the attributes of interventions that work for children as clients are, we contend, the same attributes that can work for MICA clients. We list some of these attributes of successful service interventions as follows:

1. Programs which are successful in reaching and helping the most disadvantaged children and families offer a broad spectrum of services. (MICAs require a similar broad spectrum—the more "one stop" services we can provide at one site the better).
2. Successful programs recognize that they cannot respond to people's "untidy basketfuls" of needs without regularly crossing traditional, professional, and bureaucratic boundaries.
3. Staff members and program structures are fundamentally flexible.
4. Programs see the child in the context of the family and the family in the context of its surroundings. (MICAs also need to be seen in the context of their families—they are not all alone in the world.)
5. Successful programs describe their staffs as skilled and highly competent.
6. Programs serving a large number of multiproblem families see to it that services are coherent and easy to use. (MICAs are all too often shifted from one agency to another, getting lost in the shuffle.)
7. The programs find ways to adapt or circumvent traditional, professional, and bureaucratic limitations when necessary to meet the needs of clients.
8. Professionals are able to redefine their roles in order to meet client needs.

(Adapted from Schorr 1988:256–59)

Our own experiences in the three fields have shown us that the best work is usually done by people who

- are clear about their own roles but extend themselves to their colleagues
- have a deeply felt empathy for clients
- really listen to clients
- aren't afraid to say "I don't know"
- have a learning attitude
- mobilize resources for clients
- like recognition but aren't hung up on status
- offer hope to clients
- have a "can do" approach to problem solving
- can be real people with clients which includes sharing their feelings
- have a sense of humor
- take their clients seriously, but usually don't take themselves too seriously

- acknowledge mistakes
- try to acquire new skills
- make good use of clinical supervision
- enjoy a good debate, but don't have to put the other guy down
- don't "bad rap" other staff or clients

Learn, Baby, Learn—Staff Training. Views and recommendations about training staff seem to fall into two categories: 1) we need well-informed generalists and/or 2) we need well-informed specialists. We think what is needed is for as many people as possible, regardless of their discipline or job title, to receive comprehensive, holistically oriented training. Several times in this book we have mentioned the phenomenon of the "lone ranger." This refers to a single, appointed specialist—a substance abuse counselor in a mental health treatment setting or a mental health specialist in a substance abuse treatment setting—who is called in when the need arises. How many of you remember this old joke?

> The Lone Ranger and Tonto suddenly find themselves surrounded by hostile Indians. Faced with no possibility of escape, the Lone Ranger turns to Tonto and plaintively asks: "Tonto, what are we going to do about all these Indians?" To which Tonto replies with a grin, "What you mean, *we* . . . white man?"

This estrangement has all too often been the fate of the appointed specialist. We do not object to the use of specialists. However, in order for their role to have meaning to clients, it must also have meaning to other staff. When the entire staff is: 1) open to and receives training about the issues (either substance abuse or mental health); 2) when the dynamics and logistics of how the new specialist will work with others is discussed; and 3) when both parties test out the reality of this new position—only then can the role really become viable. Otherwise it just becomes the sources to whom we "send all the crazies" or "send all the druggies."

Koop (1972) says one cannot change attitudes with facts, so the training form must allow for an actual exchange of views (attitudes, beliefs, and feelings). Let's consider a real life example. In the late 1970s when Dr. Levy was heading up the Alcoholism Treatment Program (ATP) at Beth Israel Medical Center in New York City, a decision was made to accept methadone-maintenance patients with alcohol dependence onto the fifty-bed detoxification unit at the ATP. Historically, these patients had been detoxed from alcohol on the drug detox unit. The problem was that there was no educational program about alcoholism or referral to other services after detoxification. The ATP detox staff was gravely concerned about what might happen when the "junkies" hit the unit. There were fears that pocketbooks would have to be locked up, that the methadone patients would intimidate the "regular" patients. (All patients were people who needed either physical detoxification or simply to get off the street and interrupt their cycle of drinking.)

Several months before the admission of any MMTP patients, the staff received didactic training from the chief and assistant clinical chief of the methadone program (Dr. Harold Trigg and Dr. Stewart Nichols, both psychiatrists). The training could have been called "Everything you wanted to know about methadone but were afraid to ask." A lot of myths and misconceptions were dispelled. It was decided that the MMTP patients would be given the same daily dose of methadone that they received in their clinics (no dose changes were negotiable except in a medical crisis). The second part of the training involved our internal discussions. This took place more at the gut level. Staff let each other hear and feel their anxieties and worries. We listened to one another and made decisions based on respect for both patient and staff.

At first, we only admitted one or two patients at a time. As things progressed smoothly, we opened the doors all the way. There was no stealing, there was no intimidation of any other patients. In fact what happened was in some ways truly remarkable. For the first time these alcohol-dependent MMTP patients were learning about drugs, alcohol, and the problematic consequences of their use. They learned that drinking a lot of alcohol lowered their serum levels of methadone—they needed less alcohol, not more methadone. They began to hear about sobriety instead of just recycling through detox after detox. We did not give them mixed messages. Stay on methadone and stop drinking (and using other drugs) and life will improve. In the first two months, four patients actually sent thank-you notes to the staff. By using training as a forum for information exchange, an examination of stigmata and prejudice, and a mutual planning process, we opened the way for service to a sorely underserved population. Some of these MMTP patients were MICAs as were some of our "regular customers." This was not a problem for us: the detox unit chief was a psychiatrist, the internist was committed to quality care for all patients, several nurses had psychiatric experience, and the social workers and counselors were well-trained professionals. It was very rewarding to watch staff go from feelings of high anxiety to a real sense of pride. This never could have been accomplished by a single specialist.

We also don't think that training that simply provides new "layers" of information is very helpful. That is, a guest lecturer comes in and speaks about a topic, such as the uses of psychotropic medication. Who will help process this new information? What is its meaning in terms of the actual service delivery system? Was this just another interesting lecture or is there an intention to make programmatic changes? It's like the difference between members of a staff engaging in passive learning as when members attend grand rounds versus an active learning process where a trainer works with an entire staff on team building and program planning.

In the state of New York mandates and initiatives were decreed for training in the late 1980s. At the request of the governor in 1986, a task force was established to investigate the problem of patients dually diagnosed for addiction and general psychiatric disorders. This task force was organized by the Office of Mental Health and had representation from all three state agencies. It made lots of recommendations in its two annual reports. A coordinating body called the IOCC was formed. Jackie Cohen was the first MICA trainer in the New York State Division of Substance Abuse Services system and attended a number of the IOCC meetings. Only a handful of their ambitious training goals were met. For example, very little team training was done by trainers from the three agencies. Although the logistics were planned in advance, the training curriculum was never a multidisciplinary, multiperspective endeavor. Information was layered and not integrated. Trainers never truly team-trained. Each supplied a layer. Jackie's suggestions for cross systems training went unheeded. At the writing of this book, only a small audience has been reached. Integrated training is still not a reality, and several pilot programs in the state psychiatric centers which grew out of the training have ended owing to budget cuts. Very few of the recommendations trickled either up or down the systems and most had little system impact. There is a need for integrated, comprehensive, holistic training. There is an equal need for administrative support for this type of training.

Destigmatizing Drug Use. If all practitioners had the same sympathy and empathy for substance abusers as they have for mentally ill people, then substance abusers would receive far fewer stigmatizing communications and would be able to get more support from the fields. In fact, the heart of the problem is whether or not habitual drug use is a form of mental illness. It is hard to conceptualize a person whose life is organized around addictive behaviors being totally free from mental illness. The problem and any attempt at dialogue are caused by a tendency of many people to conceptualize mental illness as only the most profound and debilitating types of illness—the bizarre, hallucinating, ranting-and-raving-in-the-street kind of behavior. The challenge presented by Dr. Thomas Szasz is that mental illness is a myth created to enforce social control by mental health professionals. To those of us working with patients their illness is no myth. But we are often guilty of a failure to understand cultures and life-styles different from our own middle-class orientation toward life and to label such manifestations as deviant. Racism, classism, sexism, ageism, and homophobia are real and so is psychiatric name-calling. But this does not mean that alcoholics and drug addicts are psychologically well-adjusted people. We need to see them as they are: people who do not handle life well. Our goal must be to help them do that without resorting to intoxicants, which are so harmful to them and our society.

In our opinion, this can not be done unless we come to grips with the fact that drug use is utilitarian. It serves a purpose in people's lives—namely, the alteration of mood and consciousness to achieve both positive feeling states and flight from physical and psychic pain. Ultimately, all drugs—caffeine, nicotine, alcohol, prescription medicine, over-the-counter drugs, and street drugs—all are taken in an effort to either feel good or to feel better (Levy 1983). Addicted people do not manage their lives well and they have a difficult time handling their affective states (Khantzian 1985). And as individuals they range across all the diagnostic entities in the *DSM–IIIR*. They are not normal people suffering only from the vagaries of unknown genetic and/or psychological anomalies. They are members of families, they have an individual psychology, they have a spiritual self, they are shaped and molded by their society and react to it, and they have strengths and weaknesses. Their character flaws and defects may or may not neatly fit into diagnostic nosology but they are, nevertheless, people in pain.

When clinicians learn to be nonjudgmental and nonpunitive toward drug use, viewing it as an attempt to cope, no matter how ill conceived, then the quality of care for MICA clients will advance. The time has come for practitioners to work on their countertransferential issues in the area of drug use and abuse. Others will have to work out similar issues about mental illness.

Temporal Aspects of Diagnosis. In the best of all worlds there would exist diagnostic centers in which comprehensive holistic workups could be done before referring clients to the best and most appropriate treatment modality. Complete past and current histories (medical, psychological, substance use/abuse, and so forth) would be taken. Everyone would have urine, blood, and breath samples analyzed to objectively detect the presence of substances. A thorough physical examination would be performed and appropriate diagnostic tests ordered and analyzed. Neuropsychological test batteries would be administered and interpreted. Family members would be interviewed. In short, a soup to nuts evaluation and assessment process would be employed. And only then would the staff, with a full and complete knowledge of the clients, refer them to care and treatment.

Meanwhile, back in the real world, we recommend that clinicians in all systems make careful note of the temporal (time) factors involved in doing careful and accurate diagnoses. We have taken great pains to explain how the toxic effects of various substances can cause behaviors that resemble symptoms of a wide variety of mental disorders. When clients are known to be drug free for a period of days or weeks and these symptoms remit, it is safe, for the moment, to rule out the disorder which the symptoms mimicked. However, if the symptoms persist, then the clients must be considered for concurrent treatment of substance abuse and mental illness.

Beyond this initial diagnosis, clinicians should consider the assessment process as continuing and be alert to any changes in a client's status. As sensoriums clear, as memory returns, as feelings resurface, as issues are faced, a client's mental status will fluctuate along with other aspects of functioning. Therefore, the initial treatment plan should be considered temporary in nature.

Conservative practitioners have stated that clients should not be diagnosed until six months of abstinence have been achieved. The reason for this is that beyond the "post-acute withdrawal" period the clinical picture has often been observed to improve, or at least change. For example, one residential MICA program in California routinely rediagnoses their clients at six-month intervals and has found that the diagnosis has changed and the overall clinical picture has improved. Such improvement may not indicate that the client's mental illness is in remission. Rather it may show that the illness was the result of a substance ingestion. Crucial to such judgments are toxicological analysis upon admission and good history taking, including past psychiatric and substance treatment episodes (inpatient, outpatient, and self-help groups).

Staff should be prepared to make appropriate changes, including referral to a more appropriate modality of care when indicated. By starting out with a real awareness of changes over time, the clinician's hunches must remain open to further education. This means the clinician must hold his/her biases in check and not make unilateral interpretations. Comprehensive and holistic training can help to insure this. Such training asks clinicians to get to know themselves as well as the literature. This type of clinician has an open mind, a learning attitude, and a recognition of his/her own humanity and frailty. Sorry, there's not much room left for staff omnipotence in doing quality work with MICA clients.

Integrated Care. At this point, you should be thinking: "Wait a minute, didn't you just get finished arguing that most serious substance abuse reflects, in the broadest sense, a form of mental illness? And if that is true, shouldn't everyone be enrolled in concurrent treatment?" "Aha," we say, "You are beginning to catch on." Clients in alcohol and drug abuse treatment programs are in need of mental health therapeutic services. The best such programs we know deliver these services. They are also staffed by both professionals and paraprofessionals, all of whom have received comprehensive, holistic training. In these programs clients are not receiving concurrent treatment, they are actually receiving integrated treatment. These are not mere hybrid programs in which treatments are layered on top of one another; rather, the substance use issues are part and parcel of the whole therapeutic thrust of an attempt to address the whole person. Everything else that is done is just a matter of treatment technology. Decisions are made about which tools are to be applied: psychotherapy, counseling, chemotherapy, case management, self-care, mutual help groups, training in independent living, family counseling, educational programs, housing, educational and vocational training and placement, and so on.

An important aspect of integrated care is a kind of "behavioral prophylaxis." In this day and age, we all have to face certain realities. Many millions of Americans drink and use drugs of all kinds. Sexually transmitted diseases, including HIV and AIDS, can be transmitted and received by anyone. Mental patients are uniquely vulnerable to substance misuse. Drug addicts and alcoholics suffer from a wide variety of mental problems. The NIMH Epidemiological Catchment Area (ECA) study in 1990 revealed that 30 percent of adults who have ever had a mental disorder have had a diagnosable alcohol and/or other drug abuse problem during their lives, and 53 percent of adults who have had drug abuse disorders have had one or more mental disorders. What this and similar studies raise is the tantalizing, unanswered question: "Which came first—the mental illness or the substance abuse?" Those substance abusers in treatment who are not diagnosed with mental disorders (other than the substance abuse) usually do not encounter trained professional staff who are on the lookout for such problems. Funding streams and admission criteria often have more to do with diagnosis upon admission to treatment than with clinical criteria.

The behavioral prophylaxis we are speaking about has to do with educating clients about their total humanity, which is comprised of their physical, psychological, spiritual, vocational, educational, and social selves. Thus, all clients receiving mental health services should be taught about the potential dangers of substance ingestion. All clients receiving substance abuse services should be learning about other aspects of themselves besides those directly related to drug issues. In integrated care these issues would not be considered separate or antithetical.

We would like to make an even more emphatic point regarding substance abuse treatment agencies. Their failure to address psychological and life-style issues that predate addictive behavior, is part of the whole *setup* for client relapse. The unwillingness to provide individual psychotherapy along with drug counseling and a failure to use psychotropic medications when indicated are probably the major reasons for clients' leaving programs prematurely and for relapses. Methadone programs' failure to address alcohol, marijuana, cocaine, and tranquilizer use and abuse and the therapeutic communities' failure to address drinking issues also contribute to client failure (although we think it's treatment agency failure). Some TCs are beginning to change this practice in recognition of the harm done in the past to staff and client alike. Without adequate psychotherapeutic and medication services, it is easy to see how the client's "dread of distress," so well described by Dr. Ed Khantzian, can prompt a return to drugs even after months or years of treatment. It is not enough to deal with the manifest characterological distortions through behavioral conformity. People need to work through the issues that brought shame, sorrow, and despair into their lives before addiction. The lack of sensitivity to female clients has been the most glaring of all omissions. Women are wisely loathe to reveal the pains associated with their lives in a group with men present. Women-only groups are not enough either. One-on-one therapy is needed as well. In the Rockland County Crack/Cocaine Program, attendance figures for individual sessions were far superior to group therapy or group educational sessions. In very recent months Jackie Cohen actually received several referrals of reentry candidates from several major drug-free therapeutic communities which are beginning to acknowledge that many of their clients need such help. And how many clients could have benefitted from psychotherapeutic services if psychotropic medications had allowed them the freedom from the most disturbing symptoms long enough for them to benefit from therapy?

Agencies with integrated care have staff members with solid professional training. We don't believe that just because a person formerly drank or drugged with negative consequences imparts any clinical expertise. By achieving their own recovery, they have assumed a healthier posture for themselves. However, this alone is woefully inadequate preparation for helping others in any but a mutual help peer group. To become part of a professional agency dedicated to the assessment and treatment of mental illness and/or addictive behaviors must require formal academic and clinical training. By this we mean that one should acquire academic training—at a minimum securing a baccalaureate degree (we really think a master's degree is more like it) to assure mastery of fundamental skills. The creation of the certified alcoholism counselor (CAC) credential is a step in the right direction for a specialty certification but most states require only a high school diploma. The American Academy of Health Care Providers in Addictive Disorders confirms the title of certified addiction specialist (CAS) to those who can document two full years of supervised clinical work in addictive disorders such as alcohol, drugs, and eating disorders, in addition to providing other appropriate endorsements. The CAS provides a mechanism for those of us with advanced degrees and who are members of licensed professions (medicine, nursing, psychology, and so forth) to be recognized for our work experience with addictive disorders.

It's time to raise staff credentialing standards across the board. All disciplines need to learn about both substance abuse and mental health. They are inextricably bound together in the bond of humankind. The problems facing our society grow worse and the numbers of dollars are finite. We have seen numerous examples of the cost-effectiveness of an integrated approach. It's good science, it's good treatment, and it's validating for the clients and staff alike.

Special Recommendations for Each Field

The Substance Abuse Treatment Field

Methadone Maintenance Programs

1. Insist on regular, weekly individual and group counseling sessions.
2. Assess for alcohol abuse and dependence and refer to or provide needed services.
3. Be willing to discharge clients who refuse services other than methadone medication.
4. Address clients' use of non-opiate drugs.
5. Help clients to find gainful employment.
6. Provide psychotherapy services or referrals for same.
7. Consider what psychotropic medications might work with methadone.
8. Help clients start their own mutual help groups.
9. Provide family-oriented services.
10. Do more AIDS assessment and counseling. Don't rely solely on a belief that a client is no longer doing intravenous drugs. New York State now mandates an HIV coordinator in every clinic.
11. Form linkages with acute care psychiatric services.
12. Create twenty-four-hour emergency services for all clients (MICAs need this). Have consultant psychiatrists on staff.
13. Help clients who wish to try to make it drug-free. Do real maintenance-to-abstinence supportive counseling.
14. Address housing issues.
15. Understand that doing the above will cause a tremendous boost in staff morale and a change in the poor public perception that you suffer.
16. Train staff in death, dying, and bereavement issues (particularly in regard to HIV and AIDS).

Drug-Free Therapeutic Communities

1. Need to be less punitive and ego damaging.
2. Realize that not all suicidal ideation is manipulation.
3. Hire and integrate mental health professionals into your structure.
4. Realize that what appears to be laziness or resistance may also be depression, organic brain syndromes, or developmental disabilities.
5. Seriously raise the standards for staff. College training and beyond and certification in addiction counseling can only work to enhance programming.

6. Get rid of the concept of drinking privileges. Why should renunciation of one type of drug be rewarded with yet another drug?
7. Provide one-to-one counseling to help clients work through their issues. Not everything can or should be dealt with in a group.
8. Find new approaches. If you can open a door with a key, why kick it down? Try methods of group therapy that are not as harsh as the encounter groups' (known as the Synanon game).
9. Leave rigid rules to management. Sound clinical judgment cannot prevail when rules are more important than individual problems.
10. Realize that if you really want to help women residents, first have the staff deal their own sexist attitudes and practices.
11. Realize that if you really want to help lesbians and gay men, first have staff deal with their own homophobia.
12. Staff need to understand the continuum of behavior that constitutes psychopathology. Everything can't be explained by the simple-minded notion that every client is a "dope fiend."
13. Consider an integrative model (such as Harbor House's) that will allow the inclusion of seriously mentally ill clients.
14. Provide staff with real clinical supervision.
15. Provide staff with inservice training.
16. Make available emergency psychiatric care on a twenty-four-hour basis.
17. Have a consultant psychiatrist on staff.
18. Have staff trained in death, dying, and bereavement issues (particularly in regard to HIV and AIDS).
19. Provide individualized assessment and treatment planning.

Outpatient Drug-Free Programs

1. Hire mental health professionals as counselors.
2. Provide holistic, integrated training for all staff.
3. Make sure staff receive regular clinical supervision.
4. Form linkages to acute care mental health services.
5. Take clients who need psychotropic medication and help them with medication compliance. Make sure they learn about alcohol-to-drug and drug-to-drug interactions.
6. Consider making home visits.
7. Make use of case management concepts.
8. Help clients negotiate systems that are frightening to them (social services, probation, and so forth).

9. Do not expect compliance with total abstinence.
10. Help clients who can't/won't attend 12-step meetings to start their own peer support network.
11. Work with clients' families.
12. Help clients deal with their child care issues.
13. Make linkages with halfway houses.
14. Address educational and vocational issues.
15. Address housing issues.
16. Help clients to recreate and socialize.
17. Make available emergency psychiatric care on a twenty-four-hour basis.
18. Have a psychiatrist as a staff consultant.
19. Train staff in death, dying, and bereavement issues (particularly in regard to HIV and AIDS).

The Alcoholism Treatment Field

Recommendations for All Modalities of Care

1. Give more equal weight to the multiple factors that give rise to alcohol abuse and alcohol dependence.
2. Be open to the reality that mental illness can cause alcoholism and vice versa.
3. Provide staff with comprehensive, holistic training.
4. Be open to models of problem drinking other than the disease concept.
5. Consider other forms of peer support since not all MICA clients are comfortable at 12-step meetings.
6. Learn about psychopharmacology and the interactions between psychotropic medications and alcohol (and other drugs).
7. Hire mental health professionals and integrate them into the program as key staff, not just ancillary personnel.
8. Study the sociocultural and psychological literature on alcohol problems.
9. Establish residential services for MICA clients.
10. Become knowledgeable about organic mental states since alcohol can cause long-term as well as acute problems. This is especially true for MICA clients who may have also sustained head injuries in the street.
11. Stress educational and vocational assessment, training, and placement.
12. Provide clients with psychotherapy services.
13. Raise the educational standards of alcoholism counselors.

14. Help clients to understand that not everything that goes on in their lives is a result of alcoholism.
15. Strongly consider working from the compensatory model as it enables MICA clients to feel more in control of some aspects of their lives.
16. Set up double trouble groups for clients.
17. Provide emergency psychiatric services on a twenty-four-hour basis.
18. Work with families around mental health issues.
19. Help clients with practical issues of housing, nutrition, and child care.
20. Have staff trained in death, dying, and bereavement issues (particularly in regard to HIV and AIDS).

The Mental Health Treatment Field
Recommendations for All Modalities of Care

1. Establish concrete survival services for seriously mentally ill clients. These include housing, nutrition, and basic health care.
2. Develop among staff more optimistic perspectives on clients' possible growth and change. If clients are not capable of change, why bother addressing the whole substance abuse issue?
3. Don't work from only a strict abstinence model.
4. Use educational forums to open up client discussions of drug use. Present information at a level clients can understand. Repetition and discussion is important.
5. Don't be afraid to confront clients who drink and drug, but have clear policies for how to actually handle this. Clients need to know that you expect them to avoid harmful substances as part of their care plan. Also help clients to do this with one another as part of their therapeutic socialization.
6. Integrate staff with substance abuse expertise with the general staff.
7. Provide entire staff with comprehensive holistic training.
8. Set up double trouble groups so clients can participate in 12-step meetings.
9. For those clients who are not comfortable with such participation as 12-step meetings call for, consider other forms of peer support.
10. Help clients avoid those 12-step meetings at which they are encouraged to stop taking all mood-altering drugs (if they are taking psychotropic medications).
11. Provide additional services. When clients stop abusing substances, their mental illness may improve to the point where they can benefit from psychotherapy. Make therapy available to them.

12. Take substance abuse histories on all clients. As they move into more lucid periods when memory returns, try to get more accurate information.
13. Do drug screening and use breathylyzers. This is very important in outpatient settings and when clients go out on pass from inpatient settings.
14. Have staff trained in death, dying, and bereavement issues (particularly in regard to HIV and AIDS).
15. Rediagnose all clients routinely after six months of abstinence.

References

ADAMHA. 1989. *Alcohol, Drug Abuse, and Mental Health Administration News: The First 15 Years* (U.S. Dept. of Health and Human Services, Office of Communications and External Affairs): 15(2).

Alcoholics Anonymous. 1984. *The AA member—medications and other drugs: Report from a group of physicians in AA.* New York: AA World Services.

Alexander, F.G., and Selesnick, S.T. 1966. *The history of psychiatry: An evaluation of psychiatric thought and practice from prehistoric times to the present.* New York: Harper & Row.

Alibrandi, L.A. 1985. "The folk psychotherapy of AA." In *Practical approaches to alcoholism psychotherapy.* 2d ed., eds. S. Zimberg, J. Wallace, and S.B. Blume. New York: Plenum Press.

American Psychiatric Association. 1987. *Diagnostic and statistical manual of mental disorders.* 3d ed. rev. Washington, D.C.: American Psychiatric Association.

Arella, L.R.; Deren, S.; Randell, J.; and Brewington, V. 1990. Vocational functioning of clients in drug treatment; exploring some myths and realities. *Journal of Applied Rehabilitation Counseling* 21 (2):7–18.

Armor, J.M.; Polich, J.M.; and Stambul, H.B. 1978. *Alcoholism and treatment.* New York: Wiley.

Attia, P.R. 1988. Dual diagnosis: Definition and treatment. *Alcoholism Treatment Quarterly* 5 (3/4): 53–63.

Bachrach, L.L. 1982. Young adult chronic patients: An analytical review of the literature. *Hospital and Community Psychiatry* 33:189–97.

Baekland, F.; Lundwall, L.K.; and Kissin, B. 1975. "Methods for the treatment of chronic alcoholism: A critical approach." In *Research advances in alcohol and drug problems.* ed. Y. Israel. vol. 2. New York: Wiley.

Bandura, A. 1977. Self-efficacy: Toward a unified theory of behavior change. *Psychological Review 84*: 199–215.

Bargman, E.; Wolfe, S.M.; Levin, J.; and the Public Citizens Health Research Group. 1982. *Pills that don't work.* New York: Warner Books.

Barr, H., and Cohen, A. 1979 *The problem drinking drug addict.* Administrative Report, Services Research Branch, National Institute on Drug Abuse. Rockville, Md.: National Institute on Drug Abuse.

Bender, M.G. 1986. Young adult chronic patients: Visibility and style of interaction in treatment. *Hospital and Community Psychiatry* 37(3):265–68.

Berg, M. 1986. Toward a diagnostic alliance between psychiatrist and psychologist. *American Psychologist* 41, (1): 52–59.

Bergman, H.C., and Harris, M. 1985. Substance abuse among young adult chronic patients. *Psychosocial Rehabilitation Journal* IX(1): 49–54.

Blane, H.T., and Leonard, K.E. 1987. *Psychological theories of drinking and alcoholism.* New York: Guilford Press.

Bootzin, R.R., and Acocella, J.R. 1988. *Abnormal psychology: Current perspectives.* 5th ed. New York: Random House.

Bourgois, P. 1989. In search of Horatio Alger: Culture and ideology in the crack economy. *Contemporary Drug Problems* 16:619–49.

Brandsma, J.M.; Maultsby, M.C.; and Welsh, R.J. 1980. *The outpatient treatment of alcoholism: A review and comparison study.* Baltimore: University Park Press.

Bratter, T.E.; Pennacchia, M.C.; and Gauya, D.C. 1985 "From methadone to abstinence: The myth of the metabolic disorder theory." In *Alcoholism and substance abuse: Strategies for clinical intervention,* eds. T.E. Bratter and G.G. Forrester. New York: Free Press.

Breakey, W.R., et al. 1974. Hallucinogenic drugs as precipitants of schizophrenia. *Psychological Medicine* 4:255–61.

Braginsky, B.M.; Braginsky, D.D.; and Ring, K. 1969. *Methods of madness: The mental hospital as a last resort.* New York: Holt, Rinehart and Winston.

Brecher, E.M., and the editors of *Consumer Reports.* 1972. *Licit and illicit drugs.* Boston: Little, Brown & Co.

Brickman, P.; Rabinowitz, V.C.; Karuza, J.; Coates, D.; Cohn, E.; and Kidder, L. 1982. Models of helping and coping. *American Psychologist* 37(4):368–84.

Brown, D. 1985. *The transfer of care: Psychiatric deinstitutionalization and its aftermath.* Boston: Routledge and Kegan Paul.

Brown, V.B.; Ridgely, M.S.; Pepper, B.; Levine, I.S.; and Ryglewicz, H. 1989. The dual crisis: Mental illness and substance abuse: Present and future directions. *American Psychologist* 44(3):365–69.

Burglass, M.E., and Shaffer, H. 1981. "The natural history of ideas in the treatment of addictions." In *Classic contributions in the addictions,* ed. H. Shaffer and M.E. Burglass. New York: Brunner/Mazel.

Califano, J.A. 1982. The 1982 report on drug abuse and alcoholism: A report to Hugh L. Carey, Governor of the State of New York. Albany, N.Y., Executive Chamber.

Carroll, J.F.X.; Malloy, M.A.; and Kenrick, F.N. 1977 Alcohol abuse by drug dependent persons: A literature review and evaluation. *American Journal of Drug and Alcohol Abuse* 4(3):293–315.

Casriel, D. 1963. So fair a house: The story of Synanon. Englewood Cliffs N.J.: Prentice-Hall.

Cermak, T. 1985. A primer on adult children of alcoholics. Pompano Beach, Fla.: Health Communications.

Chamber, C.D. and Inciardi, J.A. 1972. Some aspects of criminal careers of female narcotic addicts. Paper presented at the Southern Sociological Society, Miami Beach, Florida.

Chein, I.; Gerard, D.L.; Less, R.S.; and Rosenfeld, E. 1964. *The road to H: Narcotics, delinquency and social policy.* New York: Basic Books.

Chiauzzi, E. 1989. Breaking the patterns that lead to relapse. *Psychology Today,* Dec: 18–19.

Clark, W.B. and Midanik, K.L. 1982. "Alcohol use and alcohol problems among U.S. adults: Results of the 1979 national survey." In *Alcohol consumption and related problems.* Alcohol and Health Monograph, no. 1, NIAAA, DHHS Publication no.(ADM) 82–1190.

Cohen, J. 1989. Assessment curriculum. Training Institute, Narcotic and Drug Research, Inc., New York, N.Y.

Cox, W.M. 1987. "Personality theory and research." In *Psychological theories of drinking and alcoholism,* eds. H.T. Blane and K.E. Leonard. New York: Guilford Press.

Daley, D.C. 1987. Relapse prevention with substance abusers: Clinical issues and myths. *Social Work* (March-April):138–42.

DeAngelis, T. 1991. DSM being revised, but problems remain. *The American Psychological Association Monitor* 22(6):12–13.

DeLeon, G. 1989. Psychopathology and substance abuse: What is being learned from research in therapeutic communities. *Journal of Psychoactive Drugs* 21(2):177–87.

Deren, S. 1986. Children of drug abusers: A review of the literature. *Journal of Substance Abuse Treatment* 3:77–94.

Devlin, J.J. 1975. Treatment of the addictions: A territorial imperative? *The Addiction Therapist* 1:25.

Dividio, J.F.; Evans, N.; and Tyler, R.B. 1986. Racial stereotypes: The contents of their cognitive representations. *Journal of Experimental Social Psychology* 22:22–37.

Dole, V.P. 1980. Addictive behavior. *Scientific American* Dec.

Dole, V.P., and Nyswander, M.E. 1968. Successful treatment of of 750 criminal addicts. *Journal of the American Medical Association* 206:2711.

Drake, R.E., and Wallach, M.A. 1989. Substance abuse among the chronically mentally ill. *Hospital and Community Psychiatry* 40(10):1041–46.

Egri, G., and Caton, C.L. 1982. "Serving the young adult chronic patient 1980s: A challenge to the general hospital." In *New Directions for mental health services: The young adult patient* 4, eds. B. Pepper and H. Ryglewicz. San Francisco: Jossey-Bass.

Emrick, C.D., and Hansen, J. 1983. Assertions regarding effectiveness of treatment for alcoholism. *American Psychologist* 38(10):1078–88.

Enright, J.B. 1970. "Synanon: A challenge to middle-class views of mental health." In *Community psychology and mental health: Perspectives and challenges,* eds. D. Adelson and B.l. Kalis. Scranton, Pa.: Chandler Publishing Co.

Fingarette, H. 1988. *Heavy drinking: The myth of alcoholism as a disease.* Berkeley: Univ. of California Press.

Frank J.D. 1961. *Persuasion and healing: A comparative study of psychotherapy.* Baltimore: The Johns Hopkins University Press.

Freudenberger, H. J., and Richelson, G. 1980. Burn out: The high cost of high achievement. Garden City, N.Y.: Anchor Doubleday.

Galanter, M. 1989. Task force on combined psychiatric and addictive disorders, 2nd annual report. Albany: New York State Office of Mental Health.

Galanter, M.; Castaneda, R.; and Ferman, J. 1987. Substance abuse among a general psychiatric population: A review of the "dual diagnosis" problem. In New York State task force for combined psychiatric and addictive disorders, Interim report, First year, ed. M. Galanter. New York: New York University School of Medicine: 1-29.

Gardner, S.E. 1980. National Drug/Alcohol Collaborative Project: Issues in multiple substance abuse. Services Research Branch, NIDA, DHEW, Publication no. (ADM) 80–0157. Rockville, Md.: NIDA

Glaser, F.B.; Annis, H.M.; Pearlman, S.; Segal, R.L.; and Skinner, H.A. 1985. "The differential therapy of alcoholism: A systems approach." In *Alcohol and substance abuse: Strategies for clinical intervention.* eds. T.E. Bratter and G.G. Forest. New York: Free Press

Glueck, S., and Glueck, E. 1950. Unraveling juvenile delinquency. New York: The Commonwealth Fund.

Glueck, S., and Glueck, E. 1968. Delinquents and non-delinquents in perspective. Cambridge, Mass.: Harvard University Press.

Goodwin, D., et al. 1973. Alcohol problems in adoptees raised apart from alcoholic biological parents. *Archives of General Psychiatry* 28: 238–42.

Gordon, J.S. 1981. "The paradigm of holistic medicine." In *Health for the whole person,* eds. A.C. Hastings, J. Fadiman, and J.S. Gordon. New York: Bantam Books: 3–31.

Gorski, T., and Miller, M. 1982. *Counseling for relapse prevention.* Independence, Mo: Independence Press.

Gottheil, E., and Waxman, A.M. 1982. "Alcoholism and schizophrenia." In *Encyclopedic handbook of alcoholism,* eds. E.M. Pattison and E. Kaufman. New York: Gardner Press: 636–46.

Gottlieb, M.S. 1991. AIDS—the second decade: Leadership is lacking. *New York Times,* Wednesday, June 5, op-ed, A29.

Graedon, J. 1980. *The people's pharmacy–2.* New York: Avon Books.

Griffith, H.W. 1987. *Complete guide to prescription and non-prescription drugs.* Tucson, Ariz.: HP Books.

Group for the Advancement of Psychiatry [GAP]. 1986. Committee on psychopathology. Interactive fit: A guide to nonpsychotic chronic patients. Manuscript.

Hall, R.C.W.; Popkin, M.K.; DeVaul, R.; and Stickeny, S.K. 1977. The effect of unrecognized drug abuse on diagnosis and therapeutic outcome. *American Journal of Drug and Alcohol Abuse* 4(4):455–65.

Halleck, S.L. 1971. *The politics of therapy.* New York: Science House.

Hanson, B.; Beschner, G.W.; Walters, J.M.; and Bovelle, E., eds. 1985. *Life with heroin: Voices from the inner city.* Lexington, Mass.: Lexington Books.

Harkness, S.R. 1984. *Drug interactions handbook.* Englewood Cliffs, N.J.: Prentice-Hall.

Harrison, P.A., et al. 1985. Conjoint treatment of dual disorders. In *Substance abuse and psychopathology,* ed. A. Alterman. New York: Plenum Press.

Hastings, A.C.; Fadiman, J.; and Gordon, J.S. (eds.). 1980. *Health for the whole person.* Boulder: Bantam Books.

Hayes, S.C.; Nelson, R.D.; and Jarrett, R.B. 1987. The treatment utility of assessment: A functional approach to evaluating assessment quality. *American Psychologist* 42 (11):963–74.

Heather, N., and Robertson, I. 1981. *Controlled drinking.* New York: Methuen.

Hollingshead, A.B., and Redlich, F.C. 1958. *Social class and mental illness.* New York: Wiley.

Hubbard, R., et al. *Drug abuse treatment: A national study of effectiveness.* Chapel Hill: Univ. of North Carolina Press.

Jaffe, J.H. 1984. "Evaluating drug abuse treatment: A comment on the state of the art." In *Drug abuse treatment evaluation: Strategies, progress and prospects,* Research Monograph, no. 51. eds. F.M. Tims and J.P. Luford. Rockville, Md.: NIDA.

Janowsky, D. and Davis, J. 1976. Methylphenidate, dextroamphetamine and levamphetamine: Effects on schizophrenic symptoms. *Archives of General Psychiatry* 33:304–08.

Jellinek, E.M. 1952. Phases of alcohol addiction. *Quarterly Journal of Studies on Alcohol* 13(4):673–84.

Jellinek, E.M. 1960. *The disease concept of alcoholism.* New Haven: Hillhouse Press.

Johnson, L.D.; O'Malley, P.M.; and Bachman, J.G. 1987. *National trends in drug use and related favors among American high school students and young adults, 1975–1986.* DHHS Publication no. (ADM) 87–1535. Rockville, Md.: NIDA.

Johnson, D.L. 1989. Schizophrenia as a brain disease: Implications for psychologists and families. *American Psychologist* 44(3):553–55.

Jones, M. 1952. *Social psychiatry: The therapeutic community.* London: Tavistock Publications.

Jones, R.T. 1973. "Mental illness and drugs: Pre-existing psychopathology and response to psychoactive drugs." In *Drug use in America: Problems in Perspective,* Appendix, vol. 1. Washington, D.C.: National Commission on Marijuana and Drug Abuse.

Katz, S.J., and Liu, A.E. 1991. *The codependency conspiracy: How to break the recovery habit and take charge of your own life.* New York: Warner Books.

Kennedy, E.M. 1990. Community-based care for the mentally ill: Simple justice. *American Psychologist* 45 (11): 1238–40.

Khantzian, E.J. 1982. "Psychopathology, psychodynamics and alcoholism." In *Encyclopedic handbook of alcoholism,* eds. E.M. Pattison and E. Kaufman. New York: Gardner Press: 581–95.

Khantzian, E.J. 1985. The self-medication hypothesis of addictive disorders: Focus on heroin and cocaine dependence. *American Journal of Psychiatry* 142 (11) 1259–64.

Khantzian, E.J. 1987. Psychological suffering and substance dependence; Unravelling the cause/consequence controversy. Paper presented at symposium Diagnosis and Treatment, New Perspectives on Old Dilemmas. Tenth Annual Alcoholism Symposium, 7 March, Cambridge Hospital, Cambridge, Massachusetts.

Khantzian, E.J., and Treece, C. 1985. *DSM–III* psychiatric diagnoses of narcotic addicts. *Archives of General Psychiatry* 42:1067–71.

Koop, S.B. 1972. *If you meet the Buddha on the road, kill him!* Palo Alto, Calif.: Science and Behavior Books.

Kreek, M. J. 1978. Medical complications in methadone patients. *Annals of the New York Academy of Sciences* 311.

Laing, R.D. 1964. Is schizophrenia a disease? *International Journal of Psychiatry* 10:184–93.

Lamb, H.R. 1982. Young adult chronic patients: The new drifters. *Hospital and Community Psychiatry* 33(6) 465–68.

Levy, S.J. 1974. Milieu therapy and individual differences: Some social and clinical variables. Paper presented at the eighty-first Annual Convention of the American Psychological Association, 28 August, Montreal, Canada.

Levy, S.J. 1975. A survey of drug and alcohol use among patients at the Community Center for Mental Health, Dumont, New Jersey. manuscript.

Levy, S.J. 1977. *Clients and staff view their methadone clinics.* Trenton, N.J.: Division of Narcotic and Drug Abuse Control, New Jersey Department of Health.

Levy, S.J. 1982. Multiple substance abuse: Implications for treatment. *Bulletin of the Society of Psychologists in Substance Abuse* 1(3): 110–13.

Levy, S.J. 1983. Managing the drugs in your life: A personal and family guide to the responsible use of drugs, alcohol and medicine. New York: McGraw-Hill Book Company.

Levy, S.J., and Broudy, M. 1975. Sex role differences in the therapeutic community: Moving from sexism to androygyny. *Journal of Psychedelic Drugs* 7(3): 294–97.

Levy, S.J., and Doering, G.R. 1990. Rockland County Crack/Cocaine Program; Third Annual Report, submitted to the New York State Division of Substance Abuse Services, Ramapo Counseling Center, Spring Valley, N.Y.

Levy, S.J., and Doyle, K. 1974. Attitudes toward women in a drug abuse treatment program. *Journal of Drug Issues* (Fall): 428–34.

Levy, S.J., and Doyle K. 1976. Treatment of women in a methadone maintenance treatment program. In *Women in treatment: Issues and approaches,* ed. A. Bauman. Rockville, Md.: National Drug Abuse Center for Training and Resource Development, NIDA.

Levy, S.J., and Rutter, E. 1992. *Children of drug abusers.* New York and Lexington, Mass.: Lexington Books.

Lyons, J.S., and McGovern, M.P. 1989. Use of mental health services by dually diagnosed patients. Hospital and Community Psychiatry 40 (10): 1067–69.

Mandel, W. 1973. *Interdrug final report: An evaluation of treatment programs for drug abusers.* Baltimore: Johns Hopkins University School of Hygiene and Public Health.

Marlatt, G.A. and Fromme, K. 1988. Metaphors for addiction. In *Visions of addiction,* ed. S. Peele. Lexington, Mass.: Lexington Books.

Marlatt, G.A., and Gordon, J.R. 1985. *Relapse prevention: Maintenance strategies in the treatment of addictive behaviors.* New York: Guilford Press.

Marlatt, G.A., and Rohsenow, D.J. 1980. "Cognitive processes in alcohol use: Expectancy and the balanced placebo design." In *Advances in substance abuse,* vol. 1, ed. N.K. Mello. Greenwich, Conn.: JAI Press.

May, R. 1961. "Existential bases for psychotherapy." In *Existential psychology,* ed. R. May. New York: Random House.

McAuliffe, W.E., and Ch'ien, J.M.N. 1986. Recovery training and self help: A relapse prevention program for treated opiate addicts. *Journal of Substance Abuse Treatment* 3:9–20.

McCarrick, A.K.; Manderscheid, R.W.; and Bertolucci, D.E. 1985. Correlates of acting-out behaviors among young adult chronic patients. *Hospital and Community Psychiatry* 36(8):848–53.

McLellan, A.; Woody, G.E.; and O'Brien, C.P. 1979. Development of psychiatric illness in drug abusers. *New England Journal of Medicine* 301(29): 1310–14.

Meek, P.S.; Clark, H.W.; Solana, V.L. 1989. Neurocognitive impairment: The unrecognized component of dual diagnosis in substance abuse treatment. *Journal of Psychoactive Drugs* 21(2): 153–60.

Mendelson, J.H., and Mello, N.K. 1985. *The diagnosis and treatment of alcoholism.* New York: McGraw-Hill Book Company.

Mescavage, A. 1989. Co-existing not secondary: Alcoholism in the mentally ill. *New York Federation of Alcoholism Counselors Newsletter* (Albany, N.Y.; April/May).

Meyers, J.K., and Bean, L.I. 1968. *A decade later: A follow-up of social class and mental illness.* New York: Wiley

Milkman, H., and Shaffer, H. 1988. *The addictions: Multi-disciplinary perspectives and treatments.* Lexington, Mass: Lexington Books.

Milkman, H., and Sunderwirth, S. 1983. The chemistry of craving. *Psychology Today* (Oct.): 36–44.

Miller, W.R., and Hester, R.K. 1986. Effectiveness of alcoholism treatment: What research reveals. In *Treating addictive behaviors,* eds. W.R. Miller and N. Heather. New York: Plenum Press.

Minkoff, K. 1987. Resistance of mental health professionals to working with the chronically mentally ill. In *Barriers to treating the chronic mentally ill,* ed. A.T. Meyerson. San Francisco: Jossey-Bass.

Mondanaro, J. 1989. *Chemically dependent women: Assessment and treatment.* Lexington, Mass: Lexington Books.

Moore, R.A. 1982. The involvement of two private psychiatric hospitals in alcoholism treatment. In *Encyclopedic handbook of alcoholism,* eds. E.M. Pattison and E. Kaufman. New York: Gardner Press.

Moynihan, D.P. 1989. Yes, we do need a methadone clone. *New York Times,* February 26.

National Institute of Mental Health. 1986. Unpublished data, Division of Biometry and Applied Sciences, Washington, D.C.

New York Times. 1990. U.S. returns to 1820s in care of mentally ill, study asserts. Sept. 12.

Orford, J. 1985. *Excessive appetites: A psychological view of addictions.* New York: John Wiley and Sons.

Osher, F. 1989. The dually depressed patient: Characteristics and treatment strategies. *Community Support Network News* 5 (4): 1–11.

Osher, F.C., and Kofoed, L.L. 1989. Treatment of patients with psychiatric and psychoactive substance abuse disorders. *Hospital and Community Psychiatry* 40 (10) 1025–30.

Pattison, E.M. 1982. "A systems approach to alcoholism treatment." In *Encyclopedic handbook of alcoholism,* eds. E.M. Pattison and E. Kaufman. New York: Gardner Press.

Pattison, W.M.; Sobell, M.B.; and Sobell, L.C. 1977. *Emerging concepts of alcohol dependence.* New York: Springer.

Peele, S. 1985. *The meaning of addiction: Compulsive experience and its interpretation.* Lexington, Mass: Lexington Books.

Peele, S. 1989. *Diseasing of America: Addiction treatment out of control.* Lexington, Mass.: Lexington Books.

Pepper, B. 1985. Adult chronic patients: Population overview. *Journal of Clinical Psychopharmacology* 5 (3): 3S–7S

Pepper, B.; Kirshner, M.C. and Ryglewicz, H. 1981. The young adult chronic patient: Overview of a population. *Hospital and Community Psychiatry* 32 (7): 463–69.

Pepper, B., and Ryglewicz, H. 1984. The young adult chronic patient and substance abuse. *T.I.E. Quarterly Bulletin* [New York, N.Y.], July.

Persons, J.B. 1986. The advantages of studying psychological phenomena rather than psychiatric diagnoses. *American Psychologist* 41 (11): 1252–60.

Pinsker, H. 1983. Addicted patients in hospital psychiatric units. *Psychiatric Annals* 13 (8): 619–23.

Polich, J.M.; Armor, D.J.; and Braiker, H.B. 1981. *The course of alcoholism*. New York: Wiley.

Progress. 1991. Patient motivation, individualized treatment may play vital role in Holliswood's dual diagnosis unit. Vol. 2 (3: Winter).

Rachal, V.J.; Maisto, S.A.; Guess, L.L.; and Hubbard, R. 1982. "Alcohol use among youth," In *Alcohol consumption and related problems*. Alcohol and Health Monograph, no. 1, NIAAA, DHSS Publication No. (ADM) 82–1190.

Ralph, N., and Barr, M. 1989. Diagnosing attention-deficit hyperactivity disorder and learning disabilities with chemically dependent adolescents. *Journal of Psychoactive Drugs* 21(2): 203–15.

Rangel, C.B. 1990. The killer drug we ignore. *New York Times,* August 14.

Reiber, R.W., and Salzinger, K., eds 1980. *Psychology: Theoretical and historical perspectives*. New York: Academic Press.

Reinarman, C., and Levine, H.G. 1989. Crack in context: Politics and media in the making of a drug scare. *Contemporary Drug Problems* (Winter), Federal Legal Publications: 535–78.

Richard, M.A. et al. 1985. Recent psychostimulant use in hospitalized schizophrenics. *Journal of Clinical Psychiatry* 46(3):79–83.

Ridgely, M.S.; Goldman, H.H.; and Talbott, J.A. 1986. *Chronic mentally ill young adults with substance abuse problems: A review of relevant literature and creation of a research agenda*. Baltimore: University of Maryland School of Medicine, Mental Health Policy Studies Center.

Ridgely, M.S.; Osher, F.C.; and Talbott, J.A. 1987. *Chronic mentally ill young adults with substance abuse problems: Treatment and training issues*. Baltimore: University of Maryland School of Medicine, Mental Health Policy Studies Center.

Robins, L.N. 1982. "The diagnosis of alcoholism after *DSM–III*." In *Encyclopedic handbook of alcoholism,* eds. E.M. Pattison and E. Kaufman New York: Gardner Press.

Rochefort, D.A., ed. 1989. *Handbook on mental health policy in the United States*. New York: Greenwood Press.

Rockland Journal News. 1991. Drinking habits don't always run in families, April 31, A4.

Rogers, C.R. 1980. *A way of being*. Boston: Houghton Mifflin.

Rounsaville, B. et al. 1986. Proposed changes in *DSM–III* substance use disorders: Description and rationale. *American Journal of Psychiatry* 143(4): 463–68.

Rounsaville, B.J.; Weissman, M.M.; Kleber, H.; et al. 1982. Heterogeneity of psychiatric diagnosis in treated opiate addicts. *Archives of General Psychiatry* 39: 161–66.

Safer, D.J. 1987. Substance abuse among young adult chronic patients. *Hospital and Community Psychiatry* 38(5); 511–14.

Salzman, B.; Kurian, M.; Demirjian, A.; Morant, E.; Davell, S.; Miller, I.; and Royo,

W. 1973. The paranoid schizophrenic in a methadone maintenance program. New York University Medical Center, manuscript.

Sandmaier, M. 1980. *The invisible alcoholics: Women and alcohol abuse in America.* New York: McGraw-Hill Book Company.

Sargent, M. 1989. Update on programs for the homeless mentally ill. *Hospital and Community Psychiatry* 40 (10): 1015–16.

Saxe, L; Dougherty, D.; and Esty, K. 1985. "The effectiveness and cost of alcoholism treatment: A public policy perspective." In *The diagnosis and treatment of alcoholism,* 2d ed., eds. J.H. Mendelson and N.K. Mello. New York: McGraw-Hill Book Company.

Saxe, L; Dougherty D.; Esty, K.; and Fine, M. 1983. Health technology case study number 20: The effectiveness and costs of alcoholism treatment. Washington, D.C.: Office of Technology Assessment, U.S. Congress.

Schacht, T.E. 1985. *DSM–III* and the politics of truth. *American Psychologist* 40 (5): 513–21.

Schorr, L.B. 1988. *Within our reach: Breaking the cycle of disadvantage.* New York: Anchor Books.

Schwartz, S., and Goldfinger, S. 1981. The new chronic patient: Clinical characteristics of an emerging subgroup. *Hospital and Community Psychiatry* 32(7): 470–74.

Sciacca, K. 1987. Alcohol/substance abuse programs at New York State Psychiatric Centers develop and expand. *AID Bulletin,* Winter.

Segal, S. et al. 1977. Falling through the cracks: Mental disorders and social marginality in a young vagrant population. *Social Problems* 24:387–400.

Septimus, A. 1989. Psychological aspects of caring for families of infants infected with human immunodeficiency virus. *Seminars in Perinatology* 13 (1): 49–54.

Shaffer, H., and Jones, S.B. 1989. *Quitting cocaine: Struggle against impulse.* Lexington, Mass.: Lexington Books.

Shaffer, H., and Kaufman, J. 1985. The clinical assessment and diagnosis of addiction: Hypothesis testing. In *Alcoholism and substance abuse: Strategies for clinical intervention,* eds. T.E. Bratter and G.G. Forest. New York: Free Press.

Sheets, J.; Provost, J.A.; Reihman, J. 1982. Young adult chronic patients: Three hypothesized subgroups. *Hospital and Community Psychiatry* 33(3): 197–203.

Slaby, A.E.; Leib, J.; and Tancredi, L.R. 1975. *Handbook of psychiatric emergencies.* New York: Medical Examination Publishing Company.

Smith, S. 1983. *Ideas of the great psychologists.* New York: Harper & Row.

Snowden, L.R. and Cheung, F.K. 1990. Use of inpatient mental health services by members of ethnic minority groups. *American Psychologist* 45(3): 347–55.

Solomon, P., and Gordon, B. 1986. The psychiatric emergency room and follow-up services in the community. *Psychiatric Quarterly* 58(2):119–27.

Sorensen, J.L. 1990. Addictions and AIDS in the 1990s. *Psychology of Addictive Behaviors* 4(1):50–51.

Spotts, J.V., and Shontz, F.C. 1980. Cocaine users: A representative case approach. New York: Free Press.

Sturz, E.L. 1991. *First annual report of February 1, 1990 through March 31, 1991 for the U.S. Department of Labor on the New Leaf Work Experience Project,* Argus Community, Inc., Bronx, N.Y.

Styron, W. 1990. *Darkness visible: A memoir of madness.* New York: Random House.

Sunderwirth, S.G. 1985. "Biological mechanisms: Neurotransmission and addiction." In *The addictions,* eds. H.B. Milkman and H.J. Shaffer. Lexington, Mass.: Lexington Books.

Szasz, T. 1961. *The myth of mental illness.* New York: Harper & Row.

Thacker, W., and Tremaine, L. 1989. Systems issues in serving the mentally ill substance abuser: Virginia's experience. *Hospital and Community Psychiatry* 40(10): 1046–49.

Torrey, E.F. 1988. *Nowhere to go: The tragic odyssey of the homeless mentally ill.* New York: Harper & Row.

Torrey, E.F.; Flynn, L.; Wolfe, S.; and Erdman, K. 1990. *Care of the seriously mentally ill.* Washington, D.C.: National Alliance for the Mentally Ill and the Public Citizen Health Research Group.

Trice, H. M. 1983. "Alcoholics Anonymous." In *Alcoholism: Introduction to theory and treatment,* ed. D.A. Ward. Dubuque, Iowa: Kendall/Hunt.

U.S. Congress. Senate. 1986. *Barriers to Health Care for the Mentally Ill.* U.S. Senate Hearings 99–393, October 9. Washington, D.C.: GOP.

Valliant, G.E. 1966. A twelve year follow-up of New York narcotic addicts: Some characteristics and determinants of abstinence. *American Journal of Psychiatry* 123: 573–84.

Valliant, G.E. 1983. *The natural history of alcoholism: Causes, patterns and paths to recovery.* Cambridge: Harvard Univ. Press.

Valliant, G., and Milofsky, E.S. 1982. The etiology of alcoholism: A prospective viewpoint. *American Psychologist* 37 (5): 494–503.

Waldorf, D. 1973. *Careers in dope.* Englewood Cliffs N.J.: Prentice-Hall.

Wallace, J. 1985. "Working with the preferred defense structure of the recovering alcoholic." In *Practical approaches to alcoholism psychotherapy,* 2d ed., eds. S. Zimberg, J. Wallace, and S.B. Blume. New York: Plenum Press.

Wallen, M.C., and Weiner, H.D. 1989. Impediments to effective treatment of the dually diagnosed patient. *Journal of Psychoactive Drugs* 21 (2): 161–68.

Waller, P.F. 1982. Alcohol and highway safety. In *Encyclopedic handbook of alcoholism,* ed. E.M. Pattison and E. Kaufman. New York: Gardner Press.

Way, B.B. and McCormick, L.L. 1990. *The mentally ill chemical abusing population: A review of the literature.* Albany: Bureau of Evaluation and Services Research, New York State Office of Mental Health.

Weller, R.A., and Preskorn, S.H. 1984. Psychotropic drugs and alcohol: Pharmacokinetic and pharmacodynamic interactions. *Psychosomatics* 25, (4): 301–09.

Wender, P.H., and Klein, D.I. 1981. *Mood, mind and medicine: A guide to the new biopsychiatry.* New York: Meridian.

Wepner, R.S. 1973. The role of the ex-addict. *Drug Forum* 2:103.

Wilsnack, S.C. 1982. "Alcohol abuse and alcoholism in women." In *Encyclopedic handbook of alcoholism,* ed. E.M. Pattison and E. Kaufman. New York: Gardner Press.

Woititz, J. 1983. *Adult children of alcoholics.* Deerfield, Florida: Health Communications, Inc.

Wolfe, H. L., and Sorensen, J.L. 1989. Dual diagnosis patients in the urban psychiatric emergency room. *Journal of Psychoactive Drugs* 21(2): 169–75.

Wolfe, S.M.; Coley, C.M.; and the Health Research Group. 1980. *Pills that don't work*. New York: Farrar Straus Giroux.

Zimberg, S.V. 1971. *New York Law Journal*, 6 Dec.: 43.

Zimberg, S. 1982. *The clinical management of alcoholism*. New York: Brunner/Mazel.

Zucker, R.A., and Gomberg, E.S. 1986. Etiology of alcoholism reconsidered: The case for a biopsychosocial model. *American Psychologist* 41 (7): 783–93.

Zweben, J.E. 1986. Recovery-oriented psychotherapy. *Journal of Substance Abuse Treatment* 3 (4): 255–62.

Zweben, J.E., and Smith, D.E. 1989. Considerations in using psychotropic medication with dual diagnosis patients in recovery. *Journal of Psychoactive Drugs* 21 (2): 221–28.

Index

About the Authors

Jacqueline Cohen, M.S.W., has been a social worker for fifteen years in the fields of addiction treatment and mental health. She has done extensive group work in the areas of women's issues, relapse prevention, and the treatment of the mentally ill chemical abuser, and she has been a clinical supervisor in both methadone maintenance and mental health settings. She was the first MICA trainer for the state of New York, researching, developing, and providing training for professionals in the fields of mental health, alcoholism, and substance abuse. In addition, she was program supervisor for a newly developed model of providing outpatient drug treatment for women and children, funded by the New York City Child Welfare Administration.

Currently Ms. Cohen is a consultant, providing training, clinical supervision and assessments, and program development. She continues to do individual and group work in her private practice, specializing in women's treatment, sexual abuse, incest, addictions, and relapse prevention.

Stephen Jay Levy, Ph.D., C.A.S., is a psychologist who specializes in the treatment of addictive disorders and has served as director of several leading drug abuse programs, including the Division of Drug Abuse, New Jersey College of Medicine and Dentistry; the Alcoholism Treatment Program, Beth Israel Medical Center, New York City; the Koala Center of Nyack Hospital; and the Rockland County Crack Cocaine Program. Dr. Levy is a certified addiction specialist with the American Academy of Health Care Providers in Addictive Disorders and provides critical incident stress debriefing for emergency service personnel as a mental health consultant to the Emergency Assist Team of Rockland County. He maintains a private practice in Nanuet, New York.

Dr. Levy has served on the faculty of New York University, Hunter College, Empire State College, John Jay College of Criminal Justice, Jersey City State College, New Jersey College of Medicine and Dentistry, and the Mount Sinai School of Medicine. He has been organizing workshops and conferences on addictive behaviors for twenty-four years. In addition to writing numerous professional articles, Dr. Levy is the author of *Managing the Drugs in Your Life* (McGraw-Hill, 1983), editor of *Addictions in the Jewish Community* (Federation of Jewish Philanthropies of New York, 1986), and coauthor with Eileen Rutter, C.S.W., of *Children of Drug Abusers* (Lexington Books, 1992).